Key Issues for Teaching Assistants

This book is designed to support Teaching Assistants in the important and unique role they play in the education of children. This new edition includes a range of additional material and reflects developments in the recent UK context and legislation that relates to participation and diversity. It raises issues concerning values and professional practice for Teaching Assistants, emphasising inclusive approaches and the importance of understanding the perspectives of learners throughout. Each chapter contains an overview of topical debates, current research and a discussion of issues relating to values and professional practice. It raises questions and suggests reading for further reflection.

   This highly accessible resource includes contributions from leading researchers and experienced education practitioners. It introduces a range of issues, with a focus on inclusion and the key role of Teaching Assistants, such as:

- understanding inclusive education: school communities and participation;
- special educational needs and inclusive practice;
- supporting Gypsy, Roma and Traveller (GRT) children;
- ethnic diversity and attainment;
- the influence of gender on the achievement of boys and girls;
- working with teachers and parents;
- religious diversity and inclusive practice;
- including and supporting Lesbian, Gay, Bisexual and Transsexual (LGBT) students;
- welcoming and understanding asylum-seeking and refugee students;
- disability, human rights and inclusion.

This book will enable Teaching Assistants to develop a deeper understanding of the fundamental principles of inclusive education. It provides an essential resource for Teaching Assistants and all those workin

Gill Richards is Professor of Special Edu   ie School of Education, Nottingham Trent University

D1340805

Felicity Armstrong is Emeritus Professor   f Education, University College London, UK.

Key Issues for Teaching Assistants

Working in diverse and inclusive classrooms

Second edition

Edited by Gill Richards and Felicity Armstrong

Routledge
Taylor & Francis Group

LONDON AND NEW YORK

Second edition published 2016
by Routledge
2 Park Square, Milton Park, Abingdon, Oxon OX14 4RN

and by Routledge
711 Third Avenue, New York, NY 10017

Routledge is an imprint of the Taylor & Francis Group, an informa business

First edition published by Routledge 2008

British Library Cataloguing in Publication Data
A catalogue record for this book is available from the British Library

Library of Congress Cataloging in Publication Data
Names: Richards, Gill.
Title: Key issues for teaching assistants : working in diverse and inclusive classrooms / edited by Gill Richards and Felicity Armstrong.
Description: 2nd edition. | New York : Routledge, 2016. | Includes bibliographical references.
Identifiers: LCCN 2015041037| ISBN 9781138919648 (hardback) | ISBN 9781138919624 (pbk.) | ISBN 9781315687766 (ebook)
Subjects: LCSH: Teachers' assistants. | Inclusive education. | Special education.
Classification: LCC LB2844.1.A8 K49 2016 | DDC 371.14/124--dc23
LC record available at http://lccn.loc.gov/2015041037

ISBN: 978-1-138-91964-8 (hbk)
ISBN: 978-1-138-91962-4 (pbk)
ISBN: 978-1-315-68776-6 (ebk)

Typeset in Sabon
by Saxon Graphics Ltd, Derby

FSC
www.fsc.org FSC® C013604

MIX
Paper from
responsible sources

Printed and bound by CPI Group (UK) Ltd, Croydon, CR0 4YY

Contents

Contributors

Vikki Anderson has taught in schools, further education colleges and in higher education. She is currently a Learning Support Advisor at the University of Birmingham, where she works with a wide range of students with specific learning difficulties and delivers continuing professional development. Her research interests include listening and responding to the voice of the learner, transition to higher education and the inclusive curriculum.

Felicity Armstrong is Professor of Education at the Institute of Education, University College London. She has a life-long commitment to supporting the development of policies and practices for inclusive education. She is on the editorial board of *Disability & Society* and the *International Journal of Inclusive Education*, and has published numerous books and articles relating to equality, human rights and education.

Steve Bartlett is Professor of Education Studies and current honorary lecturer at the University of Wolverhampton. He has published in the areas of education studies, practitioner research and teacher professionalism and is editor of *Educationalfutures: e-journal of the British Education Studies Association* (BESA). He chaired the recent QAA Education Studies Benchmarking Committee.

Len Barton is Emeritus Professor of Inclusive Education at the Institute of Education, University College London. He is the founding editor of the prestigious journals *Disability & Society* and *British Journal of Sociology of Education*. He has published extensively on disability and inclusive education issues. He has a particular research interest in cross-cultural issues and the implications for policy and practice which have also been translated into innovatory postgraduate teaching programmes.

Diana Burton is part-time Professor of Education at the University of Wolverhampton, leading education research in the Faculty of Education, Health and Wellbeing. She has held executive leadership positions in a number of universities and has published widely in the areas of education studies, practitioner research, learning and teaching, and teacher professionalism.

Mano Candappa is Senior Lecturer in Sociology of Education at UCL Institute of Education, University College London. Her research focuses on childhoods, migration and forced migration, and issues around social marginalisation and human rights. She has collaborated with EU partners on research on human trafficking and asylum, and directed UK research for a range of funders, including research councils, national and local government and voluntary sector organisations around the experiences of refugees and asylum-seeking children and families. Recent publications include *Education, Asylum and the 'Non-Citizen' Child: the politics of compassion and belonging* (with Halleli Pinson and Madeleine Arnot).

Chris Derrington is Founder and Director of the EQualities Award. Her previous career spans 35 years of teaching pupils with learning disabilities, hearing impairment and emotional and behavioural difficulties. In 1990 she established the first Traveller Education team in Northamptonshire and went on to manage a large Race Equality Service. She has also been a Head Teacher, Ofsted inspector and a Senior Researcher for the NFER before joining the University of Northampton as a Senior Lecturer in Inclusive Education. Chris has a PhD in Cultural Psychology and Education and has published widely in the field of Traveller education.

Neil Duncan qualified as a teacher of Art from Bretton Hall College (Leeds University) in 1977. He became a Residential Child Care Officer in a secure unit for young people in Cumbria, then held a number of posts in special residential schools in the North of England, before settling in the West Midlands where he was Head of Year and Head of Behaviour at a local high school. While working as a teacher, Neil gained a PhD with his research into sexualised and gendered forms of bullying. Since then, Neil has appeared on TV and radio both in the UK and overseas, and published several books and papers which take a unique view of bullying in schools as an institutional problem rather than an individual child problem. He is currently Reader in Education for Social Justice at the University of Wolverhampton.

Linda Lyn-Cook has had long-standing experience teaching and managing in both mainstream and special schools. Her specialist expertise is in Autism, Special Educational Needs, Inclusion and Teacher Professional Development. She was employed for twelve years as a Local Authority Consultant Teacher leading a team of specialist staff. She is a visiting lecturer at Nottingham Trent University and lectures on the National Award for SENCOs as well as other post-graduate programmes. Linda is an additional school inspector and currently works independently as a school improvement advisor.

Michele Moore is a Professor of Inclusive Education. She is editor of the world-leading journal *Disability & Society* and on the Editorial Board of *Medicine, Conflict & Society*. Her work is concerned with advancing the global agenda for inclusion working with governments, teachers, disabled people, their families and representative organisations, most recently in the Middle East and Africa.

She works on numerous international projects to develop inclusion in schools and communities.

Bill Myers is a senior lecturer and the Pathway Leader for PGCE Psychology at the University of Wolverhampton. He has been involved in research on cyberbullying, perceptions of self-harm in secondary schools and the locus of control and its role in trainee teacher professional development. Prior to his current post he graduated from the Queen's University of Belfast, trained in teaching at the Institute of Education, London and taught in secondary schools in London, Leicestershire and Birmingham holding numerous roles including Head of Psychology and Health & Social Care, Head of Year, and Head of Mentoring.

Sheine Peart has worked in education since 1986 and is a senior lecturer in Education at Nottingham Trent University. She is the Post Graduate Research Tutor for the School of Education and teaches on education doctorate courses and other post-graduate programmes. Her principal research interests are working with marginalised and excluded groups, and she has a strong interest social justice and community cohesion. She has served as a Justice of the Peace since 1991.

Michael J. Reiss is Professor of Science Education at UCL Institute of Education, University College London, Visiting Professor at the Universities of Leeds and York and the Royal Veterinary College, Honorary Fellow of the British Science Association and of the College of Teachers, Docent at the University of Helsinki, a Fellow of the Academy of Social Sciences, a Priest in the Church of England, President of the International Society for Science & Religion and President of the International Association for Science and Religion in Schools.

Gill Richards is Professor of Special Education, Equity and Inclusion at Nottingham Trent University. Prior to this, she taught pupils identified as having special educational needs. At NTU, she has designed courses in Special and Inclusive Education and for the National SEN Co-ordination Award, led Government SEN projects in schools and a European project in Greece with teachers, and carried out a longitudinal study of disadvantaged girls. She currently teaches national courses for SENCOs and Head Teachers, and supervises PhDs. Her research, publication and international conference presentations focus on issues of equity and inclusion.

Raphael Richards is a director of a Learning Trust and Chair of Governors at a primary school in Nottingham. He retired in 2014 from Sheffield City Council where he worked for the last twelve years in the Children, Young People and Families (CYPF) Department as Head of their Ethnic Minority Travellers Achievement Service (EMTAS). Before that he held senior positions in private, community and voluntary sectors. He attained an MA in Equal Opportunities from University of Central England and has been a visiting lecturer in several universities, specialising in a range of equality issues.

David Ruebain is the Chief Executive of the Equality Challenge Unit. Prior to this, he was a practicing solicitor for twenty-one years. He was Director of Legal Policy at the Equality and Human Rights Commission of Great Britain, and before that he was a Partner and Founder of the Department of Education, Equality and Disability Law at Levenes Solicitors.

Jackie Scruton has spent most of her career working with children and young people for whom inclusion might be an issue. This has been in a range of settings, from special schools to further education. Her special interest is in communication skills and she is a Makaton regional tutor. She currently works as a senior lecturer at Nottingham Trent University and is a specialist member of the Special Educational Needs and Disability Tribunal (SENDIST).

Colin Slater's teaching career spans over twenty-five years during which he has worked in a wide variety of educational settings. He was awarded an MA in Inclusive Education at the Institute of Education in in 2004. By undertaking this he was determined to broaden the notion of inclusion to apply to other marginalised groups and in particular to give a voice to young Lesbian, Gay, Bisexual and Transgender people in our schools. He is passionate about the right of all to be included and for us to live in a more inclusive society.

Acknowledgements

We would like to thank Alison Foyle (Senior Publisher) and Rebecca Hogg (Editorial Assistant), and the team at Routledge, for their encouragement and invaluable support in the production of this book. We would also like to thank Michele Taylor, Subject Administrator in the School of Education at Nottingham Trent University, for vital support with the administrative work associated with the final stages of this book.

Introduction

Gill Richards and Felicity Armstrong

This book is about inclusive education, diversity and participation. We hope it will be a valuable resource for all those involved in teaching and learning, and the development of inclusive schools and colleges. In the process of editing and contributing to this book we have focused, in particular, on the diverse roles of Teaching Assistants in supporting inclusion. However, we have become more aware than ever of the importance of collaboration and discussion between all those involved in the development of inclusive learning communities. We hope this book will be of great value to Teaching Assistants and teachers working together, and support co-operative working and shared opportunities for discussion and planning.

In some respects it is a contradiction to produce a book about inclusive education with a focus on one group of professionals (in this case, Teaching Assistants), because inclusion has to be about partnership and the building of shared understandings and democratic collaboration. The kind of deep cultural transformation involved in developing inclusive education in terms of relationships, values and practices cannot be brought about by individuals acting on their own – although the work of individuals is important in the process of change. Inclusive education has to be concerned with all members of the school or college community, and must be responsive to the diversity and interests of the wider community too.

Our decision to think in a focused way about Teaching Assistants was based on the recognition that they have often been left out of debates about inclusion, and treated in instrumental ways, without understanding or recognition of their knowledge and experience and the crucial and active role they play in many aspects of the life of schools and colleges. Our view, and that of the contributors to this book, is that Teaching Assistants are often 'at the coal face' in terms of the interpretation of values and policies, and – most importantly – are often in a position to understand and respond to the rich diversity of experience, expectations and concerns of children and young people.

This book is underpinned by an interest in issues and values and their relationship to the processes and practices of inclusive education. In exploring values and the possible differences and contradictions in policies and beliefs, we hope that a deeper understanding will emerge of the fundamental principles of inclusive education and the way these work their way through different relationships and practices in schools and colleges.

In editing this book we have been confronted by a range of different interpretations and perspectives about the meaning of inclusive education, and the underlying causes of barriers to participation and the ways these may be overcome. Inevitably, we all bring our own values and perceptions to our work, and this is very much the case for the contributors to this book. We do not all speak with one voice and it has not been our intention to iron out differences or impose a uniform interpretation of inclusion. To do this would be to deny the richness and diversity in perspective and experience of the individual contributors. However, we *did* ask authors to provide in some form:

- An overview of topical debates, current research and initiatives.
- Some discussion of issues relating to values and professional practice for Teaching Assistants, emphasizing inclusive approaches and the importance of understanding the perspectives of others.
- Some issues and questions for further reflection.

In general, many – if not all – of our contributors are 'insiders'. In all cases they have direct professional experience and knowledge of the issues they are writing about, and in many cases they are themselves closely connected to, or members of, the different groups which provide the focus for different chapters. In editing the book we have engaged with a number of questions that have arisen in relation to the varied interpretations, values and experiences of contributors. We have had numerous discussions – usually by email – about the arguments put forward or the reasons for particular positions. This has been a learning experience for us as we have sometimes had to reflect critically on our own assumptions and values. We hope the different chapters in the book, and the questions they raise, will be a rich resource and basis for critical debate for independent readers as well as groups working together on professional development and academic courses.

Teaching Assistants are a rapidly growing group of paraprofessionals (over 240,000 currently employed within education settings), with a keen interest in professional development. Despite national cuts in funding for this, increasing numbers are attending university foundation degrees and courses to validate the Higher Level Teaching Assistant (HLTA) status. All of these programmes require underpinning with knowledge of education values and their impact on practice.

In this book, there is an emphasis on support for inclusion of all learners and the promotion of positive values and attitudes about diversity, through challenging stereotypes and all forms of exclusion. It explores a range of issues, intending to provide a resource for all those working in education and, in particular, for Teaching Assistants. We hope that the book will be interesting to read and enhance personal-professional understanding as well as providing a useful course text for those following a route to professional qualifications.

Clearly, with increasing government initiatives and policy directives, as well as the perspectives of campaigning groups with different interests and ideals, parents and communities, there is a wide range of issues that can be seen as competing in importance for a book on 'current issues of diversity and inclusion'. We have not been able to cover all possible topics of this vast area in a book of this size and we regret, in particular, the absence of chapters that specifically relate to the effects of poverty on questions of inclusion and exclusion in education, and the ways in which communities can work together to develop inclusive cultures and practices.

The structure and contents of the book

Key Issues for Teaching Assistants: Working in diverse and inclusive classrooms is made up of 15 chapters – all addressing different aspects and issues concerning diversity and inclusive education. In general, there is a common view of inclusive education as being concerned with the participation of all learners in education on a basis of social justice and equal recognition. Many of the ideas and arguments put forward are related and overlap. We hope that the book will be interesting and enjoyable to read as a whole, but that it will also be useful to dip into to find chapters on topics of particular interest or current concern. Each chapter ends with a number of questions or statements which we hope will stimulate critical reflection and debate, followed by some suggested key readings.

In Chapter 1 Felicity Armstrong explores some of the background and principles relating to inclusive education and the way the concept of inclusion in education and 'inclusive' terminology are used in different ways and in different contexts. The chapter raises some issues presented by policy developments and considers some of their implications for inclusive education. The chapter suggests some fundamental principles which will inform the development of inclusive schools and briefly discusses research issues and findings in relation to the role of Teaching Assistants in the teaching and learning process and in the life of the school.

Chapter 2 by Gill Richards argues that inclusive education must involve listening to the voices of learners as a means of facilitating meaningful participation and the development of inclusive practices involving all those concerned. Teaching Assistants play a key role in establishing good communication with learners and accessing their perspectives. Drawing on relevant research and reports, and making links with policy developments, the chapter stresses the importance of learning from the voices of children and young people to inform the process of change.

Chapter 3 by Chris Derrington provides insights into some key cultural considerations and draws upon a body of research to suggest ways of effectively supporting the particular needs of Gypsy, Roma and Traveller (GRT) children and improving their educational outcomes. It explains some of the cultural and social background to the position of these children and young people in schools and raises some issues relating to their attainment and participation. She discusses the crucial part Teaching Assistants can play in building trust, promoting social inclusion and supporting the academic progress of children from GRT communities.

Chapter 4 by Raphael Richards explores the background of Black minority ethnic (BME) groups and links this discussion to individualized experiences within education settings. It reflects on current education initiatives that support these groups, raising achievement and promoting inclusive practice. Recent research studies are used to reflect on BME perspectives, identifying areas for development in schools and colleges, and the role of Teaching Assistants in contributing to change.

Chapter 5 by Steve Bartlett and Diana Burton is concerned with the influence of gender on achievement as part of a wider concern with inclusive education. It covers a brief review of research and initiatives on boys and girls' achievement and explores a range of gender specific initiatives supported by the government, and current curriculum and social issues that affect participation and achievement. The chapter argues that Teaching Assistants, and all practitioners, need to understand issues relating to gender and their implications for inclusive education, so that they can be more effective in their practice.

In Chapter 6 Michael J. Reiss explains some of the background to the broad topic of 'religion' in schools in the UK and explores some issues which school communities need to consider and engage with in positive ways. Inclusive schools welcome the diversity represented by their neighborhood communities and regard differences as sources for enriching teaching and learning and for fostering harmonious, respectful relationships and mutual understanding. Teaching Assistants, like teachers, need to be aware of the kinds of issues which arise in relation to religious and cultural diversity so that they can play a key role in supporting all learners, regardless of differences in culture and belief.

Chapter 7 by Vikki Anderson and Linda Lyn-Cook briefly traces the historical development of Teaching Assistants in education settings. It explores the working relationship that Teaching Assistants have with teachers, using key research studies and current policy initiatives. It draws on a study of Teaching Assistants' views concerning the experience and practice of working with teachers and examines ways in which this key relationship may affect the quality of practice with learners and identifies implications for the role of Teaching Assistants.

Chapter 8 by Michele Moore explores the perspectives of Teaching Assistants about the role they can play in helping schools develop positive relationships and effective communication with parents. It focuses on the facilitative role of Teaching Assistants in discussions with parents and teachers. Reflections are drawn from a range of in-schools observations made in the context of research projects, and from continuing professional development activities.

Chapter 9 by Gill Richards traces the historical development of special schools with reference to key legislation. It presents a range of perspectives on the current role of special schools, drawing on research concerning personal experiences and educational practice. It reflects on new initiatives and government policy on diversity and inclusion, and discusses the position taken by those who support full inclusion for all. This raises some important issues about the different and often conflicting values underpinning contrasting positions on the future of special schools.

Chapter 10 by Mano Candappa focuses on asylum-seeking and refugee children, their experiences, and how schools can support their participation and their learning in the country of refuge. Schools have a duty to support these children so that they can fully enjoy their right to education under the UN Convention on the Rights of the Child. The refugee experience makes these children resilient, but they are among the most marginalized in our society. Mano Candappa argues that the inclusive school, which has a culture that celebrates diversity, is the most supportive environment for asylum-seeking and refugee students. The nature of Teaching Assistants' work places them in a key position to support these young people in their learning and in rebuilding their lives in Britain.

Chapter 11 by Colin Slater is about the experiences of Lesbian, Gay, Bisexual, Transsexual (LGBT) children and young people in school. It discusses the wider policy context in relation to the position of LGBT students in education, and draws on the findings of a small qualitative study. The underlying focus of the chapter is on the perspectives of young people themselves and on the importance of listening to the voices of LGBT young people as a means of understanding their experiences. These 'insider' perspectives are crucial in gaining understanding of issues of inclusion and exclusion in schools. They are also a potentially valuable starting point in rethinking and strengthening the role Teaching Assistants can play in sensitively supporting inclusive education for all students, and – in particular – for LGBT children and young people.

Chapter 12 by Jackie Scruton explores a brief review of research, legislation and policies concerning students that are perceived as challenging within educational settings. It explores some of the barriers that contribute to young people's disenfranchisement and considers the role of Teaching Assistants and schools within this. The chapter draws on a range of initiatives currently available for schools to respond to behaviour that is seen to be difficult, reflecting on ways that Teaching Assistants can use these to work positively with learners and other professionals.

In Chapter 13 Neil Duncan and Bill Myers open a discussion on the difficult issue of bullying and draw out questions concerning the ways schools may respond to bullying. The chapter provides a brief overview of research on bullying and how it has become an area of national and international concern. It explores the multiple forms of bullying, including cyberbullying, and the potential role of school ethos and adult relationships as contributors to levels of bullying in schools. Different approaches to dealing with bullying are reviewed, drawing out implications for Teaching Assistants' practice.

Chapter 14 by David Ruebain and Sheine Peart covers key legislation relating to meeting diverse needs in education settings. It discusses a range of legislation and its effects, including the 1981 Education Act and the Special Needs and Disability Act (SENDA), statementing procedures, the Disability Equality Duty and other key legislation relating to Race and Gender, drawing out implications for education practice and professional responsibilities. The chapter argues that Teaching Assistants have an important role to play in ensuring equality in the classroom and this will be strengthened through familiarity with the legal rights of children and young people in education.

Chapter 15 by Len Barton draws together some of the overriding concerns of the book relating to social justice and inclusive education, making connections with issues of democracy and the values which underpin policies and practices in education. The chapter emphasizes the importance of building positive relationships between all those involved in working together for inclusive education, raising some contentious issues for reflection. The chapter confirms the important role of Teaching Assistants in developing inclusive cultures and practices in education.

Chapter 1

Inclusive education

The key role of Teaching Assistants

Felicity Armstrong

Inclusive education is one of the key ideas and driving forces to emerge in education both nationally and internationally over the past 30 years or so. In this chapter we begin to explore the idea, and origins, of inclusive education and some of the very different ways the term is used in different contexts. We will consider the possible meanings and values which underpin these different interpretations, and how these relate to the lives of schools and their communities.

The term 'communities' is used here to mean both the communities of people who make up the internal life of the school, and to refer to a wider concept of community which encompasses the lives, cultures, practices and interests of those in the neighbourhoods associated with the school. This discussion will be linked to the often contradictory demands made on all those implicated in the complex relationships involved in the lives of colleges and schools, learning and teaching. Teaching Assistants, teachers and pupils are at the sharp edge of where these contradictions are most keenly felt – in the day-to-day life of the classroom. In the course of the discussion the chapter will draw on some examples of research to raise some issues about the role of Teaching Assistants in teaching and learning and in developing inclusive relationships and practices. It will end with some issues and questions which may be helpful in making connections between some of the points raised in the chapter and the particular challenges faced by Teaching Assistants and others, such as learning mentors, in developing inclusive education. There are many different interpretations of the terms 'inclusion' and 'inclusive education', so it is important to consider the ways we use language, and the need to recognize that inclusion means different things to different people. These differences are reflected in the kinds of policies, practices and attitudes which governments, schools and practitioners adopt.

The starting point in this chapter is that there is a dynamic relationship between schools, communities and the broader social context. Tony Booth describes participation in the inclusive classroom in the following terms:

> It … implies learning alongside others and collaborating with them in shared lessons. It involves active engagement with what is learnt and taught and having a say in how education is experienced. But participation also means being recognised for oneself and being accepted for oneself: I participate

with you when you recognise me as a person like yourself and accept me for who I am.

(Booth 2003: 2)

These ideas go to the heart of the principles of inclusive education: being respected and recognized as an equal member of the school community; having equal access to learning and full participation in all aspects of school and college life; being together, not apart. These principles have important implications for the physical organization of the school, for relationships between members of the school community, for the way in which the curriculum and teaching are understood and for the wider culture and practices of the school.

Inclusive education is a continuous and changing process, which is deeply affected by changes in society – both short- and long-term. Thus, the kinds of issues which a school needs to engage with may change dramatically in the face of changes in context, such as the following: the closing down of a local factory; the outbreak of hostilities with another country; the closure of a local special school; a change in the political complexion of the country or the local council; the arrival of Travellers in the local community; the introduction of new structures and measures relating to testing and assessment; or the government-led revision of an aspect of the curriculum.

Inclusive education, then, is related to the notions of context and community, and raises questions for schools about the way in which they respond to change and diversity at both national and local levels.

Inclusive education: origins and rights

Education is recognized as a basic human right by a number of United Nations instruments, from the Universal Declaration of Human Rights (1948) to the UN Convention on the Rights of the Child (1989). Different countries and cultures all have their own unique characteristics and challenges, but these international instruments do provide a vision, a set of goals and expectations, which we can try to interpret in ways that reflect the barriers and opportunities relating to education within our own changing settings. If we value all our citizens equally, and recognize their fundamental rights to equal participation and access to social well-being, we must ensure that all have equal access to education. However, it is apparent that national education systems exclude many children and young people, either by making inadequate or inappropriate provisions, or sometimes by excluding them from education altogether. We need to explore the extent to which failure to participate fully in education is an outcome of policies and practices in education systems and in schools themselves, as well as broader questions relating to attitudes, resources and wider inequalities in society.

In 1990 the challenge of exclusion from education was first taken up on a global level by world leaders at The World Conference on Education for All: Meeting Basic Learning Needs held in Jomtien, Thailand and the World Summit on Children (New York 1990) which adopted the goal of Education for All by the Year 2000 as one of the key Millennium Goals. The World Declaration on Education for All emanating from the Jomtien conference specifically refers to the need to provide equal access to education for all children, including those who have impairments or experience disadvantages. The Framework for Action adopted by the conference provided a set of principles in support of promoting 'inclusive education':

- the right of all children to a full cycle of primary education;
- the commitment to a child-centred concept of education in which individual differences are accepted as a source of richness and diversity – a challenge not a problem;
- the improvement of the quality of primary education including improvements in professional training;
- the provision of a more flexible and responsive primary schooling, with respect to organization, processes and content;
- greater parental and community participation in education;
- recognition of the wide diversity of needs and patterns of development of primary school children, demanding a wider and more flexible range of responses; and
- a commitment to a developmental, intersectoral and holistic approach to education and care of primary school children.

The emphasis on primary education reflects the fact that in many countries of the world education may be restricted to the primary level, or even denied to some groups of children altogether. It is interesting to reflect on the principles listed above in the light of our own policies and practices, and to ask: To what extent are we fulfilling, or falling short of, these principles in our own contexts? How should these principles be interpreted, and what would be the implications for changes in school cultures and practices?

The UNESCO World Conference on Special Needs Education: Access and Quality held in Salamanca, Spain in 1994 focused on the practical requirements that need to be fulfilled in order for inclusive education to become a reality. It produced the Salamanca Statement which formulated a new Statement on Inclusive Education and adopted a new Framework for Action based on the principle that ordinary schools should welcome all children, regardless of difference. It proclaimed that

> regular schools with this inclusive orientation are the most effective means of combating discriminatory attitudes, creating welcoming communities, building an inclusive society and achieving education for all; moreover, they provide an effective education to the majority of children and improve the efficiency and ultimately the cost-effectiveness of the entire education system.

> (UNESCO 1994: ix)

The Salamanca World Conference called upon all governments to:

- give the 'highest policy and budgetary priority' to improve education services so that all children could be included, regardless of differences or difficulties;
- adopt as a matter of law or policy the principle of inclusive education and enrol all children in ordinary schools unless there were compelling reasons for doing otherwise;
- ensure that organizations of disabled people, along with parents and community bodies, are involved in planning and decision making;
- put greater effort into preschool strategies as well as vocational aspects of inclusive education; and
- ensure that both initial and in-service teacher training address the provision of inclusive education.

In particular, the Framework for Action is based on the belief that 'inclusion and participation are essential to human dignity and to the enjoyment and exercise of human rights. In the field of education this is reflected in bringing about a 'genuine equalization of opportunity'. Inclusive education

> assumes human differences are normal and that learning must be adapted to the needs of the child, rather than the child fitted to the process. The fundamental principle of the inclusive school is that all children should learn together, where possible, and that ordinary schools must recognise and respond to the diverse needs of their students, while also having a continuum of support and services to match these needs. Inclusive schools are the 'most effective' at building solidarity between children with special needs and their peers.
>
> (The UNESCO Salamanca Statement [1994: 7],
> as summarized by the Centre for Studies in Inclusive Education)

The UN 2009 Global Conference on Inclusive Education, *Confronting the Gap: Rights, Rhetoric, Reality? Salamanca 15 years On,* adopted a resolution which stated:

> We understand inclusive education to be a process where mainstream schools and early year's settings are transformed so that *all* children/students are supported to meet their academic and social potential and involves removing barriers in environment, attitudes, communication, curriculum, teaching, socialisation and assessment at all levels.
>
> (Inclusion International 2009, Rieser 2016: in press)

More recently the United Nations issued the Incheon Declaration at the Global Forum in South Korea (2015), which reiterated the commitments made by the global Education for All (EFA) movement.

Inclusive education: meanings and interpretations

In this chapter, the use of the term 'inclusive education' reflects the principle that inclusion concerns everybody – all learners, and all members of the school, college and wider community. This view is reflected in the different chapters in the book and is based on the principle that inclusion is

> fundamentally about issues of human rights, equity, social justice and the struggle for a non-discriminatory society. These principles are at the heart of inclusive policy and practice.
>
> (Armstrong and Barton 2007: 6)

It is based on the belief in the rights of all to equal recognition, respect and treatment, regardless of difference. This does not mean that particular interests, learning styles, knowledge, and cultural and linguistic heritage shall not be recognized. On the contrary – inclusion recognizes, and is responsive to, diversity and the right 'to be oneself ' – in an open and democratic community. This interpretation of inclusive education implies the right for all to be equal members of their neighbourhood school and college communities. This is rather different from the concept of 'integration', which focuses on the question of how an individual child, or group of children, might 'fit in' to a school or a class, rather than focusing on the need for a fundamental transformation in the social, cultural, curricular and pedagogic life of the school, as well as its physical organization. '*Integration*' has, traditionally, referred to a concept and practices associated with learners identified as having special educational needs. Paradoxically, the term '*inclusion*' is often used in the same way as integration. For example, it is common to hear children referred to as 'being included' in a certain activity for part of the week, or to mean they attend a special school or unit but attend a mainstream school or class as visitors on particular days. In some schools it is possible to find an 'Inclusion Room' – or something similar – which may actually be the reverse if it is really a place where students are sent when they are disturbing the class or 'not getting on with their work'. These varied and contradictory uses of terminology create confusion; integration and inclusion represent very different values and practices.

An important contributor to changing understanding of impairment and disability, and to the development of the principles of inclusive education, has been the 'Social Model' of disability. According to the Social Model,

> a person's impairment is not the cause of disability, but rather disability is the result of the way society is organised, which disadvantages and excludes people with impairments. It follows from this that the focus should not be on the person with impairment and how they can be made to 'fit' into schools (individual model of disability), but rather on removing any barriers within schools that disable the person with impairment.
>
> (Armstrong, Armstrong and Spandagou 2010: 27)

The Social Model is a powerful approach to understanding the processes of exclusion which affect a wide range of other groups who experience discrimination and exclusion. It shifts attention away from the individual, towards the social context, conditions and attitudes of others as the elements creating barriers to equality and participation.

Muddles over terminology are also created by the way policy documents sometimes adopt the language of inclusion to refer to issues such as 'raising standards' in terms of improving exam results which, in turn, is linked to 'widening participation', although the term 'inclusion' is notably absent from policy documents in recent years. Much of the legislation introduced by recent governments has been concerned with measurable performance and raising attainment as part of an overall strategy for school improvement. The pressures of a highly competitive global economy are one factor in creating this climate of 'performativity'. Unfortunately, when 'high standards' in education are measured primarily by levels achieved in public tests and examinations, other broader educational and creative concerns and projects become marginalized and create perceptions of 'failure' in relation to children and young people whose attainment is deemed unacceptably low. The implications for students who experience difficulties in learning in the present educational regime and climate relate to low-self esteem, marginalization and a lack of recognition in terms of who they are and what they have to contribute.

Ainscow *et al.* (2006) demonstrated, through their research, how the pressure to improve scores on national tests may distort the work of schools – including those which have shown a strong commitment to developing inclusive policies and practices. However, Florian and Rouse (2001: 403) found in their research that "many schools committed to the development of inclusive practice have been able to mediate these tensions, and work creatively and successfully" to build schools which are 'effective' in terms of developing inclusive cultures and practices, and also 'effective' in terms of raising levels of attainment. Another example of possible conflicts in values relating to the 'raising standards' agenda lies in the increase in assessment procedures and setting in primary and secondary schools, with children being categorized and labelled at an increasingly young age, and placed in different groups according to perceived ability. A recent example of this is the introduction of baseline assessments of children when they start school at the age of four or five, leading some schools to use these assessments as a basis for grouping children according to 'ability'. This policy has been severely criticized by teachers and their organizations as encouraging the labelling and separation of children at a very young age. The author and teacher Michael Morpurgo commented,

> When you test children, whether you like it or not you create successes and failures. I feel the greatest danger you can put children in is making them feel they are not worthwhile.
>
> (*Times Educational Supplement*, 15 May 2015)

In contrast, the Department for Education (DfE) put forward the argument that baseline assessment of children when they enter school enables schools to identify the strengths and weaknesses of individual children and ensure that they do not 'fall behind' and are 'secondary ready' (DfE 2014, OfSTED 2014). Assessment of young children when they arrive in school is just one example of the introduction of a policy which can have an impact on the life of the school, and the positioning of children within it.

The position and role of Teaching Assistants: what does research tell us?

Teaching Assistants often work with children who experience difficulties in the classroom and may find themselves placed alongside them in 'bottom sets'! Interestingly, some research suggests that grouping students for English, Maths and Science according to perceived ability is not necessarily effective in raising standards of attainment overall (Ireson, Hallam and Hurley 2005). Other within-school factors which may have an impact on student attainment include the type and quality of learning and teaching opportunities provided, curriculum differentiation, teacher attitudes and expectations – as well as pupils' own sense of self-worth and confidence. These factors all have an impact on school cultures and their values and practices.

The rapidly increasing number of Teaching Assistants working in schools over recent years, and the emphasis on work-based learning as part of professional development, has led to a greater interest in this neglected area on the part of researchers. In this section some of this work will be discussed particularly with reference to the question of the development of inclusive schools and classrooms. In order for Teaching Assistants to work effectively and comfortably with other adults and with children and young people, their work and their diverse wider role, and the particular skills and knowledge which they contribute, need to be recognized. The work of those working in a 'support' role has been marginalized both in schools and in research. Sometimes even the language used to refer to those who work in a support role is devaluing or instrumental. It is quite common to come across the terms 'deployment' or 'use' of Teaching Assistants or learning support staff in policy documents, reports, academic articles and professional literature (although rarely, I suspect, in schools themselves).

Significantly, there is increasing recognition of the crucial role played by Teaching Assistants in developing inclusive practices and cultures (Moran and Abbott 2002; Bosanquet, Radford and Webster 2016). This will come as no surprise to those who actually work in schools! Democratic collaboration and teamwork is essential in developing inclusive practices and planning, and this involves everybody being able to express their views and recognition given to the knowledge and experience of all participants. This is not easily accomplished in schools where professional relationships are deeply hierarchical or where there is no tradition of consultation and debate.

The question of the nature of 'support' provided by both Teaching Assistants and teachers themselves has been the subject of much debate. Should support for learning be provided on an individual basis or does this encourage dependency and lack of motivation among pupils, as well as creating barriers to social interaction with other learners? In her study of working practices of Learning Support Assistants (LSAs) working with students identified as having 'severe learning difficulties' and 'profound and multiple learning difficulties', Lacey (2001) concluded that the most effective practices in developing 'inclusive learning' involved the following:

- allowing opportunities for social interaction to take place between students;
- making time available for LSAs and teachers to plan together; and
- supporting groups of children, rather than individuals.

In this study, the importance of recognizing and drawing on the knowledge and experience of LSAs emerged as an important requirement for inclusion. Much of the research relating to learning support assistants and classroom assistants highlight the crucial importance of the relationships which are formed between the different groups involved in the life of the school and in teaching and learning. Hammett and Burton (2005) observed that the failure to value, and ensure the participation of support staff can lead to feelings of demoralization and demotivation. Their research was carried out in an 'improving' 11–18 secondary school in which 'Learning Support Assistants' (the term used in the article) are seen as "prime supporters of the renewed emphasis on improving teaching and learning" (2005: 299). They argued that there needs to be more opportunities for communication between teachers and Learning Support Assistants and this means providing time and resources to make this possible.

In their in-depth study, Webster and Blatchford (2013, 2014) found that students who have Statements of special educational needs spent the equivalent of more than a day a week away from the classroom and during most of their time in class they were accompanied by a Teaching Assistant. They reported that the students had far more interaction with Teaching Assistants than with teachers. Webster found that Teaching Assistants had the main responsibility for teaching Statemented students and planning their work and modifying the curriculum, and argued that these students "had a lower quality pedagogical diet" compared to other students (Webster 2014: 233). Finally, the study found that teachers seemed to devolve responsibility for Statemented students, deferring to the Teaching Assistant as "the expert on the child and their SEN" (Webster 2014: 232).

These research findings have important implications for inclusion. They provide a valuable basis for critical reflection on roles of teachers and Teaching Assistants, the need for a rolling programme of staff development, a questioning of the values and practices of the school and the ways students identified as having special educational needs are seen in terms of their learning and right to participation. One recommendation coming out of the research is that a far greater emphasis should be placed on the quality and kind of support for learning and the overall experience of education received by students, rather than focusing primarily on the number of hours allocated for support from a Teaching Assistants. It should be stressed that, far from underrating the role of Teaching Assistants, the study is concerned with ways of enhancing their role so that TAs and teachers have a greater understanding of inclusive practices in teaching and learning. There is also a need for a heightened awareness of the social and psychological consequences, particularly in terms of friendships and self-image, for students if they are removed for the ordinary class and have a Teaching Assistant constantly attached to them (the 'velcroed on' model).

The question of how support workers relate to individual students and the wider class is certainly an important one. The narrow interpretation of inclusive education as being concerned with learners identified as having special educational needs is supported by a view of the role of support staff as supporting individual students, or groups of students, identified as having difficulties. Yet, research suggests that there is a general awareness amongst teachers, learning support staff, pupils and researchers that the practice of individual support presents a number of difficulties and barriers to inclusion. Vincent, Cremin and Thomas (2005) pointed out that concentration of attention on students who have been identified as having special educational needs, can encourage social, academic and physical dependence. It can also prevent interaction between students, leading to the isolation of the 'supported' student and the possible creation of negative perceptions.

Bosanquet *et al.* stressed the importance of understanding the clear differences between the role of the teacher and the role of the TA. They argued that

> the TA role must be seen as making a distinct contribution to teaching and learning.... Since TAs work with small groups and individuals, they are in the unique position of being able to constantly monitor the step-by-step progress pupils make towards achieving learning goals. From this vantage point, TAs can provide immediate feedback and give targeted support with parts of the task the pupils find difficult. This is called *scaffolding* and it is the key to ensuring that pupils become able to work more independently.
>
> (2016: 19)

'Scaffolding' is a process in which learning is developed through interaction between the learner and the 'more experienced other'. Ideally, the teacher or teaching assistant carefully intervenes or collaborates in a given learning activity in ways which help children understand and consolidate concepts and processes so that they can move on in their learning. The image of 'scaffolding' is a good one because it suggests a process of gradual and careful construction, rather than the acquisition of isolated 'blocks of learning'. Scaffolding can also take place when children work together in groups, with the children supporting each other in the development of learning through 'exploratory talk' (Littleton and Mercer, 2013). Once again we come across the importance of interaction and collaboration, already mentioned as a part of the development of inclusive and equal relationships.

Conclusion

We cannot overestimate the important role Teaching Assistants have to play in developing inclusive practices through their own work and their participation in the life of the school. As well as creating positive relationships with children and young people so that they feel confident and full members of the school community, an important part of the role of Teaching Assistants is their contribution to teaching and learning with individual children and small groups through a process of collaboration and support. This aspect of their role, and the many possibilities and opportunities it opens up, is highlighted in many chapters of this book, from different perspectives.

Reflections on values and practice

Inclusive education is both a set of ideals and a project based on values and practices which recognize the right of all to belong. The inclusive school will, for example, try and counter oppressive beliefs and behaviours relating to racism, sexuality, class and narrow notions of conformity. It will attempt to learn as a community to understand and overcome inequalities, bullying and marginalizing practices which are part of the everyday life of many school communities. The inclusive school is democratic, so everybody has a voice and contributes to decision making and the planning of teaching and learning.

The values and principles discussed in this chapter raise questions about the policies, practices and relationships which might foster inclusive schools and colleges. With this in mind it may be helpful to reflect on the following questions:

1   What kinds of changes are needed in your own work context or local school in order to develop an inclusive community in which all students and staff are valued equally, and participate fully in life of the school?
2   What contribution can Teaching Assistants make to creating inclusive education?
3   How do you see your role in the teaching and learning process? What would help you to be more effective in this role?

Suggested further reading

Ainscow, M., Booth, T. and Dyson, A., with Farrell, P., Frankham, J., Gallannaugh, F., Howes, A. and Smith, R. (2006) *Improving Schools, Developing Inclusion*. London: Routledge.

Armstrong, F. and Moore, M. (eds) (2004) *Action Research for Inclusive Education: Changing Places, Changing Practices, Changing Minds*. London: RoutledgeFalmer.

Booth, T. and Ainscow, M. (2002, 2011) *The Index for Inclusion*. Bristol, UK: CSIE.

Bosanquet, P., Radford, J. and Webster, R. (2016) *The Teaching Assistant's Guide to Effective Interaction: How to Maximise Your Practice*. London: Routledge.

Vincent, K., Cremin, H. and Thomas, G. (2005) *Teachers and Assistants Working Together*. Maidenhead, UK: Open University Press.

References

Ainscow, M., Booth, T. and Dyson, A., with Farrell, P., Frankham, J., Gallannaugh, F., Howes, A. and Smith, R. (2006) *Improving Schools, Developing Inclusion*. London: Routledge.

Armstrong, A. C., Armstrong, D. and Spandagou, I. (2010) *Inclusive Education International Policy and Practice*. London. Sage.

Armstrong, F. and Barton, L. (2007) 'Policy, Experience and Change and the Challenge of Inclusive Education: The Case of England' in L. Barton and F. Armstrong (eds), *Policy, Experience and Change: Cross-Cultural Reflections on Inclusive Education*. Dordrecht, Netherlands: Springer.

Booth, T. (2002) 'Inclusion and Exclusion in the City: Concepts and Contexts' in P. Potts (ed), *Inclusion in the City: Selection, Schooling and Community*. London: Routledge-Falmer.

Bosanquet, P., Radford, J. and Webster, R. (2016) *The Teaching Assistant's Guide to Effective Interaction: How to Maximise Your Practice*. London: Routledge.

DfE. (2014) *Reforming Assessment and Accountability for Primary Schools*. Retrieved from www.gov.uk/government/uploads/system/uploads/attachment_data/file/297595/Primary_Accountability_and_Assessment_Consultation_Response.pdf

Florian, L. and Rouse, M. (2001) 'Inclusive Practice in English Secondary Schools: Lessons Learned'. *Cambridge Journal of Education*, 31(3), 399–412. doi:10.1080/03057640120086648

Hammett, N. and Burton, N. (2005) 'Motivation, Stress and Learning Support Assistants: An Examination of Staff Perceptions at a Rural Secondary School'. *School Leadership and Management*, 25(3), 299–310.

Inclusion International. (2009) Retrieved from http://inclusion-international.org/wp-content/uploads/2013/07/Newsletter-September-special-edition-clb-edits.pdf

Ireson, J., Hallam, S. and Hurley, C. (2005) 'What Are the Effects of Ability Grouping on GCSE Attainment?'. *British Educational Research Journal*, 31(4), 443–458.

Lacey, P. (2001) 'The Role of Learning Support Assistants in the Inclusive Learning of Pupils with Severe and Profound Learning Difficulties'. *Educational Review*, 53(2), 157–167.

Littleton, K. and Mercer, N. (2013) *Interthinking: Putting Talk to Work*. London: Routledge

Moran, A. and Abbott, L. (2002) 'Developing Inclusive Schools: The Pivotal Role of Teaching Assistants in Promoting Inclusion in Special and Mainstream Schools in Northern Ireland'. *European Journal of Special Needs Education*, 17(2), 161–173.

OfSTED. (2014) Are You Ready? Good Practice in School Readiness. Retrieved from www.gov.uk/government/uploads/system/uploads/attachment_data/file/418819/Are_you_ready_Good_practice_in_school_readiness.pdf

Rieser, R. (2016) 'Global Approaches to Education, Disability and Human Rights: Why Inclusive Education is the Way Forward.' In G. Richards. and F. Armstrong (eds), *Teaching and Learning in Diverse and Inclusive Classrooms: Key Issues for New Teachers*. London: Routledge.

Times Educational Supplement. 'Baseline assessments for four-year-olds are "completely absurd" and put children under excessive pressure, according to award-winning children's author Michael Morpurgo'. TES, 15/09/15.

UNESCO and Ministry of Education and Science, Spain. (1994) *The Salamanca Statement and Framework for Action on Special Needs Education*. Retrieved from www.unesco.org/education/ pdf/ SALAMA_E.PDF) Paris: UNESCO.

Vincent, K., Cremin, H. and Thomas, G. (2005) *Teachers and Assistants Working Together*, Maidenhead: Open University Press.

Webster, R. (2014) '2014 Code of Practice: How Research Evidence on the Role and Impact of Teaching Assistants Can Inform Professional Practice'. *Educational Psychology in Practice*, 30(3), 232–237.

Webster, R. and Blatchford, P. (2013) 'The Educational Experiences of Pupils with a Statement for Special Educational Needs in Mainstream Primary Schools: Results from a Systematic Observation Study'. *European Journal of Special Needs Education*, 28(4), 463–479.

Webster, R. and Blatchford, P. (2014) 'Worlds Apart? The Nature and Quality of the Educational Experiences of Pupils with a Statement for Special Educational Needs in Mainstream Primary Schools. *British Educational Research Journal*. doi:10.1002/berj.3144.

Chapter 2

Listening to learners

Whose voice counts?

Gill Richards

Introduction

Seeking children and young people's views on issues that affect them is central to the Children and Families Act 2014. This builds on the original UN Convention on the Rights of the Child (1989 Article 12) and UK initiatives such as Every Child Matters: Change for Children (2003). Taking this approach means that schools are increasingly listening to learners to discover how their pupils experience what is provided for them. This information is particularly important when it is gained from the most vulnerable children and young people, as it can then provide the basis for further developments that more accurately meet their needs and remove barriers to learning and participation (NASEN 2014). Collecting feedback from a full range of learners is an important way for education settings to demonstrate a commitment to inclusion. Being prepared to do whatever it takes to discover the views of even the most 'hard to reach' learners indicates the value that they place on each individual.

So why is this important for Teaching Assistants? First, because providing opportunities for learners to express their views and supporting feedback processes is often an important part of a Teaching Assistant's role. Second, to do this effectively requires a range of communication skills to both draw out information and ensure that what is recorded reflects accurately what the learner was trying to say. Understanding some of the tensions that exist about expression of learner voice can help Teaching Assistants use their skills more effectively, and so this chapter will explore some of the complex issues involved, drawing out implications for practice.

Listening to learners' views

> No adult can really know what it is like to be a child, a teenager or a young adult today – we do not need to make assumptions, we only need to ask.
>
> (Tashie, Shapiro and Rossetti 2006: 129)

Many education settings have well-established systems for collecting learners' views on their services. These typically include school councils, class representatives, questionnaires, focus groups, evaluation of curriculum content and involvement with staff selection procedures. In some settings these work effectively for all learners, but in others they are seen as a management tool that only seeks feedback on issues important to staff rather than identifying learners' own priorities – what Johnstone (2005) calls 'damage limitation' issues. Cullingford (2005: 210) suggests that, "we have not yet learned to listen to their voices, let alone hear them. Perhaps we do not like the implications of what they are trying to say". This is an important point for schools to consider: *how* do they listen and *what* do they do with the information they collect?

Pupil perspectives can help teachers and others understand any gaps between provision as it is intended and how it is actually experienced. Whose views are sought can affect this understanding, because as Rudduck, Chaplain and Wallace (1996) originally argued, there is a need for *all* voices to be heard, not just those who are more articulate and socially confident. Atkinson (2013) supports this view, describing the importance of engaging 'vulnerable' or 'disadvantaged' young people, even if this makes for uncomfortable listening, for it is only by doing this that schools can respond in ways that meet real rather than perceived needs:

> Research informs us we perform least well with children who have the harshest messages to give us – those with disabilities and special needs, those abused, neglected, with health difficulties, youth justice, those in poverty or isolated. They are a minority but their views matter.
>
> (Atkinson, Newman Lecture 2013)

Morrow (2006) also stresses the importance of needing to understand the 'rules of the game' within education settings; if young people do not grasp the wider picture of what is going on in schools, they will not know what is possible, what they can reasonably expect or any 'hidden school agendas'.

These points are key to helping us all listen effectively to learners about their experiences. If a learner's 'voice' is viewed as tokenistic and just 'lip service' because it does not result in action, feedback may be seen as a mechanistic chore that nobody takes seriously (Osler 2010). Similarly, feedback that is seen to just produce reams of statistical information and not result in changes is likely to affect learners' motivation to contribute and, worse still, further reinforce their feelings of disempowerment.

The way that learners' views are collected can also affect the responses they give. If questions focus on how satisfied they are about something provided, but this is done in a situation that does not offer anonymity or even confidentiality, learners are likely to only risk giving positive answers and so what they say may be of limited value for improving that service. Kaplin, Lewis and Mumba (2007: 23) describe such a situation in their study, where pupils said that they were worried that "if we say what we really think, we might get done for it". Concerns also occur when schools appear to enter into consultation while really they are still remaining firmly in control of the agenda. This results in tokenism, just as in other situations where staff 'interpret' views of learners who have difficulty in giving feedback, just to make sure they comply with policy directives, or where feedback does not receive any official response (Richards 2012).

Even where feedback mechanisms are generally effective for listening and responding to learners' voices, some individuals or groups may experience difficulties in making their views known and influence change. Traditionally, disabled learners are one such group, as they are often seen as needing to receive professional advice rather than be experts about their own lives (Mason 2005; Gwynn 2004). This perception may be further reinforced when communication is problematic, for example when specialized communication aids are used, where learners do not yet have the skills of advocacy or where a particular impairment impedes communication skills. Compounding these difficulties can be inaccessible feedback procedures such as forms individuals find impossible to physically complete independently, or are not understood. In a similar way, learner forums may be intimidating for those who are inexperienced in voicing their opinions, particularly in front of peers or staff, and this may prevent critical comment.

There is also growing awareness of wider groups of young people, identified in school as 'vulnerable' or disadvantaged, whose voices need to be heard. These young people, often referred to in the contexts of 'closing the [achievement] gap' (Ofsted 2007) or requiring Pupil Premium support, are recognized as often experiencing complex or multiple barriers to learning (Sheehan, Rhoades and Stanley 2012): enabling them to talk about their experiences will help schools to seek personalized solutions, rather than targeting them for 'one-size-fits-all' interventions (Ontario 2009). However, we need to be wary of focusing attention only on those young people with such labels and overlooking others equally vulnerable, but without a 'label', whose experiences may then be missed (Messiou 2012). Labelling can also make the focus on an individual, rather than considering the impact of wider contextual school-based issues on creating barriers and disadvantage.

Placing all learners at the heart of education services so that they can help shape their communities can provide education settings with a route towards increasingly inclusive practice (Alliance for Inclusive Education 2014). By engaging with 'hard-to-reach' learners routinely, schools and colleges may use feedback in a more sustained way, fulfilling *actual* rather than *perceived* needs (Gwynn 2004) and challenging inequalities in education (Hatcher 2012). Including the 'hardest-to-reach' learners will require all education settings to review their procedures for collecting young people's perspectives and consider how responses to these are actioned. It may be that some learners need to learn self-advocacy skills first, or appropriate school language for discussing their views. Teachers and Teaching Assistants need to recognize that some learners find it difficult to express opinions that criticize their setting because they have learned to regard themselves as powerless. Other learners may not trust staff to treat their views positively and feel generally disconnected from consultation processes. They may also be accustomed to lowering their expectations, being satisfied with provision, whatever its shortcomings, and afraid of jeopardizing what they do have through criticism (Quaglia and Corso 2014; Anderson *et al.* 2003).

Identifying the reasons why learners are unable (or unwilling) to make their views and experiences known may prove to be a complex process that requires significant skills, patience and tenacity. Having discovered these, designing more inclusive ways to listen and respond to these learners' voices may in time impact significantly on the wider day-to-day practice in many settings. Less traditional successful methods of collecting views have included analysis of children's social drawings; photos of 'children's worlds'; use of 'priority cards' such as 'Really want it', 'Want it', 'Don't want it', 'Not bothered'; 'Diary Rooms'; 'Graffiti Walls'; mobile phone texting; 'Talking Tables'; and photographs taken by learners about where they feel safe and unsafe, and where they learn best in school (Miles and Ainscow 2011; Richards, Anderson and Drury 2007). What appeared to work best in these studies was offering a *range* of methods each time to collect the information required so that all individuals have an opportunity to contribute in the way that suited them best. This of course took time and so schools have to be prepared to give this if they genuinely want to listen to what young people have to say. Otherwise, there is a danger that staff revert back to systems that target confident and articulate learners as an easy way to meet set feedback goals and in doing so, exclude learners whose experiences might be key to creating a more inclusive setting.

Conflicts about 'voice'

Returning to Cullingford's (2005) suggestion that maybe schools are not ready to hear what learners have to say, and Atkinson's (2013) point about 'harsh messages', it may be helpful for all school staff to consider how capable they feel to deal with responses made by empowered young people. For example, if learners are enabled to express views that are not restricted to issues set by staff, schools may have to cope with completely unexpected criticisms or requests. This can involve uncomfortable decision making and possible conflicts between different groups or between individuals and groups that will need resolving. It takes a very confident staff group to be both open to such feedback and to withstand pressure to automatically respond positively to suggestions, even when this is inappropriate.

Learners' views may challenge those commonly held by professionals. This can be seen increasingly in debates, for example, about disabled learners' inclusion in mainstream settings. Deciding on the success or otherwise of such placements and reviewing special education policy have traditionally been the territory of 'professionals'. Engaging with disabled learners about these matters could result in powerful changes as their fresh perspectives challenge organizations. This is not to suggest that disabled people's views are not currently available, but that they may sometimes be taken less seriously if they conflict with the views of more powerful education advocates. Similarly, further tensions can occur when professionals deal mainly with parents and prioritize their views over those of the young person. This theme is addressed in the government guidance provided for parents and carers about the Children and Families Act (2014), where it advocates increased self-advocacy for young people as they get older (DfE 2014).

A clear example of this conflict can be seen in debates about inclusive education and 'closing the [achievement] gap' (Ofsted 2007). While government documentation often states support for inclusion for most learners, it also emphasizes that the quality of the experience is more important than the location (Ofsted 2006), supporting the belief that there are still some learners for whom special or separate school provision is the only viable option, i.e. those identified in the Children and Families Act 2014 to have 'severe and complex needs' or behaviour that is viewed as too challenging for mainstream schools to deal with. In contrast, people who have been past recipients of such 'specialized' provision have found a 'voice' through organizations such as The Alliance for Inclusive Education. They have argued that it is essential for all learners to be educated together and that it is the very presence of specialized settings that prevent mainstream schools from developing the resources to fully support all pupils. For them, it is the learners seen as the most challenging who need inclusion the most. These conflicting views raise serious issues for us all about whose voice receives the greatest audience and for what reason? How are 'user' voices sought and responded to at a national level? Teachers and Teaching Assistants may have easier access to 'establishment' views by the very nature of their work, so how can they discover wider perspectives to inform decision making?

School staff are at the front line of inclusion initiatives, but often their training concentrates on meeting skills criteria rather than critically examining the multiple factors involved in classroom practice that create, or exacerbate, barriers to participation. The focus of many training courses is usually directed at legislation, professional responsibilities and practical strategies for teaching and learning. This leads us to further key questions about learner voice. If teachers and Teaching Assistants are to be prepared to listen effectively to learners at risk of exclusion from school process, when should they learn the necessary skills and how can these be incorporated into their training? What about the tutors on these programmes? They may have limited experience themselves of fully inclusive practice and limited access to the views of disadvantaged groups to share with students. Whose 'voices' do student teachers and Teaching Assistants hear on their courses, whose research do they learn about and how does this affect their views on inclusion? If they only hear the viewpoints of professionals rather than the 'recipients' of education services, how might this affect their perception of what is successful practice (Richards 2012)?

The issue of power is critical as we reflect on how and why we listen to learners' voices. A truly inclusive setting values all of its members' perspectives without placing these within a hierarchy where some are seen to be more valid or important than others. Possibly the key question for Teaching Assistants to ask themselves is: What voice do *I* have? Even skilled individuals may be unable to provide support for learners to be heard if the setting in which they work does not encourage them to give their own opinions or value their contributions. Teaching Assistants and learners may become united by a common experience of lack of power to influence change, but this situation can be frustrating for all involved.

The operation of power within settings can impact on the success of strategies used to gain all learners' views. While it might seem to be a simple training need for staff to learn specific communication skills such as British Sign Language or basic advocacy skills, wider considerations are required to change processes that have been established by particular values and attitudes. These might include reflecting on:

- Who selects someone to be an advocate? Is this genuinely the choice of the learner and how can we be sure that it is the learner's voice that is being presented by the advocate?
- Who selects which voices to hear? Do all learners have an opportunity to present their views or only a carefully selected few?
- What information is sought? Who decides? Do adult agendas override those of children and young people?
- Who controls the conversations? What language is used? Is it accessible to everyone?
- Can learners with communication difficulties express perspectives that are 'unfiltered' by staff?
- Are opportunities for giving perspectives unthreatening?
- Who listens to learners' views and who responds?
- How are conflicts of perspectives resolved?
- Do individuals have the right to refuse to give their views?

These questions focus on the core differences between 'consultation' and empowered 'learner voice'. Where learners are able to select who advocates for them and share control of the feedback agenda with staff, the process becomes more meaningful and inclusive. Being able to give opinions in non-threatening situations and knowing that what is said will be treated respectfully and responded to will encourage contributions from a broader range of learners. Of equal importance, although this may seem to be at odds with working inclusively, are individual learners' rights to refuse to be involved. It is easy to see why having the opportunity to voice an opinion is seen to be a 'good thing', but respect for 'voice' must also allow for those who choose not to be involved. Of course there may be many reasons for making such a decision and these may need resolving in the longer term, but if we believe that inclusion means valuing people for themselves rather than trying to fit everyone into set practices, even this can be a valuable starting point for change.

Conclusion

The themes explored in this chapter have attempted to show that the concept of 'learner voice' is complex. If schools and colleges really want to engage with all their learners, they need to understand the deeper issues involved and respond accordingly. A truly inclusive process is not easy and needs careful planning, adequate time allocated and a range of staff skills to make the process successful. It may even challenge traditional power relationships within the setting. Teaching Assistants have a key role to play in this process. They often have a unique relationship with the children and young people with whom they work and so are able to support learners' advocacy. Teaching Assistants do however need to consider their own position in this process. They may, for example, be too involved with a learner to be a 'detached' facilitator in feedback situations and so need to pass this role on to a colleague. In another situation they might find themselves coerced into making sure that people they support complete a particular feedback form even if they do not understand it. Such situations can create very real difficulties for Teaching Assistants, but if they are able to remain focused on the learner rather than processes, this can demonstrate a clear commitment to making everybody's voice count.

Reflections on values and practice

If you are going to support learners to have a voice about matters that are important to them, you will need to reflect honestly about your own role and skills in this process.

1   When you think about the methods that your setting use to gain the views of its whole community, are these successful or do some people get the message that they are not valued?
2   How confident are you in expressing your own views and do you feel that these are valued?
3   When working with learners, how well are you able to support them in saying what they *really* think? Are you tempted to 'interpret' what they say? Are you able to separate your own views from those of the learners and when necessary represent views that conflict with your own?
4   If someone external to your setting (for example an Ofsted inspector or Pupil Premium reviewer) asked your learners about their experiences, would these match what the school has said?
5   Are you committed to making every voice count?

Suggested further reading

Cole, M. (2012) *Education, Equality and Human Rights*, Abingdon, UK: Routledge.
Mason, M. (2005) *Incurably Human*, Nottingham, UK: Inclusive Solutions.
Miles, S. and Ainscow, M. (2011) *Responding to Diversity in Schools*, Abingdon, UK: Routledge.

References

Alliance for Inclusive Education. (2014) *The Case for Inclusive Education*, London: Alliance for Inclusive Education.
Anderson V., Faraday, S., Prowse, S. Richards, G. and Swindells. D. (2003) *Count Me in FE*, London: Learning and Skills Development Agency.
Atkinson, M. (2013) *Silent Voices*, Lecture, Newman College, 25 April 2013.
Cullingford, C. (2005) 'Lessons from Learners about Inclusive Curriculum and Pedagogy' in Nind, M., Rix, J., Sheehy, K. and Simmons, K. (eds), *Curriculum and Pedagogy in Inclusive Education* (pp. 201–210), London: Routledge.

DfE. (2014) *Special Educational Needs and Disability: A Guide for Parents and Carers*, London: Author.

Gwynn, J. (2004) 'What About Me? I Live Here Too!' in Armstrong, F. and Moore, M. (eds), *Action Research for Inclusive Education. Changing Places, Changing Practices, Changing Minds*, London: RoutledgeFalmer.

Hatcher, R. (2012) 'Social Class and Schooling', in Cole, M. *Education, Equality and Human Rights*, Abingdon: Routledge.

Johnstone, J. (2005) 'Pupil Voice and Research: A Narrative Review'. *Annual Review of Education, Communication and Language Sciences,* E-Journal, Vol 2.

Kaplin, I., Lewis, I. and Mumba, P. (2007) 'Picturing Global Educational Inclusion? Looking and Thinking Across Students' Photographs from the UK, Zambia and Indonesia', *Journal of Research in Special Educational Needs*, 7(1): 23–35.

Mason, M. (2005) *Incurably Human*, Nottingham: Inclusive Solutions.

Messiou, K. (2012) *Confronting Marginalisation in Education: A Framework for Promoting Inclusion*, London: Routledge.

Miles, S. and Ainscow, M. (2011) *Responding to Diversity in Schools*, Abingdon, UK: Routledge.

Morrow, V. (2006) 'We get played for fools. Some promises and pitfalls of community and institutional participation for children and young people'. Keynote speech, *Pupil Voice and Participation: Pleasures, Promises and Pitfalls*, National Research Conference, Nottingham University.

NASEN. (2014) *Everybody Included. The SEND Code of Practice Explained*, Tamworth: NASEN.

Ofsted. (2006) *Inclusion: Does it Matter Where Pupils Are Taught?*, London: Crown Copyright.

Ofsted. (2007) *Narrowing the Gap: The Inspection of Children's Services*, London: Author.

Ontario. (2009) *Ontario's Equity and Inclusive Education Strategy: Realising the Promise of Diversity*, Ontario: Ministry of Education.

Osler, A. (2010) *Students' Perspectives on Schooling*, Maidenhead: Open University Press.

Quaglia, R. and Corso, M. (2014) *Student Voice: The Instrument of Change*, London; Sage.

Richards, G., Anderson, V. and Drury, P. (2007) *Responding to Learners' Views*, London: Learning and Skills Network.

Richards, G. (2012) 'Perspectives on Special Educational Needs and Inclusive Practice: Whose Views Count?' in Cornwall, J. and Graham-Matheson, L. (eds), *Leading on Inclusion: Dilemmas, Debates and New Perspectives*, Abingdon: Routledge.

Rudduck, J., Chaplain, R. and Wallace, G. (1996) *School Improvement: What Can Pupils Tell Us?*, London: David Fulton.

Sheehan, R., Rhoades, H. and Stanley, N. (2012) *Vulnerable Children and the Law*, London: Jessica Kingsley Publishers.

Tashie, C., Shapiro, S. and Rossetti, Z. (2006) *Seeing the Charade: What We Need to Do and Undo to Make Friendships Happen*, Nottingham: Inclusive Solutions.

Chapter 3

Gypsy, Roma and Traveller pupils

Underachievement and building relationships for inclusion

Chris Derrington

Introduction

Supporting Gypsy, Roma and Traveller (GRT) children in schools can be one of the most interesting and rewarding roles that Teaching Assistants can undertake. As a group, children and young people from GRT communities have historically had the lowest attainment and engagement of all in our education system (Ofsted 1999: 7) although we know that they are capable of achieving just as well as any other child (DCSF 2008a). This pattern of underachievement is improving slowly but there is still much work to be done in order to improve the inclusion of these pupils in our schools. The Teaching Assistant can play a crucial part in building trust, promoting social inclusion and supporting their academic progress. This chapter aims to provide insight into some of the cultural considerations and draws upon a body of research to suggest ways of effectively supporting the particular needs of this diverse group of children and young people and improving their educational outcomes.

Who are Gypsies, Roma and Travellers?

It might surprise you to know that the vast majority of Gypsy, Roma and Traveller families these days live permanently on authorised sites or in houses. Some people assume, wrongly, that you can't be a Traveller if you live in a house. This poses an interesting question. If most Gypsy, Roma and Traveller children live in houses or on a permanent Traveller site (as opposed to travelling from place to place) then why should they, as a group, have the lowest educational outcomes at all Key Stages (DfE 2013, 2014a, 2014b, 2014c)? Let's look first at the different communities we are considering here.

The term 'GRT' embraces a diverse collection of communities, each with different social histories and different identities. Although there are some shared cultural characteristics, the main distinction is that some, but not all, are recognised in law as constituting a minority ethnic group. In considering whether a community is an ethnic group (as opposed to a social group), a number of criteria must be met. Two essential characteristics are:

- ancestry and a long shared history of which the group is conscious as distinguishing it from other groups and the memory of which it keeps alive; and
- a distinct cultural tradition including social customs and manners, often but not necessarily associated with religious observance.

The first three groups described below are recognised in law as having a distinct ethnicity.

Romany Gypsies

The largest group of Travellers in the UK is often referred to as 'Romany Gypsy' or 'Gypsy Traveller' although the term 'Roma' (see below) is also being increasingly adopted. It is only right that people have the freedom to describe their ethnicity in whatever way they wish and it's important that we take the lead from the parents and pupils themselves, rather than make assumptions about 'correct' terminology.

Regardless of the preferred term, this community is believed to have descended from Northwest India about a thousand years ago and began to arrive in the UK in the fifteenth century. From their appearance, it was assumed that they were pilgrims from Egypt and so were called Egyptians (from which the word 'Gypsy' is derived). Linguistic evidence however, supports the theory of their Indian origins and, although it is not widely known, Romany Gypsies have retained elements of a language known as Romanes or Romani which has its roots in ancient Sanskrit (the language used in northern India around the ninth century). A hybrid version of this language is commonly spoken by Romany families today and a number of words have been incorporated into common English usage (e.g. cushti, bloke, pal, gaff).

Many Romany Gypsies live in houses these days; others might live in trailers (caravans) or mobile homes. Wherever they live, they are Romany Gypsies by birthright and are therefore recognised in law as being a legitimate ethnic group, protected by the Equality Act 2010.

European Roma

This diverse sub-group, believed to number around ten million globally, also constitutes a minority ethnic group in the UK. The largest numbers continue to live in Eastern Europe, particularly in Romania, Bulgaria and Hungary. However, since the incorporation of countries from Eastern Europe into the European Union (EU) in 2004, more Romanian, Czech and Slovak Roma families have settled in the UK. Each Roma group has its own national identity and language and families will often identify themselves first in national terms and then as Roma, for example 'Czech Roma'. Others hide the fact that they are Roma due to the fear of hate crime and persecution.

Travellers of Irish heritage

As the name suggests, these Travellers are indigenous to Ireland and are believed to be descendants of travelling entertainers, itinerant craftsmen and metal workers. The derogatory term 'tinker' refers to the traditional occupational status of tinsmith. Although their historical and linguistic roots are different, their customs and traditions have similarities with those of Romany Gypsies.

It is important to understand that all the groups described above are legitimate minority ethnic communities and are therefore protected by the Equality Act 2010. Unfortunately, many Traveller parents and children choose not to disclose their identity for fear of bullying and prejudice. This impacts significantly on the accuracy of statistical data available and led to government guidance for schools to encourage wider practice in self-ascription (DCSF 2008a).

Pupils from Fairground or Circus (Showmen) communities, 'New Travellers' or those dwelling on the waterways, are recognised as Occupational Travellers or social groups as opposed to minority ethnic groups. However, it is important to mention these other Traveller groups in this chapter as they experience many of the same educational challenges.

Fairground Showmen

Fairground communities have a distinctive culture and lifestyle that stretches back many centuries. Today, Fairground Showmen families tend to own or rent land which serves as their base during the winter months, but spend the majority of the year following a circuit of meticulously planned events both in the UK and, increasingly, on the continent. Children from these communities tend to be enrolled at a 'base' school near their winter quarters and in many cases, remain in contact and engage in distance learning programmes during periods of travelling.

Circus communities

Like Fairground Showmen, Circus communities may describe themselves as Occupational Travellers, although some performers may also be Gypsies. Circus groups are usually diverse, typically comprising a troupe of international performers, some of whom will have children. The frequency of movement between venues can make access to school difficult for them and, although some benefit from distance learning programmes organised by their base school, other circuses employ tutors who travel and live as part of the community.

New Travellers

New Travellers (commonly referred to in the past as 'New Age Travellers') are, by definition, a more recent cultural phenomenon. Groups of younger people (known as 'hippies') opted for a nomadic lifestyle during the 1960s, but the phenomenon grew during the 1970s and 1980s with the emergence of the free festival movement as more young people bought large vehicles to transport themselves and their possessions between the summer festivals. In the late 1980s, cut-backs in social security and housing benefits made by the Thatcher government had a particular impact on young people between the ages of 16 and 25, leading to a surge in youth homelessness and young economic refugees taking to the road and an alternative travelling lifestyle (Martin 1998).

Key issues for Teaching Assistants

Having looked briefly at the various Traveller communities in the UK, let's now consider the key implications for Teaching Assistants. As mentioned previously, the underachievement of GRT pupils was attributed historically to their nomadic lifestyle, but this no longer carries weight. It has been estimated that there are over 300,000 Gypsies and Travellers in the UK; the majority are settled and as many as two thirds now live in conventional housing (Clark and Greenfields 2006). Even where pupils have relatively stable school experiences, their achievement rates are still significantly lower than those of their peers (DCSF 2009). So, how can this be accounted for?

Poor or non-attendance by Gypsy, Roma and Traveller pupils continues to be flagged up by Ofsted as significant, particularly during the secondary phase (Ofsted 2014) and, not surprisingly, this has been linked to a lack of progress in academic attainment (Reynolds, McCarten and Knipe 2003). Cultural and community influences are frequently cited in the staff room in order to explain the issue of poor attendance and lack of engagement in the education system (Thomson 2013). Such influences might be related to customs (such as attendance at traditional horse fairs) or social norms (family matters taking precedence over school). Cultural influences can also be related to core values and belief systems. For example, culturally perceived markers of infancy, childhood and adulthood within the Traveller community could mean that a five-year-old child is considered too young to leave the home and be left in the care of strangers. Similarly, a 13-year-old may be perceived by his/her community as 'too old' for formal education when they could conceivably be more productively engaged in family-based learning or economic activity.

However, it has been suggested by Wilkin *et al.* (2009) that lower attainment and engagement of this group is not as simple as that, and is more likely due to a complex web of interrelated factors. Their TARGET model (Wilkin *et al.*: 81) identified six constructive conditions that (provided they are balanced) seem to impact positively on educational outcomes for GRT pupils. They are:

- Safety and trust
- Respect
- Access and inclusion
- Partnership
- High expectations
- Flexibility

Let's take a closer look at the first three constructive conditions and consider them in terms of the Teacher Assistant (TA) role.

Safety is the top priority

Have a look at these statements. Do any of them sound familiar?

> *Our (Traveller) girls don't go to high school.*
> *She's only a baby. I'll send her (to school) when she's bigger.*
> *He won't be going to big school because he'll only get bullied (like I did when I was his age).*
> *My dad doesn't want me go on trips because coaches aren't safe.*
> *If anyone calls me names, my dad says 'hit them'.*
> *We don't like them (girls) mixing with boys as they get older.*
> *We don't use secondary schools because of all the drugs and smoking.*

It is important to appreciate that Traveller parents tend to be very child centred and highly protective, and it may take time and effort for a trusting relationship to develop between home and school. We should remember too that Gypsies, Roma and Travellers have endured a long history of persecution and rejection by the settled community and consequently many parents express anxiety about the welfare of their children in school (Derrington and Kendall 2004; Bowers 2004; Padfield 2005; Wilkin *et al.* 2009; D'Arcy 2014). Wilkin *et al.* (2009) concluded that for many GRT parents, this deep-seated anxiety and concern for the moral, physical and emotional safety of their children often dominates their thoughts and decisions about education and schooling. Although these voiced anxieties may sound familiar and therefore 'scripted', the feelings and emotions associated with them are no doubt authentic to the individual and it is sometimes hard for members of staff in schools to fully appreciate the extent of this mistrust without having a clear insight into the experiences that these families continue to face in wider society.

Gypsy, Roma and Traveller pupils probably endure more racist name calling than most educational professionals realise. Research studies repeatedly reveal this is to be a very common problem (Warrington 2006; Fremlova and Ureche 2011; Foster and Norton 2012). Derrington and Kendall (2004) found that around one in three GRT students dealt with racist name calling, not by reporting it to a member of staff, but by retaliating physically, often with the encouragement of their parents. Furthermore, when this occurred, teachers were inclined to believe that the GRT pupils themselves were the initiators of conflict as opposed to the victims of racist bullying (Wilkin *et al.* 2009; D'Arcy 2014). In her interviews with school staff, Thomson (2013) found that they tended to downplay the significance of reported name calling, perceiving it to be untrue, exaggerated or justified. Racially motivated teasing, name calling and nonverbal bullying can all go undetected until the point where the pupil being targeted takes matters into their own hands, especially if they feel too embarrassed or ashamed to report the perpetrators. As a Teaching Assistant, your ears may be 'closer to ground'. The TA role often means that you are better placed to see and hear subtle aspects of pupil behaviour in the classroom that might otherwise go unnoticed. How do you respond in those situations?

Respect

Respect is a two-way process. Schools expect pupils and their families to respect their rules and values whilst acknowledging and respecting individuals' identities and beliefs. Research suggests that GRT pupils and their parents are generally accepting of day-to-day rules (provided they are clear and simple) but are inclined to challenge imposed sanctions (e.g. detentions) that they perceive to be unfair (Derrington and Kendall 2004). Foster and Norton (2012) have observed that GRT parents are generally reluctant to come into school but if they do have concerns, these are not always communicated in the most calm and tactful way. Staff who have invested time and effort in developing good relationships with GRT parents cope better with face-to-face dialogue and generally feel more confident in explaining and justifying the school's use of sanctions and restoring trust.

Some schools have discovered that the recruitment or deployment of a member of the GRT community as a Teaching Assistant or Family Liaison Officer can be particularly effective in this regard, not only as a bilingual assistant, role model and reassuring presence but also as a mediator to whom GRT parents can relate. For example:

> When I first came, a boy in Year 6 said 'I'm not going to secondary school, we don't believe in it, but you're a Traveller so you know we don't believe in it'. I said, 'Well I send my children to secondary school'. He looked at me and said, 'Can I get my mum to come in and talk to you?' She came in, she felt comfortable because she knew I understood her. ... I told her that my kids were doing really well and were enjoying it. She agreed, and he went to school and has got his GCSEs.
>
> (Wilkin *et al.* 2009: 51)

The presence of TESS (Traveller Education Support Service) staff in schools can also be helpful as a go-between in resolving home-school disputes or impasses (Myers and Bhopal 2009). Elsewhere, mutually respectful relationships are more likely to be found in those schools where staff are perceived as having knowledge of, and respect for, Traveller culture (Parker-Jenkins and Hartas 2002; Ureche and Franks 2007; Bhopal 2011; Thomson 2013) and where GRT children are encouraged to be proud of their heritage. Schools that include cultural references and resources to engage GRT pupils and promote self-esteem will also enrich the curriculum for all pupils.

An awareness of others' values and beliefs can help us to gain a better understanding of and respect for them. For example, Traveller parents' anxiety about secondary school (in particular) is sometimes driven by the generalised belief that non-Traveller society is corrupt and lacking in moral standards. Widely publicised reports in the media of mainstream social problems related to drugs, alcohol and promiscuity are often cited by young Travellers and their parents in discussions about secondary education (Derrington 2007). This said, opposing concepts of safety and danger might be difficult for schools to understand. As mentioned previously, young Travellers are usually afforded a high level of protection by their families and it is not uncommon for them to be forbidden to go on residential trips, to parties or school discos for their own safety. However, paradoxically, once they reach middle childhood, Traveller children tend to assume 'adult' responsibilities such as taking care of domestic and childcare duties, gaining financial independence, using tools and learning to drive. Most Traveller children are therefore quite used to working and socialising alongside adults and tend to display a level of maturity that sets them apart from peers. They are often confident communicators and their conversational style with adults can be direct and can be perceived in school as rudeness and a lack of respect (MacNamara 2001). Imagine for example, a GRT pupil informing a teacher at your school (in a mildly scolding manner) that his coffee mug was a disgrace and offering to bleach it. What might be his instinctive interpretation of that?

Access and inclusion

A number of studies have concluded that many GRT children find themselves rejected or socially excluded by their classmates in school (Lloyd *et al.* 1999; Derrington and Kendall 2004; Thomson 2013). It follows that if children are unhappy in school, they may be disinclined to attend and thus limit further opportunities to establish and secure friendships. Eventually, social difficulties may lead pupils to behave in a manner that results in their exclusion or for their parents to opt for home education (D'Arcy 2014).

Interviews and focus group discussions with Gypsy, Roma and Traveller pupils have unearthed a level of social exclusion of which members of staff in 'inclusive' schools are apparently unaware. Whilst some pupils agreed that the other children in the school were friendly towards them or that they had a mixture of friends including non-Travellers, it was more common for them to say that 'other' pupils were unfriendly and that they were 'picked on'. The majority of pupils interviewed by Wilkin *et al.* (2009) maintained that their friends at school were other Travellers (including those in different year groups). The pupils also mentioned that they were not always allowed out by their parents after school to mix with non-Traveller peers or attend extracurricular activities and this limited the amount of social contact they had with their classmates. Derrington and Kendall (2004) discovered a clear link between GRT pupils' involvement in extracurricular activities and their attendance and retention in the school system. They suggested that getting involved in after-school clubs, sports teams and residential visits helped to secure a greater sense of belonging and connection (sometimes referred to as 'social capital') and those who did so were more likely to remain in school until statutory leaving age than GRT pupils who did not.

Teaching Assistants have a key role to play in supporting pupils' psychosocial development both within and beyond the classroom and often develop positive and trusting relationships with the pupils they support. Consequently, research evidence suggests that they can be highly influential in promoting social and emotional adjustment in social situations (Alborz *et al.* 2009). Think about your own school setting. Have you noticed that GRT pupils tend to 'stick together'? How is this type of behaviour generally interpreted by staff, parents and other pupils? Could there be other reasons for it? It is important to observe closely how children interact during lessons and during less structured time and be alert to subtle behaviours that might signal social exclusion. If you are tasked with teaching small groups or have a designated responsibility for developing emotional literacy and social skills (e.g. SEAL programmes) or nurture groups, there will be good opportunities for you to gain insight into the quality of peer relationships and assess the level of support required. In addition, sensitive one-to-one support can facilitate the discussion of feelings, coping strategies and the development skills on a step-by-step basis. Work on empathy with all pupils is also particularly important, and especially for those who perpetrate the problem and underestimate the unhappiness they might be causing. Younger children often respond well to a circle-time activity using a Traveller Persona Doll to explore issues of friendship and acceptance by the majority group. For older children and young people, a circle of friends approach and peer support initiatives such as mentoring or buddying schemes can also be productive.

Conclusion

Despite official guidance aimed at raising outcomes for Gypsy, Roma and Traveller pupils over the past fifteen years or so (Ofsted 1996, 1999, 2014; Bhopal *et al.* 2000; DfES 2003; DCSF 2008a, 2008b) the achievement of these groups remains unacceptably low. A major longitudinal research project, commissioned by the former Labour Government (Wilkin *et al.* 2009) explored the phenomenon in great depth and identified a number of recurring interwoven conditions that impact positively on educational outcomes for these groups of learners. These include the establishment of parental trust in the school as a perceived place of safety, evidence of mutual respect and a commitment to social inclusion. In a recent survey, over 95 per cent of school leaders said that Teaching Assistants add value to schools, in particular, as effective mediators and advocates working with vulnerable pupils and enhancing the learning environment with all pupils (Unison 2013). This chapter has suggested ways in which Teaching Assistants can use their position and repertoire of skills to support the conditions that have been shown to impact positively on GRT pupils' engagement and attainment.

Reflections on values and practice

1   It is important for everyone working with GRT children and their families to hear the message behind the 'scripts' like those described in this chapter.

We need to find ways of building trust and facilitating dialogue that challenges limiting 'scripts' and offers alternative perceptions. Constructive and gently challenging dialogue with an approachable adult can be helpful in reassuring parents and nurturing a trusting relationship. Could this adult be you?

2   It is equally important to be aware of the same scripts being replicated (and therefore perpetuated) within school by teachers and other staff. Have you ever caught yourself using parallel scripts such as 'Their parents don't really value education' or 'They won't transfer to secondary school anyway'? Research shows that aspirations within the GRT community *are* gradually changing, and parents are placing more and more value on the importance of education and formal qualifications (Bhopal *et al.* 2000; Thomson 2013). Do you listen out for positive 'scripts' and use them to re-frame or counter less helpful assumptions voiced by colleagues?

3   What other practical steps could you take to increase your own cultural awareness? Are you aware of the many websites and resources and events aimed at supporting the education of GRT pupils?

References

Alborz, A., Pearson, D., Farrell, P. and Howes, A. (2009). *The impact of adult support staff on pupils and mainstream schools.* London: Institute of Education University of London.

Bhopal, K. (2011). 'This is a school it's not a site: teacher's attitudes towards Gypsy Traveller pupils in England, UK'. *British Educational Research Journal, 37*(3), 365–483.

Bhopal, K. with Gundara, J., Jones, C. and Owen, C. (2000). *Working towards inclusive education for Gypsy Traveller pupils* (RR 238). London: Department for Education and Employment.

Bowers, J. (2004). *Prejudice and pride: the experience of young Travellers.* Ipswich: Ormiston Children & Families Trust.

Clark, C. and Greenfields, M. (eds.) (2006). *Here to stay: the Gypsies and Travellers of Britain.* Hatfield: University of Hertfordshire Press.

D'Arcy, K. (2014). 'Home education, school, Travellers and educational inclusion'. *British Journal of Sociology of Education, 35*(5), 818–835.

DCSF. (2008a). *The inclusion of Gypsy, Roma and Traveller children and young people.* London: Department for Children, Schools and Families.

DCSF. (2008b). *Raising the achievement of Gypsy, Roma and Traveller pupils.* London: Department for Children, Schools and Families.

DCSF. (2009). *Moving forward together: raising Gypsy, Roma and Traveller achievement. Booklet 1: Introduction.* London: Department for Children, Schools and Families.

DFE. (2013). *Phonics screening check and national curriculum assessments at key stage 1 in England 2012/13, (National Statistical First Release SFR 37/2013).* London: Department for Education.

DFE. (2014a). *Pupil absence in schools in England 2013/13, (National Statistical First Release SFR 09/2014),* London: Department for Education.

DFE. (2014b). *GCSE and equivalent attainment by pupil characteristics in England 2012/13, (National Statistical First Release SFR 05/2014).* London: Department for Education.

DFE. (2014c). *National curriculum assessments at key stage 2 in England 2014, (National Statistical First Release SFR 05/2014).* London: Department for Education.

DFES. (2003). *Aiming high: raising the achievement of Gypsy Traveller pupils: a guide to good practice.* London: Department for Education and Skills.

Derrington, C. (2007). 'Fight, flight and playing White: an examination of coping strategies adopted by Gypsy Traveller adolescents in English secondary schools'. *International Journal of Educational Research*, 46(6), 357–367.

Derrington, C. and Kendall, S. (2004). *Gypsy Traveller students in secondary schools: culture, identity and achievement*. Stoke-on-Trent: Trentham Books.

Foster, B. and Norton. P. (2012). 'Educational equality for Gypsy, Roma and Traveller children and young people in the UK'. *The Equal Rights Review*, 8, 85–112.

Fremlova, L. and Ureche, H. (2011). *From segregation to inclusion: Roma pupils in the UK. A Pilot Research Project*. Budapest, HU: Roma Education Fund. Retrieved from http://equality.uk.com/Education_files/From%20segregation%20to%20integration.pdf

Lloyd, G., Stead, J. and Jordan, E., with Norris, C. and Miller, M. (1999). *Travellers at school: the experience of parents, pupils and teachers*. Edinburgh: Moray House.

MacNamara, Y. (2001). 'Education on the move'. *ACE Bulletin,* 104 (December), 13.

Martin, G. (1998). 'Generational differences amongst New Age Travellers'. *Sociological Review,* 46(4), 735–756.

Myers, M. and Bhopal, K. (2009). 'Gypsy, Roma and Traveller children in schools: understandings of community and safety'. *British Journal of Educational Studies,* 57(4), 417–434.

Ofsted. (1996). *The education of Travelling children*. London: Office for Standards in Education.

Ofsted. (1999). *Raising the attainment of minority ethnic pupils: school and LEA responses*. London: Office for Standards in Education.

Ofsted. (2014). *Overcoming barriers: ensuring that Roma children are fully engaged and achieving in education*. London: Office for Standards in Education.

Padfield, P. (2005). 'Inclusive educational approaches for Gypsy/Traveller pupils and their families: an 'urgent need for progress?' *Scottish Educational Review*, 37(2), 127–144.

Parker-Jenkins, M. and Hartas, D. (2002). 'Social inclusion: the case of Travellers' children'. *Education 3-13, 30*(2), 39–42.

Reynolds, M., McCarten, D. and Knipe, D. (2003). 'Traveller culture and lifestyle as factors influencing children's integration into mainstream secondary schools in West Belfast'. *International Journal of Inclusive Education*, 7(4), 403–414.

Thomson, L. (2013). *The perceptions of teaching staff about their work with Gypsy, Roma, Traveller children and young people*. Unpublished PhD thesis. University of Birmingham, AL, USA.

Unison. (2013). *The evident value of teaching assistants*. Retrieved from www.unison.org.uk/content/uploads/2013/06/Briefings-and-CircularsEVIDENT-VALUE-OF-TEACHING-ASSISTANTS-Autosaved3.pdf

Ureche, H. and Franks, M. (2007). *This is who we are: a study of the views and identities of Roma, Gypsy and Traveller young people in England*. London. The Children's Society.

Warrington, C. (2006). *Children's voices: changing future – the views and experiences of young Gypsies and Travellers*. Ipswich: The Ormiston Children and Families Trust.

Wilkin, A., Derrington, C., Foster, B., White, R. and Martin, K. (2009). *Improving outcomes for Gypsy, Roma and Traveller pupils: what works? Contextual influences and constructive conditions*. London: Department for Children, Schools and Families.

Chapter 4

Not in my image

Ethnic diversity in the classroom

Raphael Richards

- In state-funded primary and secondary schools 29.5 per cent and 25.3 per cent of pupils respectively were classified as being of minority ethnic origin in the 2014 Schools Census.
- It is estimated that the percentage of teachers and Teaching Assistants from minority ethnic groups in the school workforce were 8.3 per cent and 12.5 per cent respectively in 2014.
- While Chinese, Indian, Irish and Mixed White and Asian pupils consistently performed above the national average for all pupils, Black, Pakistani, Bangladeshi and Mixed White and Black Caribbean pupils consistently performed below the national average for all pupils.
- Despite the above data, working class minority ethnic pupils are making better progress in secondary schools nationally than working class White British pupils.
- There are more than a million children between 5–16 years old in UK schools who are learning English as a second, third, or indeed, fourth language, in addition to the language spoken within their families and homes (NALDIC 2014).

Introduction

Imagine that throughout your years in primary school, none of the tall people interacting with you as teachers look like you. Now, imagine spending five to six hours each day in lessons doing Maths, English, Science or History without seeing or hearing positive things about adults who might reflect you. What subconscious pictures would this create for the child about the world of work and school?

On setting out to write this chapter, I asked several teachers, Teaching Assistants and parents what they would expect from an article about ethnic diversity. They said I should start by explaining what diversity and ethnicity are, why people needed to know this and how they would benefit from having the information. It was important to find out before starting, because in my experience it helps if you ask the people you are supporting, what they need. In asking the question I recognise that most of our services are about helping individuals and that people's experiences, although often similar, can be significantly different.

In schools across the country, the ethnic diversity of the classroom will vary widely depending on where you are in the country and in which city you live. In fact, the ethnic diversity of neighbouring schools can be very different. The level of single ethnic-group access and usage of educational, residential and social facilities can be stark in some communities. Analysis of the 2011 Census showed that minority groups were increasing fastest in areas where historically low numbers existed. While immigration accounted for significant levels of the increase, children born in the UK to migrant families make up most of the minority ethnic school population.

In 2006 the minority ethnic population in schools nationally stood at 18.5 per cent. In 2014 the minority ethnic population grew to 28.4 per cent. In contrast, the percentage of teachers of minority ethnic heritage grew from 7.8 per cent in 2005 to 8.3 per cent in 2014. The estimates of minority ethnic teaching assistant population vary from 10–15 per cent (Runnymede Trust 2006; DfE 2015b).

In this chapter I want to explore the varied characteristics that make up the diversity of minority ethnic children and young people likely to be in school classrooms. Much of our discussion will focus on hard facts such as data which inform us about our community and the impact of experiences in school. This I hope to achieve by highlighting some of the key issues around an ethnically diverse classroom, and then set out a sound background from which readers can expand their understanding of diversity and ethnicity.

What is 'diversity'?

The term 'diversity' has increased in usage since the mid 1990s and today, hardly a day will pass without us reading or hearing the term. However, the context within which we hear it changes regularly. You will hear on the news and elsewhere about diversity in relation to a company's workforce, about the mix of people served in a demographic area, about the pupil population in a school or the curriculum being taught and certainly about the languages in local communities.

The dictionary shows the word 'diversity' as having multiple meanings with the two most common being (a) *variety*: a variety of something such as opinion, colour or style; and (b) *social inclusiveness*: ethnic variety, as well as socioeconomic and gender variety, in a group, society or institution (Oxford University Press 2013). Our focus in this chapter is on ethnic diversity. Within the scope of ethnic diversity, there are factors that people generally cannot change about themselves, for example, ability/disability, age, ethnicity, gender, religious beliefs and sexual orientation. Recognising ethnic diversity does not detract from the reality that people are in many ways similar and that people often have more to unite than divide them.

Diversity encompasses human aspects such as culture, gender, heritage, religion, personality, thinking style, educational background, and the myriad of qualities, visible and invisible, that makes each of us different. People are diverse in other ways: we live in different places and are shaped by our environments; we have different kinds of heritage that may be multiple for an individual; and experience different cultural influences. We speak many different languages and have a variety of ethnic backgrounds and religious beliefs. That said, many believe the level of similarities between individuals, groups and communities are far greater than any differences (Rowley and Moore 2002; Ford and Heath 2013).

What is 'ethnicity'?

'Ethnicity' is measured in the UK Census and other official data sets by asking individuals to self-identify by selecting from categories that may include nationality (Chinese, Indian, Irish), broader geographic or ancestral categories (African, Asian, Arab), colour (White, Black), and combinations of these (White Irish, White British), including explicitly 'mixed' categories such as 'White and Black Caribbean' (Afkhami and Acik-Toprak 2012).

Britain has a rich mix of cultures and communities. Some of these reflect longstanding history and heritage, while others reflect more recent and ongoing social changes and new ways of life. Ethnicity is therefore, a rich balance of heritage, ancestry, religion, culture, nationality, language, region, etc. The UK Race Relations Act 1976 defined a 'racial group' as 'a group of persons defined by reference to colour, race, nationality or ethnic or national origins'. Thus the terms 'race' and 'ethnicity' are commonly interchanged. 'Ethnicity' and 'ethnic group' became more formally defined in UK law after the *Mandla v Dowell Lee* decision (House of Lords 1983) as relating to those with a long shared history and distinct culture. It also identified other relevant characteristics as including a common geographic origin or descent from a small number of common ancestors, a common language, a common literature, a common religion and being a minority within a larger community (House of Lords 1983). The ethnic groups identified by the Office of National Statistics (ONS) in the decennial UK Census are usually adopted. Comparing the categories in the 1991 Census with those of 2001, there are some significant differences, for example 'Mixed' was added to identify people having two or more ethnic origins. While the 2001 Census used the term 'Ethnic Group', it also makes it clear that this is seen as a matter of 'cultural background'. Ten years later, two new tick boxes were added in the 2011 Census: Gypsy or Irish Traveller, and Arab (ONS 2012). In recent years, attempts have been made to acknowledge that ethnicity is a characteristic of all individuals and groups, majorities and minorities alike. It is important to recognise that definitions that are 'social constructs', such as Black community, refugees or asylum seekers, can change.

The term 'minority ethnic' is mainly used to describe people who are in the minority within a defined population on the grounds of 'race', colour, culture, language or nationality. In the past, those referred to as 'ethnic minorities' were mainly identified as those groups of people who have come from the 'New Commonwealth' to live in the country since the 1950s: that is, visible minorities (people of colour). The term was less associated with the many 'ethnic minorities' from Old Commonwealth countries and Europe who settled in Britain before and since the 1950s. Currently the term 'minority ethnic' is used increasingly to refer to all who have arrived to live and/or work in Britain, including, for example, migrant workers from new European member states.

Ethnic diversity in Britain

Little is known about the first people who inhabited Britain, except that they came from somewhere else. According to historians (Nicolson 1974; Merriman 1993) early stone, bronze and ceramic findings suggest that the culture of migrants to this land shared common features with people from as far away as the Mediterranean. In the first century AD, Celtic Britain south of Hadrian's Wall became part of the vast Roman Empire which extended deep into the Middle East and North Africa. The Romans ruled Britain for 400 years, building cities, roads and ports throughout the island. Land and sea trades linking Britain to the Mediterranean were well established in this period. The demise of the Roman Empire saw many large-scale invasions from what are now our European partner countries, including Germany, Denmark and the Netherlands. They all left cultural footprints on what is Britain today (Ferguson 2003).

The British Empire, by the end of the nineteenth century, covered large parts of the globe and had 'subjects' in far-flung places (Adams 1987, Ferguson 2003). Following the end of slavery the Empire's success was sustained by over two million Indian and Chinese indentured labourers working on plantations, mines, docks, ships and railways in Commonwealth countries (Claire 1996). Their labour was crucial to the prosperity and industrial expansion Britain achieved during the nineteenth century. As British subjects, people from the Empire were expected to fight in all of Britain's wars, including in wars of colonial expansion (Fryer 1984).

Faced with the massive task of reconstruction after the Second World War, and acute labour shortages, the British Government encouraged immigration, first from amongst European refugees displaced by the war, then from Ireland and the Commonwealth countries. Before long, in some factories, mills and plants, the overwhelming majority of workers were Asian or Black. By the end of the 1970s, strict controls on immigration had been introduced and only relatives (sons, daughters and spouses) were allowed into Britain. Most immigrants to Britain today come from other parts of Europe or arrive as asylum seekers or refugees. Immigrants have often met hostility and resentment, yet even a quick study would show that they have brought skills and qualifications, set up businesses and created jobs, not only for themselves but also for local people. Many have been willing to do jobs that have been difficult to fill locally.

The ethnic diversity of local areas and nationally is always changing and is captured every ten years by the National Census. The 2011 Census showed that the White British population has stayed the same since 2001, while the non-White British population has grown over the ten years. The rise experienced in the 'Other

White' population was not simply due to Eastern Europeans moving to the UK, but also people from the old Commonwealth – countries like Australia and New Zealand. The mixed-race population has neared a million for the first time – remaining one of the fastest growing groups with an increase of nearly 50 per cent between 2001 and 2009. One third of this group is mixed Afro-Caribbean and White, followed by Asian/White (ONS 2011).

When considering the diversity of your classroom it is important to remember that this is a very small part of the over eight million school-age pupils' education that is happening in England. With that in mind, we can focus on the individual pupils who make up the school's community and reflect the local area. Every family is different; getting to know all of the families in your class means there is less chance of assumptions being made about backgrounds, cultures, faiths or practices. Asking families about their lives and culture is the best way to get to know them and what is important to them (Alborz *et al.* 2009)

Pupils' ethnicity in schools

Some 28 per cent of pupils in state primary and secondary schools are of minority ethnic heritage, according to figures collected in January 2014 using the Pupil Level Annual School Census (PLASC) – more commonly known as the School Census – published yearly by the Department for Education (DfE 2015a). This showed that in primary schools, 29.5 per cent of pupils were from an ethnic minority, compared with secondary schools which had 25.3 per cent of pupils classified as being of minority ethnic heritage.

Being born in Britain makes you British by nationality, but your ethnicity may be stated differently, such as Bangladeshi, Black Caribbean, Pakistani or White Other (DfES 2006; DfE 2013). The Schools Census captures information about children provided by their parents. This is collected when a child starts in new school and his or her parents or legal carers fill out a form declaring the child's ethnicity, first language and other information.

The 2014 Schools Census classification of 29.5 per cent (primary) and 25.3 per cent (secondary) pupils as being of minority ethnic heritage can be compared directly with the 2006 Schools Census data that showed 21 per cent (primary) and 17 per cent (secondary) of schools' population were from minority ethnic groups (DfES 2006). This indicates a sustained rise in minority ethnic population, due in part to a decreasing White pupil population and an increase in Asian, Black African and Mixed heritage pupils. In many cities the minority ethnic school population is greater than 30 per cent (for example London, Birmingham, Leeds and Manchester). In other areas such as Cumbria, Norwich and Plymouth the minority ethnic school population is less than 6 per cent. Schools with less than 5 per cent minority ethnic population are deemed 'predominantly White'. Within many schools there are what is termed 'isolated minority ethnic pupils', where teachers often have little or no experience of working with minority ethnic pupils. Regardless of the setting, the support needs of minority ethnic pupils must be met (Knowles and Ridley 2006; Arnot *et al.* 2014) and as at some point in their careers, the majority of teachers and Teaching Assistants (TAs) across Britain are likely to work with minority ethnic pupils, they should be prepared for this.

Minority ethnic attainment characteristics

The growth in the numbers of TAs has reportedly been driven by the push for greater inclusion, more work with pupils from low-income backgrounds. Indeed, expenditure on TAs is one of the most common uses of the Pupil Premium in many schools in receipt of this funding. This may suggest that the need for focussing on ethnic diversity has become redundant, particularly when schools are being encouraged to focus on the needs of the whole child. I would argue that ethnicity is an integral part of individual pupils and impact to varying degrees on how they view their environment. More importantly, they react to the way teachers and Teaching Assistants engage with them. There are high achievers in all minority ethnic groups, with Chinese and Indian pupils outperforming all groups at all Key Stages.

High achieving pupils regularly cite supportive teachers, parents or other significant adults, including Teaching Assistants and mentors. They tell of people inspiring them and believing they would achieve and talked about wanting to attain a particular goal. Some talk about overcoming adversity and defying teachers and other adults who told them they would not achieve. One of the major features of minority ethnic pupils' underachievement is 'low expectation', stemming from teachers and sometimes parents. The commonly agreed position is that the stigma of underachievement can be changed by high-quality support, tackling low expectation, creating an inclusive environment and responding to individual needs (Green 2000; Johnson and Aboud 2013).

That said, data collected over time provide useful indicators in schools as to how specific groups fare in classrooms, year groups, key stages and the wider school community. By looking at trends over time we can see if specific groups are underachieving or consistently failing to make progress. The DfE's yearly report, "School Pupils and their Characteristics", covers ethnicity, first language, gender and socioeconomic groups outcomes. In the 2015 edition, the following attainment and socioeconomic characteristics were identified:

- Minority ethnic pupils, especially Pakistani, Bangladeshi, Black African and Black Caribbean pupils, are more likely to experience deprivation than White British pupils. For example, 70 per cent of Bangladeshi pupils and almost 60 per cent of Pakistani and Black African pupils live in the 20 per cent most deprived postcode areas, compared to less than 20 per cent of White British pupils.
- Indian, Chinese, Irish and White and Asian pupils consistently have higher levels of attainment than other ethnic groups across all Key Stages. Over the last five years their performance relative to national averages has fallen.
- Despite good progress over the last five years, White Other, Pakistani, Bangladeshi, Black Caribbean, Black African and Black Other pupils have

consistently performed below the average for all pupils on every scale of the Foundation Stage profile.

- Gypsy/Roma, Travellers of Irish Heritage, Black, Pakistani and Bangladeshi pupils consistently have lower levels of attainment than other ethnic groups across all Key Stages.
- Even when allowing for prior attainment and other variables, most ethnic groups make more progress than White British pupils with similar characteristics and levels of prior attainment. However, many ethnic groups continue to perform below national averages at both Key Stages 2 and 4, namely: Black Caribbean, White and Black Caribbean, Black other, Pakistani, Gypsy/Roma and Travellers of Irish Heritage pupils.

The above data confirm the reality that while some minority ethnic groups are outperforming their White counterparts, others like Caribbean, Pakistani and Bangladeshi pupils are underperforming, relative to national averages. It is also important that we recognise that regional and local outcomes vary significantly. For example, Caribbean pupils do well in a few cities at GCSE, while in others their progress is slow throughout secondary schooling (DfE 2015a). However, the topical attainment debate in 2014–2015 focussed on pupils receiving free school meals and White working class boys' progress in secondary schools, compared with minority ethnic pupils' progress. This reflects the complex interconnectedness of issues of attainment and progression when comparing and reviewing groups by either class or ethnicity.

For teachers and Teaching Assistants, the challenge is to identify how their own individual actions and continued professional development can be shaped to impact on the underachievement of individuals and groups in their classroom, particularly those from minority ethnic communities. While Teaching Assistants rely on teachers to set pupils' learning agendas and share pupils' information, it is important to know the context for groups of children in the school and be proactive in asking for relevant data and tools needed to maximise support for individuals and groups of children. Good teachers believe in maximising the achievement of each individual child. They identify a mix of measures to help, including raising parental and school expectations of the child. What is not often highlighted is the cultural and social characteristics we bring to our schools and use to set norms and expectations.

Predominantly White staff

One of the most significant challenges in English schools in the coming years is the mismatch between the racial and ethnic diversity of their overall pupil population and that of the school workforce. Over the last 20 years, the call has been for the education workforce to become more diverse to reflect the full range of ethnic population in Britain's schools and local authorities (Ross 2002). Ross argued that the character, ubiquity, pervasiveness and duration of school make it particularly important that teaching is a profession that reflects the population of multi-ethnic Britain.

During the 2013 academic year the proportion of ethnic minority pupils was 28.5 per cent nationally and this is projected to reach 35 per cent by 2025. In comparison, teachers from ethnic minorities are certainly under-represented. The 2014 Workforce for Schools survey estimated that the percentage of teachers and Teaching Assistants from minority ethnic groups in the school workforce (2014) were 8.3 per cent and 12.5 per cent respectively.

There are several debates running, including the need for more role models from minority ethnic communities. There are many reports showing that socially disadvantaged *groups* are consistently underrepresented in areas of government policy making for Science, Technology, Engineering and Mathematics (STEM), *including* apprenticeships, teacher training and several government reviews focused on women, girls and ethnic minorities into STEM (CaSE 2014; Baez and Clarke 1990). In writing the foreword for 'Made in Britain' Gary Phillips said that "Black and minority ethnic [BME] young people, like all other young people, need role models from every area of society but in particular role models from BME background" (D'Souza and Clarke 2005: vii). Others highlight the need to challenge racism and promote diversity by having more BME representation in schools (Cline *et al.* 2002; Arora 2005; Hooks and Miskovic 2011). For the foreseeable future we are unlikely to achieve the level of BME adults' representation in the classroom that would reflect current future minority ethnic pupil population in schools. Researchers are suggesting that initial teacher training is not putting enough emphasis on the needs of pupils from different cultural, faith and linguistic backgrounds and that teachers and Teaching Assistants are often emerging from training without the knowledge, skills, understanding or attitudes needed for successful work in multicultural schools (Cole 2012; Runnymede Trust 2013).

Increasing proportions of students from minority ethnic communities are entering higher education; however, they are not studying to enter the teaching profession. In the teaching workforce, teachers from minority ethnic communities are less likely to be in the positions of headteacher or deputy than White teachers, even when allowance is made for length of service. Teachers from minority ethnic communities are more likely to be on the basic scales. The Higher Education Statistics Agency report for 2004–05 shows that universities were not attracting enough students from minority ethnic communities on to education courses. Today, while the level of application has increased, the proportion of BME students accepted does not reflect demands (HESA 2006; UCAS 2014). Teacher training and teaching assistant courses continue to indicate significant under-representation of participants from minority ethnic communities; and the poor retention and progression of minority ethnic teachers and Teaching Assistants are cause for concern (Ross 2001; CaSE 2014). In light of this, the emphasis on creating a whole school ethos where pupils from minority ethnic communities can feel included, valued and able to participate becomes increasingly important.

Gary Howard in his book *We Can't Teach What We Don't Know* (1999) suggested that teachers need to know themselves very well in order to take on knowing others in an open and respectful way. He recommended that teachers spend time getting to know the backgrounds of children they are teaching. When we explore ethnic diversity, we are mostly talking about people with origins in significantly different lifestyles and cultural experiences from us. Research shows that as significant adults in the classroom (teachers *and* Teaching Assistants), we rarely explore who we are, how we come to believe the things we take for granted and use for forming our assumptions and intuitions. In *A White Teacher Talks about Race*, Julie Landsman outlines her heritage and the influences it brings to her work in a school where 60–80 per cent of students are non-European Americans. She said, "My culture is: East Louis jazz, Southern cooking and the work ethic from my father's side; New England Puritanism, pot roast, classical music on my mother's side" (Landsman 2001: 2). Knowing what we bring to the classroom helps us to shape pupils' experiences. The debate today is not about individual or institutional racism; it is more focussed on our level of self-awareness, our ability to take ownership and responsibility for our day-to-day engagement with our environment (Hooks 1989; Delgado and Stefancic 2000). This should lead to us to never making assumptions about an individual based on the racial, ethnic, or cultural group to which he or she appears to belong. We can then get to know and treat each student first and foremost as an individual.

Conclusion

Teaching Assistants working one to one or with groups of pupils should strive to be fully inclusive within the classroom and across the school. You can give pupils a voice and learn about the worlds in which your pupils live outside of school through their own narratives and in so doing, develop your understanding of the communities within the school area.

The classroom must be an inclusive environment, where difference does not displace or undermine each individual's sense of self. Significant adults within the classroom have a duty to ensure equality of outcome for all pupils, regardless of race, gender, ethnicity, ability or sexual orientation. Teaching Assistants have an important role in ensuring pupils' equal access to an opportunity to learn and develop. To this end they must work to avoid unwittingly discriminating against individuals or groups. In promoting equality of opportunity and good race relations, the starting point is to emphasise similarities rather than differences and the strength that having things in common brings to the classroom, so that differences can be seen to provide opportunities for learning exciting and interesting things about other cultures.

Given the growing opportunities for Teaching Assistants to engage with increasing numbers of minority ethnic groups of pupils, any training and continuing professional development must include greater emphasis on what can be done to maximise outcomes for minority ethnic children and young people in the school environment. Clearly there is a challenge for Teaching Assistants on an individual level, to be reflective and build an understanding of the minority ethnic groups within their schools and classrooms where they are working. Working with pupils from diverse backgrounds is about taking a holistic approach to pupils, an approach which regards them as multifaceted and complex individuals. It is about recognising the fact of 'hidden' or not visible 'identities' amongst pupils. It is also about exploring your own assumptions and attitudes, and recognising and working with the assumptions and attitudes of others within the classroom.

Reflections on values and practice

1   Often we achieve success with one or two children through building effective rapport and just getting on well with them. Reflect on what helps you to make those successful relationships.
2   How can you make time to listen to and learn about the feelings, perceptions, stories and concerns of the communities represented in the school?
3   Pupils for whom English is an additional language (EAL) quickly acquire conversational skills in English. However helping/supporting their academic English is required for success in the national curriculum is of high importance. What might be your role in achieving this?

Suggested further reading

Commission for Equality and Human Rights: www.cehr.org.uk
Runnymede Trust: www.runnymedetrust.org/projects/education/resourcesForSchools.html
Refugee Council: www.refugeecouncil.org.uk

References

Adams, C. (1987) *Across Seven Seas and Thirteen Rivers: Life Stories of Pioneer Sylheti Settlers in Britain*. London: Eastside Books.
Afkhami, R. and Acik-Toprak, N. (2012) *Ethnicity: Introductory User Guide*. Retrieved from www.esds.ac.uk/government/docs/ethnicityintro.pdf
Alborz, A., Pearson, D., Farrell, P. and Howes, A. (2009) 'The impact of adult support staff on pupils and mainstream schools: Technical report'. In *Research Evidence in Education Library*. London: EPPI-Centre, Social Science Research Unit, Institute of Education, University of London.
Arnot, M., Schneider, C., Evans, M., Yongcan Liu, Y., Welply, O. and Davies-Tutt, D. (2014) *School Approaches to the Education of EAL Students*. University of Cambridge: Bell Foundation.
Arora, R. K. (2005) *Race and Ethnicity in Education*. Aldershot: Ashgate.
Beaz, T. and Clarke, E. (1990) 'Reading, writing and role models'. *Community, Technical, and Junior College Journal*, 60(3), 31–34.
Campaign for Science and Engineering (CaSE). (2014) *Improving Diversity in STEM*. London: Kings College.
Claire, H. (1996) *Reclaiming Our Pasts*. Stoke-on-Trent: Trentham Books.
Cline, T., de Abreu, G., Fihosy, C., Gray, H., Lambert, H. and Neale, J. (2002) *Minority Ethnic Pupils in Mainly White Schools*. Nottingham: DfES.
Cole, M. (2012) *Education, Equality and Human Rights: Issues of Gender, 'Race', Sexuality, Disability and Social Class*. Abingdon: Routledge.
Delgado, R. and Stefancic, J. (Eds) (2000) *Critical Race Theory: The Cutting Edge*. Philadelphia, PA: Temple University Press.
Department for Education (DfE). (2015a) *National Statistic: Schools, Pupils, and Their Characteristics: January 2014*. London: Author.

Department for Education (DfE). (2015b) *National Statistic: School Workforce in England: November 2014*. London: Author.

Department for Education (DfE). (2013) *National Statistic: Workforce in England: November 2012*. London: Author.

Department for Education and Skills (DfES). (2006) *Ethnicity and Education: The Evidence of Minority Ethnic Pupils Age 5–16*. Nottingham: Author.

D'Souza, S. and Clarke, P. (2005) *Made in Britain – Inspirational Role Models from British Black and Minority Ethnic Communities*. Harlow, UK: Pearson Education.

Ferguson, N. (2003) *Empire: The Rise and Demise of the British World Order and the Lessons of Global Powers*. New York: Basic Books.

Ford, R. and Heath, A. (2014) 'Immigration: A Nation Divided?' in A. Park, J. Curtice and C. Bryson (eds), *British Social Attitudes 31*. NatCen Social Research, London. Retrieved from www.bsa-31.natcen.ac.uk/read-the-report/immigration/introduction.aspx

Fryer, P. (1984) *Staying Power: The History of Black People in Britain*. London: Pluto Press.

Green, P. (2000) DIECEC *Raising the Standards – A Practical Guide to Raising Ethnic Minority and Bilingual Pupils' Achievement*. Stoke-on-Trent: Trentham Books.

Higher Education Statistics Agency (HESA). (2006) *Students in Higher Education Institutions 2004/5*. London: Author.

Hooks, B. (1998) *Taking Back: Thinking Feminist, Thinking Black*. Cambridge: South End Press.

Hooks, D. and Miskovic, M. (2011) 'Race and racial ideology in classrooms through teachers' and students' voices'. *Race Ethnicity and Education, 14*(2), 191–207.

House of Lords. (1983) *Mandla (Sewa Singh) and another v Dowell Lee and others* [1983] 2 AC 548; United Kingdom of Great Britain and Northern Ireland.

Howard, G. (1999) *We Can't Teach What We Don't Know – White Teachers, Multicultural Schools*. New York: Teachers College Press.

Johnson, P. J. and Aboud, F. E. (2013) 'Modifying ethnic attitudes in young children: The impact of communicator race and message strength'. *International Journal of Behavioral Development, 37*(3), 182–191.

Knowles, E. and Ridley, W. (2006) *Another Spanner in the Works – Challenging Prejudice and Racism in Mainly White Schools*. Stoke-on-Trent: Trentham Books.

Landsman, J. (2001*) A White Teacher Talks About Race*. Lanham, MD: Scarecrow Press.

Merriman, N. (ed) (1993*) The People of London: Fifteen Thousand Years of Settlement from Overseas*. London: Museum of London.

NALDIC. (2014) *National Audit of English as an Additional Language: Training and Development Provision*. Retrieved from www.naldic.org.uk/resources

Nicolson, C. (1974) *Strangers to England: Immigration to England 1100–1945*. London: Wayland.

Office for National Statistics (ONS). (2011) *Population Estimates by Ethnic Group 2002 – 2009, Statistical Bulletin*. Retrieved from www.ons.gov.uk/ons

Office for National Statistics (ONS). (2012). 2011 Census: Aggregate data (England and Wales) [computer file]. UK Data Service Census Support. Retrieved from www.ons.gov.uk/ons

Oxford University Press. (2013) *Concise English Dictionary*.

Ross, A. (2001) *Ethnic Minority Teachers in the Teaching Workforce*. London: IPSE Occasional Paper.

Ross, A. (2002) *Classroom Assistants Won't End Teacher Shortage*. London: Ippr.

Rowley, S. J. and Moore, J. A. (2002) 'When who I am impacts how I am represented: Addressing minority student issues in different contexts', *Roeper Review, 24*, 63–67.

Runnymede Trust. (2006) *Black and Minority Ethnic Issues in Teaching and Learning*. Briefing Paper. Universities and Colleges Admissions Service. (UCAS) (2014) *GTTR Annual Statistical Report, 2013*. Cheltenham: Author.

Runnymede Trust. (2013) *Complementing Teachers – A Practical Guide to Promoting Race and Identity on the Agenda*. Stoke-on-Trent: Trentham Books.

Chapter 5

The influence of gender on achievement

Steve Bartlett and Diana Burton

Introduction

We are all affected in some way by issues of social class, ethnicity and gender in our society. In this chapter we look specifically at the influence of gender on the achievement of pupils in our education system. We consider how, for much of the twentieth century, research concentrated on the inequality of opportunity for girls and the social changes that have attempted to rectify this. We then look at the current debates surrounding the apparently poor achievement of boys and the culture of underperformance accompanying this. We conclude by suggesting that any examination of the self-perception, motivation and achievement of children and young people needs to include a consideration of social class, ethnicity and gender issues. It is only by being aware of such factors that policies promoting social inclusion can have any hope of success. All classroom practitioners, including Teaching Assistants, need to understand these significant forces in pupils' lives in order to make their practice more effective.

Sex and gender

Before we consider the impact of gender on pupil achievement it is important to examine the terminology that is used in such debates. The term 'sex' is usually used when referring to our biological make-up. It identifies us as male or female. Biological differences include chromosomes, hormones and physical sexual characteristics such as sexual organs, body hair, physique, etc. 'Gender' refers to the social construction of masculine and feminine. It is what we expect males and females to be 'like' in terms of behaviour, appearance, beliefs and attitudes. There has been a continuing debate as to how much of our maleness and femaleness is biologically determined and how much is socially constructed.

This determinist position holds that our biological sex is significant in determining us as individuals. Thus mothering and caring are presented as female traits, and aggression and protecting as male. While we are all individuals and we live in different social environments, our biological make-up plays the major part in determining who we are and how we behave. It can be seen as underpinning many social explanations for the structure of families and the conjugal roles within them.

An alternative view is that, although there are certain biological differences between males and females, it is society and the culture that we live in that creates the notions of masculinity and femininity.

Early feminist writers such as Oakley (1975) wished to highlight the significance of cultural as opposed to biological factors in explaining the ongoing socially inferior position of women in society. Their argument was that it was the social constructions of gender and sexuality that led to the oppression of women. The biological accounts were seen as part of male social control that perpetuated the myth of male superiority. This perspective holds that masculinity and femininity are in the main socially rather than biologically determined, but the relative influence of each factor on an individual's gender construction remains unclear. There are physical differences between males and females and these become more obvious as we grow up and move through adolescence and into adulthood. However, there is a wide variation both within and across the genders in terms of individual physical characteristics. What is deemed attractive to the opposite sex is different from society to society and changes over time as fashions change. Clothing, diet and body-building (or -reducing) exercises to alter our appearance are all used and with advances in medical science people can radically alter their physical characteristics and even biological sex. In modern societies and across a range of cultures any presentation of a clear uncomplicated sexual division would be an oversimplification.

Influences upon the creation of gender

Societies throughout the ages and around the world display many differences in gender roles. In her now classic anthropological account, Mead (1935) found great variation in the roles of men and women in a study of three tribes in New Guinea. In Western culture the representation of gender as a binary split between masculine and feminine make them appear as opposites with everyone falling either side of the sexual binary line. Thus from birth we are brought up to be male or female and to be mistaken for being of the opposite sex from that with which you identify is a significant concern as we seek to maintain our self-identity.

While teenagers strive to be independent from the older generation they are also subject to strong peer pressures. Gender characteristics that stereotype appropriate physical appearance and behaviour can cause pressure to conform, particularly on young people who are coming to terms with themselves as they develop. To be identified as different or 'other' can have a significant effect upon the self-image of young people. Pupil interaction and perceptions are significant in the 'othering' process. Labels become attached to pupils and some are more difficult to resist or counter than others. Language plays a very powerful part in this process and use of sexual insults such as 'gay', 'queer' or 'slag' may have lasting repercussions on the identities, future interactions and sexual behaviour of the young people involved (Vicars 2006). Guasp (2012) reported that over half of lesbian, gay and bisexual young people have experienced homophobic bullying at school.

Masculinities and femininities

Whilst there are many forms of male identity or masculinities, Harber suggests that there are some 'dominant or hegemonic forms of male identity internationally which have traditionally preserved patriarchal power and privilege' (2014: 162). These promote perceptions and so reinforce realities of male dominance and female subordination in many societies.

Marshall (2014) points out that many girls in the developing world face significant barriers in accessing education resulting from traditional cultural beliefs linked at the same time to economic poverty. Key factors adversely affecting girls are things such as boys' education being more valued, girls being kept at home for household chores, married at a young age and being perceived as having a home-based future and not worth educating. In some regions girls report violence and sexual harassment on the way to and from school and also in school and so are more likely to stay at home. For such reasons Marshall (2014) suggests that girls in various geographical areas are unlikely to receive an education equivalent to boys and in some cases any significant formal education at all. Harber (2014) does note, however, that in a number of areas, Honduras for example, it is the boys who are more likely to drop out of school as they are needed to earn a wage to supplement the family income, whilst girls are not expected to work outside the home. As Harber (2014) points out, once again poverty is a key factor in influencing gender and schooling.

In the developed world, such as the UK, Swain (2004) and Connell (2006) speak of a range of masculinities and femininities thus allowing for greater variation. Swain says that pupils live within the context of their own communities and that these wider contexts influence individual school policies and cultures. Thus schools are influenced by local employment opportunities, housing type, religious and ethnic mix of the area. In addition, Swain says that each school also has its own *gender regime*. This "consists of ... individual personnel expectations, rules, routines and a hierarchical ordering of particular practices" (2004: 182). It is interesting to consider the integral part that gender relationships play in school life and how these vary depending upon the ethos of the school. School uniforms, lining up in the playground or outside the classroom, class lists that separate boys and girls, and how pupils and teachers are addressed are all instances where gender may or may not be highlighted in formal school procedures. There are many ways in which gender is also part of informal school processes, e.g. the arrangement of each individual classroom and where pupils sit; who children play with at break times and what they play; the number of pupils choosing different subjects at secondary school; the number of male and female adults employed by the school and their positions of responsibility. Since schools are a key part of the wider socialization process, they both influence and are influenced by gender relationships.

Stereotypical images of boys in school include loud, boisterous behaviour, lack of interest in studying and generally taking a rushed and untidy approach to work. Images of stereotypical girl behaviour include being quiet, hard working, neat and careful in appearance. If we look at real groups of young people and consider the rich and complex picture that actually exists in terms of individual beliefs, values, appearance and so on, we see how inappropriate it is to use such stereotypes. Actually the majority of boys are not disruptive in the classroom and all girls do not get on with their work quietly. We should be wary of using too rigid a definition of what constitutes female or male behaviour of young people.

A historical view of recent developments in gender relations in Britain

The way in which the roles of men and women and their relationships to each other vary over time can be illustrated by considering the comparatively short period from Victorian England to the present day. In the early 1800s Britain was very much a patriarchal society. Women were not able to vote, own property or obtain a divorce. Within the middle classes women were effectively either under the control of their father or their husband. It was men who governed the empire and the society, ran businesses and supported the family. Women did not work and were confined to a life that revolved around the home. Boys from the more affluent classes would be educated at public and grammar schools, but the education of girls would be primarily left to governesses, conducted in the home based upon the knowledge suitable for a lady. For the working classes life was much harder and both men and women worked, though women did the more menial factory work and were paid less than men. In the early educational provision for the working classes, girls were able to attend school as well as boys, though both were taught appropriately to the social expectations of the time.

It has taken many years of political and social pressure for women to attain legal equality with men. Married women over 30 gained the vote in 1918 and in the 1920s were granted the right to divorce and importantly to retain their own property upon divorce. It was not until 1928 that they gained equal voting rights with men and it took nearly a further 50 years for the Sex Discrimination Act of 1975 to outlaw discrimination on the grounds of gender.

From this date women, legally at least, had equality with men. However, there were still economic and social differences that were strongly influenced by gender. In many areas of employment the position of women has improved. Changes in attitude have continued to take place and over the years women have increasingly taken up careers that they previously could not. In spite of this progress, employment is still an area where significant differences persist between the experiences of men and women. These are likely to take a long time to change, notwithstanding the recent Equality Act of 2010. Women's employment is still shaped by family and domestic responsibilities, with mothers more likely to leave work or go part time after having children or choose jobs where the hours fit into child care. These factors result in many women taking jobs with lower pay and fewer prospects. Women in professional jobs are more likely to miss out on promotions during their enforced 'career breaks'.

Social and political attitudes are reflected in education. State education has been provided throughout the twentieth century to all pupils regardless of gender. In the early part of the 1900s elementary schools were co-educational. While primary schools have always been co-educational, the introduction of a selective secondary system saw the development of single-sex grammar schools and often, though not always, single-sex secondary modern schools. It was the development of new large comprehensive schools from the 1960s onwards that saw boys and girls taught together in their secondary education.

Gender and achievement

Being taught in the same school did not remove the impact of gender upon a pupil's experiences. In the 1960s the inequalities in society were reflected in the classroom where teachers, peers and parents treated boys and girls very differently. At that time it was usual to have gender-specific stereotypical expectations of pupils, so curricular activities were unashamedly contrived around them, e.g. needlework and typing for girls, and metalwork and technical drawing for boys.

In the 1970s and 1980s much feminist research in education was concerned with the perceived underachievement of girls and how the education process worked to maintain this through discrimination and marginalization (Oakley 1975; Whyte 1983; Spender 1982). The gender differences were maintained and highlighted through the processes of schooling, which involved the separation of the genders through school uniform, a gender-specific curriculum and differential expectations of behaviour. This was further enforced through the attitude of teachers, peers, parents and later, their usually male, employers. Feminist researchers were interested to show how the ambitions of female students remained low and how they were discouraged in a variety of ways from choosing the 'hard' mathematical and scientific subjects so important to future employment prospects in favour of the more 'feminine' arts and humanities.

Raising girls' achievement

While the raising of awareness and the development work that accompanied it were all based on the belief in the underachievement of girls relative to boys, the actual figures show that the reality was not that straightforward. Even in the 1970s girls were outperforming boys in English and modern foreign languages. Also more girls were achieving five or more O-level passes (equivalent to A*–C, GCSE) than boys. However, because these included subjects that were seen as low status, such as home economics, and because boys were doing better at maths and sciences, which were regarded as 'hard' subjects of high status, girls were perceived as underachieving (Francis 2000). Furthermore, it should be noted that the selective system of grammar and secondary modern schools, in operation before the development of the comprehensive system, had favoured boys due to the larger number of places available in boys' grammar schools as opposed to those admitting girls. Thus boys did not need to score as highly as girls in the 11+ to secure a grammar school education. It was not the case then that girls were necessarily underachieving but that their success was not being recognized and that they were not offered the same opportunities or encouragement as boys in order to pursue the more rewarding economic options. Girls' futures were still being perceived as domestically based.

The Conservative government came to power in 1979 emphasizing competition, individual achievement and success. It did not trust the liberal education establishment and sought to reform the education system. While not being particularly concerned with the promotion of equal opportunities, one of its reforms, the introduction of the national curriculum, had what is now often regarded as a significant impact on the achievements of girls (Francis 2000). From its inception all pupils were required to study the national curriculum. Thus it was no longer possible for boys or girls to 'drop' some subjects in favour of others. The Conservatives were also responsible for the introduction of testing of all pupils at different stages in their compulsory education and the production of league tables based on GCSE, A-level and the earlier Key Stage test results. These were and are used to judge overall school performance, making the achievements of boys and girls more transparent than ever. They show how the performance of both boys and girls has steadily improved. What has caught the public attention though is that the improvement in the results of girls has been greater than that of boys. While continuing to outperform boys in language subjects, girls have caught up with boys in maths and the sciences. Concern is now focused on the performance of boys.

Current performance of boys and girls

We need to exercise great caution when interpreting statistics on gender and examination performance. In terms of GCSE performance, DfE figures (www.gov.uk 2015) show that girls attain a higher percentage of five or more passes at A*–C than boys. They outperform boys in the majority of subjects, the gap being particularly noticeable in English language. There is, however, little statistical difference between the performance of boys and girls in the areas of maths and science. At A-level, pass rates and grades are comparable for boys and girls, but what still remains significant is that apart from in biology, far fewer girls are taking the STEM (science, technology, engineering and maths) subjects than boys.

Along with the increasing number of students taking A-levels, higher education has expanded over the last 30 years and become more accessible to a wider proportion of the population. As the number of students has steadily increased, women now make up the largest proportion of those studying for both undergraduate and post-graduate degrees. In 2013–14 women made up 54.7 per cent of full time undergraduate students (HESA 2015), a significant change from when university study was largely the preserve of a minority of privileged males. Women entrants now outnumber men in the majority of undergraduate courses, including medicine and dentistry, subject areas previously dominated by males. However, men remain overrepresented in most STEM subjects, most notably engineering. Adams (2015) suggests that the success of female applicants into higher education mirrors the trend in GCSE and A-level, with girls performing well but still being underrepresented in the STEM subjects. Thus, whilst this expanding education participation creates the possibility of wider career access for women, this is still not the case in areas such as construction and engineering, which require high-level qualifications in STEM. Even with the comparable academic performance of females, gender may still be having an impact upon behaviour, subject and ultimately career choices. Francis, Burke and Read (2014) noted that many students, male and female, still tended to use stereotypical constructions of gender difference even whilst rejecting the notion that gender and other structural differences impact upon their experiences

However, it is important for Teaching Assistants to realize that though girls' overall average scores have perhaps always been higher than boys', the difference in performance is not that great with high percentages of boys continuing to perform well. To see all boys as underachieving is misleading as some groups of boys do achieve highly whilst some groups of girls do not. Richards and Posnett (2012), for instance, notice that overall, whilst girls' academic achievement appears to be better than or equal to boys, low aspirations continue to affect the performance of working-class girls. Thus, amongst both boys and girls there is a wide range of achievement with many young people continuing to experience academic and behavioural difficulties at school. It is these pupils who need the support of education professionals.

Explanations for boys' underachievement

Over the last 20 years the debate has shifted from being about the creation of equal opportunities and improving the educational experiences of girls to concerns about male underachievement and disadvantage (Elwood 2005: 377). The panic surrounding the underachievement of boys has been rather an overreaction. The media has portrayed boys as falling behind and homed in on an apparent growth of a 'laddish' culture among teenage boys that is anti-study, against school values and leads to underachievement (Smith 2012). Various explanations have been offered to explain why girls are performing better than boys.

Genetic differences

Historically, the assumption has been, perhaps due to male-dominant views, that women were the weaker and thus the inferior sex that needed to be protected. The consistently higher level of achievement by girls academically may now lead some to the conclusion that this is due to genetic differences, i.e. the intellectual superiority of women. Evidence supporting this is currently very thin. The difference in achievement between genders is not that large and more importantly great variations in achievement occur *within* the genders. Feminist analysts would suggest that the 'moral panic' that has accompanied this perceived failure of boys and the demand to rectify the situation is a reflection of the fear within the male-dominated political establishment.

Social and economic change

In recent decades there have been enormous changes in the economy that have had repercussions on how people earn their living, the organization of the family and the amount of leisure time and disposable income available. The traditional occupations based upon heavy industry dominated by male workers that involved strength and training in traditional skills have largely disappeared. This has had significant effects upon communities based around industries such as mining, ship building, steelworking and deep-sea fishing. Newer forms of employment are service based and seen as being more traditionally female. The male is now no longer the only nor even the major 'breadwinner' in the family. Thus the traditional masculine image in working-class communities is no longer applicable as it was even 30 years ago and many working-class boys see no particular role for themselves. They see no need to work hard at school as it will make little difference to their future. At the same time these boys emphasize and play out their masculinities at school where it is important to be seen as 'hard', 'cool', not a 'poof' or a 'swot' (Ward 2014). It can of course be argued that working-class boys could always get masculine jobs in the past and so have never really had reason to work hard at school. Significantly, Connolly suggests that masculinities and femininities are not just about gender alone but must be seen as combining with social class and ethnicity to 'produce differing and enduring forms of identity' (2006: 15). It is this complex mix that teachers and Teaching Assistants need to be aware of.

School culture

It is suggested that schools have become more female-oriented in recent decades and that school culture now works in favour of girls and against the achievement of boys. It is assumed that assessment regimes have developed to privilege girls with more emphasis on coursework rather than final exams. However, this trend has reversed in recent years with no significant falling back of girls' performance.

The curriculum is said to reflect girls' interests with little to excite boys; some feel the type of learning does not suit boys' learning approaches. However, whilst DCSF (2009) finds no overall bias towards girls in the curriculum this point ignores the many areas of the curriculum where the content has been specifically chosen to attract boys. In any case, learning approaches vary amongst girls as well as between boys and girls. Arnot and Miles (2005) suggest that the increasing emphasis on a performative school system has led to greater resistance from working-class boys who have a history of low achievement. This they say is being misinterpreted as a new development, termed 'laddishness'.

Beliefs about identity can inform teachers' perceptions resulting in a tendency to associate boys with underachievement and girls with high achievement. This labelling process may contribute to the low expectations of boys, thus creating a self-fulfilling prophecy. DCSF (2009) suggests that whole school strategies to raise achievement should focus on both boys and girls together.

Conclusion

In summarizing the arguments concerning gender and achievement, we can say that the performance of boys and girls overall has improved throughout the 1990s and the 2000s, that girls have been improving faster than boys and that they are now outperforming boys in many subjects and are at least performing more or less equally in all. However, to portray girls as achieving and boys as underachieving is too simplistic a view (Smith 2012; Richards and Posnett 2012). It should be noted that the differences in overall performance of boys and girls are not that great. It is the improvement in performance of girls from the more middle-class backgrounds in all subjects that has caused the rise in girls' performance overall. Boys from middle-class backgrounds continue to generally perform well. Boys and girls from the lower socioeconomic groups continue to underperform when compared to their more affluent peers. Thus, as Connolly (2006) says, while gender does exert an influence on GCSE attainment, this is overshadowed by the effects of social class and ethnicity.

In conclusion we can say that there are many influences on the achievement of pupils, with social background, ethnicity and gender all being significant. Effective Teaching Assistants must take account of these while endeavouring to treat pupils as the individuals they are.

Reflections on values and practice

1   Reflect on the different jobs done by adults in your school and the gender of those who do them. What conclusions can you draw from the results of this exercise in terms of gender and employment in your school? Do your findings have any policy implications?

2   Keep a log of all the pupils you work with on an individual basis during one school day. In this record note the age and gender of the pupil, why you were working together, and what you both did. When analysing your log are there any gender-related factors that you notice? If this exercise was extended over a longer period of one week, would this impact upon your findings? What strategies might you need to consider in light of your finding?

3   Observe pupils working in class. How do different groups and individuals work differently over a period of time? How long is spent on tasks, in cooperative behaviour and what is the quality of work produced? Is gender a factor in any of the variations you notice? How might you intervene to change things?

Suggested further reading

DCSF. (2009) *Gender and education – Mythbusters. Addressing gender and achievement: Myths and realities.* Retrieved from http://dera.ioe.ac.uk/9095/1/00599-2009BKT-EN.pdf

Affiliated to the Gender and Education Association, the *Gender and Education Journal* grew out of feminist politics and is committed to developing critical discussions of gender and education in its broadest sense. Retrieved from www.tandfonline.com/loi/cgee20#.VewzZEmFPIU

Oakley, A. (1975) *Sex, Gender and Society.* London: Temple Smith.

References

Adams, R. (2015) 'Gender gap in university admissions rises to record level'. *The Guardian*, 21 January 2015.

Arnot, M. and Miles, P. (2005) 'A reconstruction of the gender agenda: The contradictory gender dimensions in New Labour's educational and economic policy', *Oxford Review of Education*, *31*(1): 173–189.

Connell, R. W. (2006) 'Understanding men: Gender sociology and the new international research on masculinities', in Skelton, Francis and Smulyan (eds), *The Sage Handbook of Gender and Education*. London: Sage.

Connolly, P. (2006) 'The effects of social class and ethnicity on gender differences in GCSE attainment: A secondary analysis of the youth cohort study of England and Wales 1997–2001', *The British Educational Research Journal*, *32*(1): 3–21.

DCSF. (2009) *Gender and education – Mythbusters. Addressing gender and achievement: Myths and realities*. Retrieved from http://dera.ioe.ac.uk/9095/1/00599-2009BKT-EN.pdf

Elwood, J. (2005) 'Gender and achievement: What have exams got to do with it?' *Oxford Review of Education*, *31*(3): 373–393.

Francis, B. (2000) *Boys, Girls and Achievement: Addressing the Classroom Issues*. London: Routledge.

Francis, B. Burke, P. and Read, B. (2014) 'The submergence and reemergence of gender in undergraduate accounts of university experience', *Gender and Education*, *26*(1): 1–17.

Gov.uk. (2015) Accessed 19/04/2015. Retrieved from www.gov.uk/government/statistics/revised-gcse-and-equivalent-results-in-england-2013-to-2014

Guasp, A. (2012) *'The school report: The experiences of gay young people in Britain's schools in 2012'*. University of Cambridge: Stonewall. Retrieved from www.stonewall.org.uk/atschool.

Harber, C. (2014) *Education and International Development: Theory, Practice and Issues*. Oxford: Symposium Books.

Higher Education Statistics Agency (HESA). (2015) *'Free online statistics – students and qualifiers'*. Retrieved from https://www.hesa.ac.uk/stats

Marshall, J. (2014) *Introduction to Comparative and International Education*. London: Sage.

Mead, M. (1935) *Sex and Temperament in Three Primitive Societies*. London: Routledge & Kegan Paul.

Oakley, A. (1975) *Sex, Gender and Society*. London: Temple Smith.

Richards, G. and Posnett, C. (2012) 'Aspiring girls: Great expectations or impossible dreams?', *Educational Studies*, *38*(3): 249–259.

Smith, E. (2012) *Key Issues in Education and Social Justice*. London: Sage.

Spender, D. (1982) *Invisible Women: The Schooling Scandal*. London: Writers and Readers.

Swain, J. (2004) 'The resources and strategies that 10–11-year-old boys use to construct masculinities in the school setting', *British Educational Research Journal*, *30*(1): 167–185.

Vicars, M. (2006) 'Who are you calling queer? Sticks and stones can break my bones but names will always hurt me', *British Educational Research Journal*, *32*(3): 347–361.

Ward, M. (2014) "I'm a geek I am': academic achievement and the performance of a studious working-class masculinity'. *Gender and Education*, *26*(7): 709–725.

Whyte, J. (1983) *Beyond the Wendy House: Sex-Role Stereotyping in Primary Schools*. York: Longman.

Chapter 6

Religious diversity and inclusive practice

Michael J. Reiss

Introduction

Until perhaps ten to twenty years ago, there was a widespread assumption that religion was increasingly becoming less important for schools in Britain. However, this has not proved to be the case. While there are many people for whom religious belief, practice and experience are not important, there are many for whom these are significant. Furthermore, the numbers for whom religion is personally relevant have been swelled both by immigration, including children born in such families, and by a tendency found in many religions in recent decades for some religious believers to have become more fundamentalist/literalist. In addition, religious matters now seem more evident in the public arena – whether we are talking about the wearing of religious dress (e.g. the burqa) or religious symbols (e.g. a cross), attitudes to gay marriage, the rise of militant atheism or religious terrorism. In education, the situation is complicated by new forms of faith schooling (Chapman *et al.* 2014; Parker-Jenkins, Glenn and Janmaat 2014).

This chapter examines such issues from the perspective of Teaching Assistants and others (e.g. parents, mentors) who work in school classrooms alongside teachers. I start from the belief that the right to hold a particular belief, religious or secular, should be accepted as part of a wider spectrum of rights to equal participation in education, regardless of difference – and this point applies to Teaching Assistants and teachers as well as to students. So, I am not making any assumptions about the religious beliefs of you, the reader.

Inclusive schools welcome the diversity represented by members of their neighbourhood communities and regard differences as sources for enriching teaching and learning and for fostering harmonious, respectful relationships and mutual understanding (e.g. Mirza and Meetoo 2012). However, there are times when such well-intended sentiments are easier to state than to put into practice! A general point is that it is not appropriate for Teaching Assistants, teachers and other adults in school to attempt to convert students to or away from any particular religion.

One way of thinking of religion is to see it as a part of culture. In one sense there is nothing specific to religion for a school dealing with issues of inclusion. By way of analogy (though analogies are always risky as some people treat them too literally), having a religious faith is in certain respects analogous to being a vegetarian. Some vegetarians believe passionately in the importance of vegetarianism and argue strongly that for anyone to eat meat is wrong; other vegetarians, while equally passionate about not eating meat themselves, believe strongly in the right of others to eat meat if they so choose; still other vegetarians are more laid back about their own eating habits and not averse sometimes to eating fish. In other words, vegetarians vary in their views about vegetarianism and religious people vary in their views about religion. What we want a school to do is to be respectful of the diversity of religious views within it, without giving the impression that discussion about religion is off limits.

The historical context in the UK

Until the introduction of the National Curriculum in 1988, religious education was the only subject that schools in England and Wales were required to teach. This requirement dates back to the 1870 Elementary Education Act which stipulated that 'No religious catechism or religious formulary which is distinctive of any particular denomination shall be taught in the school' (Section 14). At that time, the assumption was that the education would be Christian (hence 'denomination' rather than 'religion') but thus began the long tradition in England that religious education was not to be a nurturing in the state religion (Barnes *et al.* 2012).

This contrasts with the situation in most countries where state schools often promote the official or majority state religion, though there are countries, notably France, Turkey and the USA, where no religious education takes place in state schools. Also included in the 1870 Act was the right, which persists to this day, of parents to remove their children from religious instruction (as the subject was then called).

The legal situation concerning religious education and such things as collective worship in schools is quite complicated and fast moving; there are important differences among the four UK nations and among the various types of school. In particular, the law does now allow for certain state schools with a religious character to favour one religion over others. Nevertheless, the key features of a religious education in state schools – that it is a core part of the curriculum, has provision for student withdrawal, must be part of a broad and balanced curriculum and must have regard to community cohesion – means that the position of religious education in UK schools is often held to be a much healthier one than in many other countries. This is despite quite frequent calls that religious education be either abolished or made optional, perhaps to be replaced by lessons in philosophy, in citizenship or in personal, social and health education.

The importance of religion to people

For people for whom religion is important, it can be important in two main ways: for belief and for practice. In addition, people often report religious experiences whether these are once in a lifetime ones (e.g. a religious conversion) or more frequent ones (e.g. daily prayer). Worldwide, religion remains of significance to many people, including young people; a survey undertaken in 2011 in twenty-four countries found that 73 per cent of respondents under the age of 35 (94 per cent in primarily Muslim countries and 66 per cent in Christian majority countries) said that they had a religion/faith and that it was important to their lives (Ipsos MORI 2011; see also Smyth, Lyons and Darmody 2013).

For some people, their religious faith is absolutely the core of their being: they could no more feel comfortable acting or thinking in a way that conflicted with their religious values than they could feel comfortable not eating. One way of expressing this is to say that for such people their worldview is a religious one; another way is to say that religion plays a central part in their identity. Of course, for other people, religious faith is either an irrelevancy – an historical anachronism – or positively harmful with many of the ills that befall humankind being placed at its door (Halstead and Reiss 2003).

It can be difficult for those who have never had a religious faith, or have only had one rather tenuously, to imagine what a life is like that is lived wholly within a religious ordering. For Teaching Assistants and others who work in school classrooms alongside teachers, the skill is to be open minded about the importance of religion for each student. Of course there can be external markers of religion – for example, a Jewish skullcap ('kippah' in Hebrew; 'yarmulke' in Yiddish) – but these are only worn by Orthodox males. Similarly, it can be a mistake to conclude too much because a female wears a hijab or someone wears a cross. These often indicate Islam and Christianity respectively but crosses, in particular, can be worn by those with of no religious persuasion. The safest, most respectful and helpful way forward is to try to keep in mind that religion may or may not be important for any student and to listen to what, if anything, they say to you about themselves. Classroom assistants often find that children and young people want to chat to them informally about things which they might not feel able to talk to a teacher about, or bring up in front of the class, and 'listening' in these circumstances can be an important part of their role. However, we shouldn't interrogate students about their religious beliefs, practices or experiences but nor should we avoid talking with them about these if they seem to want to.

Of course, having a secular or atheistic approach to life can be as important for some people as having a religious approach to life is for others. John White and I have argued that atheism should be studied in schools (Reiss and White 2009). Young people may well find themselves reflecting on the existence of God, especially when confronted by the debates about belief and religious practice which have assumed such importance nationally and globally. This points to discussing the standard arguments for and against the existence of God and such questions as the possibility of life after death. Students also need to discuss whether human lives can have any meaning outside of a religious framework and whether people can live a morally good life that is not dependent on religious belief.

The particular place of religious education lessons

The aims and content of religious education lessons have varied far more in recent decades than has been the case for many other subjects. When I think back to my own schooling in the 1960s and 1970s, my religious education was terrible. We were fed a watered-down, bible-based and historical account of Christianity. With hindsight I think there was a vague hope that this might make us better people though what we were offered seems more likely to put one off religion than attract or inspire one. 'Scripture', as it was called, was the one subject that I once managed to come bottom in in any school test or examination, 27th out of 27.

The idea of confessional religious education – i.e. that teaching the subject might lead to the development or strengthening of religious faith – was pretty much abandoned in the 1970s, largely as a result of the publication by School Council (1971) of Working Paper 36: Religious Education in Secondary Schools. Two main arguments against confessional religion were advanced: first, that confessional education entails indoctrination; second, that confessional education is inappropriate within an increasingly secular and pluralist society. The first argument has been controversial and there are those who continue to maintain that a confessional religion need not entail indoctrination, indeed that to abandon confessionalism is to submit to a form of liberal indoctrination that makes the implicit assumption that fostering any religious belief is educationally indefensible.

The second argument is widely accepted (Barnes 2012). It is generally agreed that school religious education needs to take account of life in a diverse society where Christianity is much less central than it once was both because of a large increase in the number of people with no religious faith and because of increasing numbers of adherents of other faiths. Religious education responded in a number of ways. Particularly popular was a 'world-religions' approach. The expectation was that at the least students during their schooling would study what are often referred to as the six 'world religions' of Buddhism, Christianity, Hinduism, Islam, Judaism and Sikhism. Furthermore, the influential Qualifications and Curriculum Authority Non-Statutory National Framework recommended the study of further traditions "such as the Bahá'í faith, Jainism and Zoroastrianism . . . and secular philosophies such as humanism" (Qualifications and Curriculum Authority 2004: 12).

Although well-meaning, this multi-faith approach ran into a number of difficulties. For a start, studying so many religions rarely inspired students, leading instead to shallow learning of miscellaneous facts (the five pillars of Islam, the five, eight or ten precepts of Buddhism, etc.). Other objections were that such teaching failed to connect to students' needs, gave a false impression of religion by denying diversity within religions, created a divide between how religion is experienced by those for whom it is important and how it is presented in the classroom, failed to engage students critically with claims about religious truth and underplayed the historical and contemporary importance of Christianity in British society (Watson 2012).

More recent curricula have reduced the number of religions that are studied, placing more emphasis on those that are relevant to the students in a school and in the local communities from which they come. An additional feature of successful religious education curricula is that they contain a substantial amount of material on values and ethics. While ethics can be taught in many subjects, teachers of religious education often have particular expertise in this area. At a time when much of the school curriculum is often criticised for being fact-heavy, good teaching about ethics can be both popular and educationally valuable. It can introduce students to ways in which fundamental questions about human meaning and existence have been addressed while giving students considerable autonomy to develop their own thinking. There are, for example, no single, universally agreed 'right answers' to such questions as whether abortion is permissible, whether we have duties to the environment and if/when war is morally right.

Teaching Assistants and others who work in school classrooms alongside teachers can therefore play an important role in helping students to talk about what they believe, think and do. Many students benefit when working in small groups from having an adult with them to help ensure that everyone gets a chance to speak and that certain views are not ridiculed. The skill as an adult is to do this only when necessary, otherwise one can easily end up dominating the conversation.

School-wide issues

There are many issues to do with religion and inclusion aside from religious education lessons. For a start, it remains the case, for community schools in England and Wales, that the law states that a collective act of worship must take place daily and be wholly or mainly of a Christian character. This is a requirement far more honoured in the breach than in the observance. In their efforts not to offend students and to provide for assemblies that 'work' in school terms, few secondary schools other than faith schools nowadays provide true collective worship.

More generally, the task of a school, whether of a religious nature or not, includes affirming in its ethos the value of diversity. This seems to me a key point in respect of the place of religion in a pluralist society. It is increasingly acknowledged that one cannot prove or disprove the validity or worth of religious faith. Given that both religious faith and atheism/secularism/agnosticism are widely represented in society, it is important that schools help students of all persuasions to live and work together respectively both now in school and in the future beyond school (cf. Starkey 2015).

This is not to imply that schools should accept every view about religion. Schools have a role to play in tackling extremism, including religious extremism. Savage (2013) has shown how education can help people to be less polarised in their thinking. It can make people less likely to see things as 'black or white', instead helping them to appreciate that there can be many sides to an argument. Importantly, being less likely to see controversial matters as straightforward and clear-cut is associated with less advocacy of violence. Extremist ideologies, whether religious or not, avoid complexity.

More generally, Teaching Assistants and others, both by what they say and by their actions, can play a major role in helping students to be tolerant and respectful of difference, including religious difference. Much of this can be done by encouraging students to talk about their actions and their views, thus helping to develop students' reasoning and their ownership of learning (Bosanquet, Radford and Webster 2015).

Teaching Assistants, parents, dinner ladies, midday supervisors and adult helpers often witness instances of bullying, whether in classrooms, in the playground, at mealtimes and on other occasions. Every school should have a policy on bullying, whether this is verbal bullying, physical bullying, relational bullying (excluding a fellow student from activities) or cyberbullying. Bullying in relation to religion should be dealt with as with any other type of bullying. The first thing to do is to stop the bullying and calmly to make it clear to all who have witnessed the bullying that it is not acceptable, and to do so, if possible, in a way that is respectful both of the bully and the one who is bullied. The second thing is to report the bullying to a teacher or some other designated adult in the school.

Teaching Assistants and others can be an important link between the school and the wider community. By drawing in, and going out to, the local community and working with local organisations (including faith groups) schools can develop their inclusive cultures in terms of sharing, accepting, celebrating and understanding (Armstrong and Barton 2010). Developing these kinds of relationships with parents of school students and with the wider community can take time and effort but prove to be mutually rewarding.

Science education

One place within schools where religion not infrequently rears its head outside of religious education lessons is in science. Issues to do with religion seem increasingly to be of importance in science lessons. To many science teachers and others involved in science even raising the possibility that religion might be considered within school science lessons raises suspicions that this is an attempt to find a way of smuggling religion into the science classroom for religious rather than scientific reasons. This is not the intention here! Considering the scope of religion (or art or music or ethics) in a science lesson can be, on occasions, useful simply for helping learners better understand why science has things to say about certain matters but not others (Reiss 2014).

Another argument for considering religion within science lessons is like the argument for considering history in science lessons. While science can be learnt and studied in an historical vacuum, there are a number of reasons for examining science in its historical contexts. For a start, this helps students understand better why certain scientific advances were made at certain times. Wars, for instance, have sometimes led to advances in chemistry, physics and information science (e.g. explosives, missile trajectories, code breaking), while certain botanical disciplines, such as the classification and naming of plants, have flourished during periods of colonisation. Then it is the case that many learners find it motivating to learn science in its historical context.

Similarly, while many students enjoy learning about the pure science of genetics and evolution, otherwise are motivated and come to understand the science better if they know something of the diversity of religious beliefs held by such important scientists as Charles Darwin, Thomas Huxley and Gregor Mendel. Such teaching is even better if students come to appreciate the religious views (including the diversity of religious views) of the cultures in which such scientists lived and worked.

There are a number of places where religion and science intersect. Consider, first, the question of 'authority' and the scriptures as a source of authority. To the great majority of religious believers, the scriptures of their religion (e.g. the Tanakh, the Christian bible, the Qur'an, the Vedas, including the Upanishads, the Guru Granth Sahib, the various collections in Buddhism) have authority by very virtue of being scripture. This is completely different from the authority of science. Newton's *Principia* and Darwin's *On the Origin of Species* are wonderful books but they do not have any permanence other than that which derives from their success in explaining the material world. Indeed, as is well known, Darwin knew almost nothing of the mechanism of inheritance despite the whole of his argument relying on inheritance, so parts of *The Origin* were completely out of date over a hundred years ago.

Then consider the possibility of miracles, where the word is used not in its everyday sense (and the sense in which it is sometimes used in the Christian scriptures), namely 'remarkable', 'completely unexpected' or 'wonderful' (as in the tabloid heading 'My miracle baby'), but in its narrower meaning of 'contrary to the laws of nature'. Scientists who do not accept that miracles take place can react to this 'contrary to the laws of nature' definition of miracles in one of three ways: (i) miracles are impossible (because they are contrary to the laws of nature); (ii) miracles are outside of science (because they are contrary to the laws of nature); (iii) miracles are very rare events that haven't yet been incorporated within the body of science but will be (as rare meteorological events, e.g. eclipses, and mysterious creatures, e.g. farm animals with two heads or seven legs, have been).

The relationship between science and religion has changed over the years (Brooke 1991; Al-Hayani 2005); indeed, the use of the singular, 'relationship', risks giving the impression that there is only one way in which the two relate. Nevertheless, there are two key issues: one is to do with understandings of reality; the other to do with evidence and authority. Although it is always difficult to generalise, most religions hold that reality consists of more than the dependable, material world that science studies and many religions give weight to personal and/or (depending on the religion) institutional authority in a way that science generally strives not to.

For example, there is a very large religious and theological literature on the world to come, i.e. life after death (e.g. Hick 1976/1985). However, although some people (notably Atkins 2011) have argued that science disproves the existence of life after death, it can be argued that science has little or nothing to say about this question because life after death exists or would exist outside of or beyond the realm to which science relates.

Sex education

Most of the world's religions have a great deal to say about sexual values. Of course, those with a religious faith also need to understand something of secular reasoning about sexual ethics: it is still too often the case that those with a religious faith assume that only they really know what sexual behaviours are morally acceptable.

In recent years there has been an increasing acknowledgement from all sex educators, whether or not they themselves are members of any particular religious faith, that religious points of view needs to be taken into account, if only because a significant number of children and their parents have moral values strongly influenced by religious traditions.

The first major attempt in the UK among believers from a number of religious traditions to agree a religious perspective on sex education resulted in an agreed statement by members of six major UK religions (Islamic Academy 1991). This statement examined contemporary sex education, listed principles which it was felt ought to govern sex education and provided a moral framework for sex education. This framework "enjoins chastity and virginity before marriage and faithfulness and loyalty within marriage and prohibits extramarital sex and homosexual acts", "Upholds the responsibilities and values of parenthood", "Acknowledges that we owe a duty of respect and obedience to parents and have a responsibility to care for them in their old age and infirmity" and "Affirms that the married relationship involves respect and love" (Islamic Academy 1991: 8).

Another early UK project to look at the important of religion and ethnicity for sex education was the Sex Education Forum's 'religion and ethnicity project'. A working group was set up which "was concerned to challenge the view that religions offer only negative messages around sex, wanting to explore the broader philosophy and rationale behind specific religious prescriptions" (Thomson 1993: 2). Each participant was sent a total of twenty-eight questions (e.g. 'Are there different natural roles for men and women, if so why?' and 'What is the religious attitude towards contraception and/or 'protection' for example, safe sex re: STDs, HIV?') and the project chose to present a range of views, rather than attempting to reach a consensus. The outcome was a pack that had chapters on Anglican, Hindu, Islamic, Jewish, Methodist, Roman Catholic, Sikh and secular perspectives.

At the same time as Rachel Thomson was compiling her pack, Gill Lenderyou and Mary Porter of the Family Planning Association were putting together a booklet arising from the 'Values, Faith and Sex Education' project (Lenderyou and Porter 1994). At a four-day residential event in this project, a bill of pupils' rights was drawn up by twenty-two people of different religious faiths, and agreed statements on sex education were produced under the headings of: Respect and difference, Faith and change in society, Male and female equality, Relationships and marriages, Homosexuality, Cohabitation, Disability and sexuality, and Celibacy. The bill of pupils' rights is more liberal and the agreed statements are more tentative than the contents of Islamic Academy (1991). For example, included in the bill of pupils' rights are the statements that pupils have the right to sex education that "provides full, accurate and objective information about growth and reproduction on topics including puberty, parenthood, contraception, child care and responsible parenthood" and that pupils have the right "to be consulted about the manner in which sex education is implemented in the classroom in connection with issues such as whether it takes place in single sex or mixed groups or which topics can be included in the programme" (Lenderyou and Porter 1994: 37).

Subsequently, Shaikh Abdul Mabud and I edited an academic book titled *Sex Education and Religion* which concentrated on Christian and Muslim views about sex education (Reiss and Mabud 1998), and publications have resulted from projects funded by the Department of Health's former Teenage Pregnancy Unit including 'Supporting the Development of SRE [sex and relationships education] within a Religious and Faith Context' (Blake and Katrak 2002). Since that time, an increasing number of publications have considered the importance of religion for sex education (e.g. Rasmussen 2010; Smerecnik *et al.* 2010; Yip and Page 2013).

Conclusions

Schools are diverse communities yet UK schools have mostly been slow to consider religion as an inclusion issue. Done poorly, which it all too often is (Ofsted 2013), education about religion can bore students and achieve little. Done well – and not just through formal religious education lessons but in other subjects and in the life and ethos of the whole school – it can engage students, build knowledge, sharpen ethical thinking, contribute to community cohesion (Hess 2009; Woodward 2012) and make religious extremism less likely (Savage 2013).

However, this isn't always easy! For one thing, Teaching Assistants and others (e.g. parents, mentors) who work in school classrooms may find themselves holding very different views about the importance, relevance and messages of religion to those held by the students. There are various ways of dealing with this – schools typically have policies about such matters as religious dress and time for prayers. It is also important not to equate cultural practices concerning arranged marriages or female genital mutilation with religious positions. More generally, religion can be thought of as a controversial issue, namely as one where a range of positions may validly be held. In most instances the cardinal rule is for teachers, Teaching Assistants and others who work in school classrooms to respect students – and vice versa – even if they don't agree with them. As students grow older, they can benefit from adults who disagree with them talking with them, helping them to think of the implications of their views, so long as this is always done in a non-confrontational manner that doesn't appear to attack religion and doesn't abuse the authority that adults in schools almost inevitably have over students.

Reflections on values and practice

1 Is it realistic to expect Teaching Assistants to develop relationships with adults and others in the community beyond the school gate?
2 How might you support a student who felt that their views on sex and relationships were being ridiculed by their classmates on account of their religious beliefs?
3 What might you do if a student with whom you were working felt that their views about religion were not being taken seriously by their teacher?

Suggested further reading

Barnes, L. P. (ed) (2012) *Debates in Religious Education*. London: Routledge.
Hess, D. E. (2009) *Controversy in the Classroom*. New York: Routledge.
Mirza, H. S. and Meetoo, V. (2012) *Respecting Difference: Race, Faith and Culture for Teacher Educators*. London: IOE Press.

References

Al-Hayani, F. A. (2005) 'Islam and science: contradiction or concordance', *Zygon*, 40: 565–576.
Armstrong, F. and Barton, L. (2010) 'Inclusive education and diversity: developing innovative strategies. A case study of an English primary school', in Bélanger, N. and Duchesne, H. (eds), *Des Écoles en Mouvement*. Ottawa: Presses de l'Université d'Ottawa, 275–306.
Atkins, P. (2011) *On Being: A Scientist's Exploration of the Great Questions of Existence*. Oxford: Oxford University Press.
Barnes, L. P. (2012) 'Diversity', in Barnes, L. P. (ed.), *Debates in Religious Education* (pp. 65–76). London: Routledge.
Barnes, L. P., Lundie, D., Armstrong, D., McKinney, S. and Williams, K. (2012) 'Religious education in the United Kingdom and Ireland', in Barnes, L. P. (ed), *Debates in Religious Education* (pp. 22–51). London: Routledge.
Blake, S. and Katrak, Z. (2002) *Faith, Values and Sex & Relationships Education*. London: National Children's Bureau.
Bosanquet, P., Radford, J. and Webster, R. (2015) *The Teaching Assistant's Guide to Effective Interaction: How to Maximise your Practice*. London: Routledge.
Brooke, J. H. (1991) *Science and Religion: Some Historical Perspectives*. Cambridge: Cambridge University Press.
Chapman, J. D., McNamara, S., Reiss, M. J. and Waghid, Y. (eds) (2014) *International Handbook of Learning, Teaching and Leading in Faith-Based Schools*. Dordrecht, Netherlands: Springer.
Halstead, J. M. and Reiss, M. J. (2003) *Values in Sex Education: From Principles to Practice*. London: RoutledgeFalmer.
Hess, D. E. (2009) *Controversy in the Classroom*. New York: Routledge.
Hick, J. (1976/1985) *Death and Eternal Life*. Basingstoke, UK: Macmillan.
Ipsos MORI. (2011) *Religion and Globalisation*. London: Author.
Islamic Academy. (1991) *Sex Education in the School Curriculum: The Religious Perspective – An Agreed Statement*. Cambridge: Islamic Academy.
Lenderyou, G. and Porter, M. (eds) (1994) *Sex Education, Values and Morality*. London: Health Education Authority.
Mirza, H. S. and Meetoo, V. (2012) *Respecting Difference: Race, Faith and Culture for Teacher Educators*. London: IOE Press.

Ofsted. (2013) *Religious Education: Realising the Potential*. Manchester: Author.

Parker-Jenkins, M., Glenn, M. and Janmaat, J. G. (2014) *Reaching In, Reaching Out: Faith Schools, Community Engagement, and 21st-Century Skills for Intercultural Understanding*. London: IOE Press.

Qualifications and Curriculum Authority. (2004) *Religious Education: Non-Statutory National Framework*. London: Author.

Rasmussen, M. L. (2010) 'Secularism, religion and "progressive" sex education', *Sexualities*, 13: 699–712.

Reiss, M. J. (2014) 'What significance does Christianity have for science education?', in Matthews, M. R. (ed), *Handbook of Historical and Philosophical Research in Science Education* (pp. 1637–1662). Dordrecht, NE: Springer.

Reiss, M. J. and Mabud, S. A. (eds) (1998) *Sex Education and Religion*. Cambridge: Islamic Academy.

Reiss, M. and White, J. (2009) 'Atheism needs to be studied in schools', *The Independent, Education*, 16 July: 4.

Savage, S. (2013) 'Head and heart in preventing religious radicalization', in Watts, F. and Dumbreck, G. (eds), *Head and Heart: Perspectives from Religion and Psychology* (pp. 157–193). West Conshohocken, PA: Templeton Press.

Schools Council. (1971) *Working Paper 36: Religious Education in Secondary Schools*. London: Evans/Methuen.

Smerecnik, C., Schaalma, H., Gerjo, K., Meijer, S. and Poelman, J. (2010) 'An exploratory study of Muslim adolescents' views on sexuality: implications for sex education and prevention', *BMC Public Health*, 10: 533.

Smyth E., Lyons, M. and Darmody, M. (eds) (2013) *Religious Education in a Multicultural Europe*. Basingstoke: Palgrave Macmillan.

Starkey, H. (2015) *Learning to Live Together: Struggles for Citizenship and Human Rights Education*. London: IOE Press.

Thomson, R. (ed) (1993) *Religion, Ethnicity & Sex Education: Exploring the Issues – A Resource for Teachers and Others Working with Young People*. London: National Children's Bureau.

Watson, B. (2012) 'Why religious education matters', in Barnes, L. P. (ed) Debates in Religious Education (pp. 14–21). London: Routledge.

Woodward, R. (2012) 'Community cohesion', in Barnes, L. P. (ed) Debates in Religious Education (pp. 132–145). London: Routledge.

Yip, A. K.-T. and Page, S.-J. (eds) (2013) *Religious and Sexual Identities: A Multi-faith Exploration of Young Adults*. Farnham: Ashgate.

Chapter 7

Teaching Assistants working with teachers

Vikki Anderson and Linda Lyn-Cook

Introduction

The move towards inclusive education has led to a greater need for additional support in the classroom, resulting in a significant rise in the number of Teaching Assistants in schools. Government initiatives aimed at raising standards and reducing teacher workloads have increased the range and complexity of tasks carried out by Teaching Assistants but research has highlighted variation in the deployment, pay, conditions and training of this body of staff. Incorporating Teaching Assistants' perspectives on working with teachers, this chapter examines how this relationship can affect the quality of inclusive practice and identifies some important implications for the role.

Working relationships: teachers and Teaching Assistants

Recent statistics show that around 243,700 full-time equivalent Teaching Assistants are employed in England – a figure that has more than trebled since 2000 (DfE 2014) – and this growth has been accompanied by marked changes in their roles and responsibilities (Whitehorn 2010). Initially they functioned as classroom auxiliaries who relieved teachers of care and housekeeping-type duties (Clayton 1993), but government approaches to inclusion, curriculum development and workforce remodelling have resulted in them taking on an ever-increasing variety of tasks, with many playing a significant part in learning and teaching (DfES 2003). Kerry (2005: 377) examined the roles of Teaching Assistants documented in the literature and proposed 11 different types, from "Dogsbody" and "Routine administrator/teacher's PA" to "Teacher support and partial substitute", and "Mobile paraprofessional", the latter being required to plan and deliver learning activities in a similar way to higher-level Teaching Assistants (Wilson *et al.* 2007). The extent to which Teaching Assistants play a role in learning and teaching was highlighted in the findings of the Deployment and Impact of Support Staff (DISS) project – a five-year, UK government-funded study which analysed the impact of teaching assistant support on the academic progress and behaviour of 8,200 pupils across seven-year groups in primary and secondary schools. Results showed that Teaching Assistants spent over half of their working day in a predominantly pedagogical role, mainly supporting lower-attaining pupils and those with special educational needs, which far outweighed time spent supporting the teacher and curriculum or performing other tasks (Blatchford *et al.* 2012). An unexpected finding was that pupils who received the most support from Teaching Assistants had less engagement with a qualified teacher and made less academic progress than similar pupils who received little or no teaching assistant support, even after controlling for factors likely to be related to more support such as prior attainment and level of special educational needs (Blatchford *et al.* 2009; Blatchford, Russell and Webster 2012).

Drawing upon a range of additional data gathered throughout the DISS project, Webster *et al.* (2011) highlight a number of 'wider factors' that could have affected the relationship between pupils' academic progress and teaching assistant support, including: insufficient paid time for joint planning and feedback; pupils becoming separated from their teachers and the broader curriculum; the ways in which Teaching Assistants interact with pupils and a lack of training for teachers in working effectively with support staff. These are key issues that have been frequently identified in the literature and should be considered by all school leaders and teachers when making decisions about how support staff are prepared for and carry out their work in the classroom. This chapter explores some of this research, focusing on studies undertaken in England that incorporated the views of Teaching Assistants themselves.

Lee and Mawson (1998) conducted a questionnaire survey of 767 classroom assistants across a range of mainstream primary schools and found that while most were satisfied with their jobs, they were unhappy about pay and the lack of time and information available to do the work properly. Many said they felt undervalued and that teachers needed to communicate with them more; include them in their lesson plans in advance and involve them in staff meetings. These findings were echoed in Farrell *et al.*'s (1999) research in which 149 learning support assistants and 113 teachers were interviewed during case study visits to twenty-one sites, including mainstream and special schools across the primary and secondary phases of education and Local Education Authority support services. The vast majority of learning support assistants was committed to their jobs and enthusiastic about their work. However, a consistent problem on the mainstream sites was the lack of time for day-to-day planning meetings when the assistant could receive advice from, and give feedback to, the teacher. An exception was in mainstream primary schools where learning support assistants supported teachers in implementing the National Literacy Strategy. Here the level of prescription resulted in everyone sharing clear objectives and the learning support assistant's role being more clearly defined.

The results of a questionnaire survey completed by 264 head teachers, 535 teachers and 568 Teaching Assistants in 327 primary and secondary schools in England and Wales (Smith, Whitby and Sharpe 2004) also revealed that a major difficulty affecting the working relationships of teachers and Teaching Assistants was lack of time to plan and prepare lessons together. Only 54 per cent of the Teaching Assistants reported that their schools had policies on their roles and responsibilities and again there were concerns about pay and conditions of service: "My job description grew, the workload doubled ... my salary stayed the same" (Smith *et al.* 2004: 8). Similar issues were highlighted in a study by Anderson and Finney (2008) which sought the views of 33 Teaching Assistants who were employed in primary, secondary and special schools whilst studying for a Foundation degree. They agreed on 30 statements they wanted to make to the teachers with whom they worked and their conversations about the reasons for their choices were recorded. Several statements referred to the lack of clarity of Teaching Assistants' roles, for example, "[We want a] clear indication of the role within the classroom" and "I'm a TA, not a PA" and were accompanied by the comment, "We sometimes assume a role and are told 'no', that is not what I want you to do" (Anderson and Finney 2008: 76).

The Teaching Assistants also made numerous statements about the need for appropriate joint planning, information sharing and effective communication with teachers:

> I am never invited to a meeting.
> I go to meetings but I'm unpaid.
> Please make time in order to plan collaboratively with me.
> Give us lesson plans.
> Give us more information [about the lessons/students' needs].

When discussing this, one Teaching Assistant said, "We are going into every lesson cold – I would like to know what I am doing for each lesson", whilst another commented, "We are expected to do more than we are paid for" (Anderson and Finney 2008: 77–78).

Ofsted (2008, 2010) reports that the quality of teaching is enhanced when teachers provide clear guidance to Teaching Assistants and involve them in planning. In effectively supported lessons, Teaching Assistants should know in advance what each pupil is expected to learn; build on prior learning; model effective approaches; enable pupils to work independently; check and review their learning at the end of the lesson and provide evidence of the impact of their support. However, the Making a Statement (MAST) study (Webster and Blatchford 2015), which explored the mainstream teaching, support and interactions experienced by 48 Year 5 pupils with statements for moderate learning difficulties or behavioural, emotional and social difficulties, revealed that in an attempt to make teaching accessible, nearly all of the Teaching Assistants explained and modified tasks set by the teacher 'in the moment', with teachers making comments such as:

> I don't plan specifically for Greg. I kind of say [to the TA], 'This is what the class are doing; this is what my more able and less able are doing. ... Use your judgement to figure out what he can access or not.
>
> (Webster and Blatchford, 2015: 334).

Some alternative approaches can nevertheless be found in the literature. For example, Fox, Farrell and Davis (2004) describe how a primary school teacher informed the Teaching Assistant about the whole day's planning, focusing on the work of the entire class, together with specific planning for a child with Down syndrome. The Teaching Assistant recorded her views in the teacher's planning and assessment book at the end of the morning and afternoon sessions, and the teacher used these to differentiate the next day's lessons. In another primary school, teachers and Teaching Assistants were allocated a weekly slot to engage in reflection and planning during whole school assembly and in a secondary school, 'Working Together' slips were created, enabling teachers and Teaching Assistants to increase communication, plan collaboratively and reflect on their work (Vincett, Cremin and Thomas 2005).

The Effective Deployment of Teaching Assistants (EDTA) project (Webster, Blatchford and Russell 2013) was a follow-up study to the DISS project that involved six primary and four secondary schools in two local authorities. Under typical circumstances and funding arrangements, the researchers collaborated with school leaders, teachers and Teaching Assistants to develop and evaluate strategies for the effective preparation, deployment and practice of Teaching Assistants. Results from pre-intervention audits showed that the quality of lesson planning was a greater issue for Teaching Assistants than teachers, with a lack of time being cited in interviews as the reason why Teaching Assistants found themselves under-prepared. Teaching Assistants in secondary schools seemed to be the most affected, with many (in a similar way to those in the DISS project) describing going into lessons 'blind' (Webster *et al.* 2013: 88). During the intervention year, primary schools found ways of arranging the school day or Teaching Assistants' working hours in order to create time with teachers, for example bringing the start and finish times of Teaching Assistants' days forward by fifteen minutes in order to allow guaranteed time for daily planning and sharing of feedback. Where creating time remained problematic in secondary schools, improving the quality and clarity of lesson plans helped prepare Teaching Assistants. By the end of the project, Teaching Assistants in both phases had benefited from teachers providing more detailed lesson plans and, in some cases, additional material in advance of lessons. Through their lesson plans, teachers not only made their expectations of Teaching Assistants clearer but avoided situations where they went into lessons blind. Concerns about the extra work this created were offset by the advantages teachers noted as a result of making the effort.

If Teaching Assistants do not have opportunities to share their ideas with, seek advice from, and give feedback to the teacher, the "voice vacuum" described by O'Brien and Garner (2001: 3) will restrict the growth of a fruitful professional partnership aimed at improving the quality of learning and teaching. It is important, however, that joint planning is not carried out at lunchtime or after school, relying on the good will of Teaching Assistants but that structured, paid time is allocated to it. The responsibility for collaborative partnership does not therefore rest solely with the class or subject teacher but is a management issue that requires a whole school approach. Unlike teachers, support staff do not have the reassurance of national pay scales and pay can vary across schools. Pay and conditions are determined by the local authority or by the school in the case of academies and salaries may differ on a regional basis, with some Teaching Assistants being paid during term time only. Although there appears to be a need for a national pay structure, the organisation working towards this, the School Support Staff Negotiating Body, was disbanded in 2010 by the Secretary of State for Education as it did "not fit well with the Government's priorities for greater deregulation of the pay and conditions arrangements for the school workforce" (Gove 2010: para. 2). Issues of pay and conditions have therefore yet to be addressed fully.

It is nevertheless clear from the perspective of Teaching Assistants that being valued does not rest solely with financial rewards. For example, learning support assistants in Mistry et al.'s (2004) research commented that they would appreciate 'being thanked occasionally'. Mistry, Burton and Brundrett (2004: 134) refer to the significance of this in human resources management, whereby "people are not going to work to their optimum level unless they feel valued and appreciated". This was reflected in statements made by the Teaching Assistants in Anderson and Finney's study, such as:

> Please ask for my opinion – it counts!;
> Don't underestimate the experience I have to offer; and
> Acknowledge our skills.

Statements such as those above show how the TAs felt that teachers should identify and make more use of their abilities and experience. This could involve giving them a role in areas of the curriculum other than core skills, for as one Teaching Assistant remarked, "I heard teachers say: 'We didn't know she could speak French fluently'" (2008: 78).

Asking Teaching Assistants to share their knowledge and expertise can have a positive effect on their confidence as well as the inclusive classroom (Symes and Humphrey 2011). They should therefore be encouraged to contribute to daily information sharing, staff meetings, INSET days, newsletters and staff intranet sites, with knowledge-sharing targets included in performance reviews (Malcolm, Hodkinson and Colley 2003). Although there is no statutory process, some schools have introduced performance management and appraisal procedures for Teaching Assistants similar to those of teachers in order to raise the professional status of support staff. This appears to have been welcomed by Teaching Assistants as a formal but supportive means of gaining recognition and appreciation for their work and engaging in discussion about professional development (Groom 2006; Balshaw 2010).

Webster, Blatchford and Russell (2013: 80) argue that Teaching Assistants have 'untapped potential', highlighting evidence that they have a positive impact on pupils' progress when they are specifically trained and prepared for curricular interventions (Alborz et al. 2009). This is augmented by the more positive findings from the DISS project on Teaching Assistants' impact on teacher workload, classroom discipline, pupils' confidence and motivation, and the quality and amount of teaching teachers are able to deliver with a Teaching Assistant present (Blatchford *et al.* 2012). Emphasising that "teaching assistant time should never be a substitute for teaching from a qualified teacher", the 2011 Green Paper, *Support and Aspiration: A New Approach to Special Educational Needs and Disability*, states: "Within schools, support staff can make a real difference to the achievement of pupils with SEN, but they need to be deployed and used effectively in order to do so" (DfE 2011a: 63). The Teaching Assistants in Anderson and Finney's study made this clear in their statements directed at the teachers they worked with:

> [We want] more differentiation – especially at secondary level.
> And there is the issue of Teaching Assistants assuming responsibility for pupils identified as having special educational needs.
> Don't assume the lower-ability group should only work with the TA.
> Why don't you use your expertise to take the lower-ability group and I'll take the rest?

The last comment came with an accompanying comment highlighting the negative effect that this could have on pupils:

> Children are often labelled because we are known to work with the 'SEN' group.

Several Teaching Assistants also expressed concerns about teachers' lack of expertise and awareness of the requirements of pupils with special educational needs:

> Teachers need more training in SEN.
> [You need] teacher training on how to use TAs effectively.
>   (Anderson and Finney 2008: 79–80)

Both the DISS (Blatchford et al. 2012) and EDTA (Webster *et al.* 2013) projects found that Teaching Assistants tended to work with low-attaining pupils and those with special educational needs, and in the MAST study (Webster and Blatchford 2015), Teaching Assistants were found to have the main responsibility for teaching pupils with statements of special educational needs. In each case it was found that teachers regarded Teaching Assistants as experts, despite both having similar limitations in their knowledge and training, and in so doing, detached themselves from these pupils.

The fact that Teaching Assistants often focus on those who are seen to need 'extra help' may reinforce "the peer-group label of 'dumb'" (Mansaray 2006: 179) and can create dependency on the part of pupil and teacher. Gerschel (2005: 71) cautions against "a 'Velcro model'" of Teaching Assistants being attached to single pupils, which can result in emotional dependency on the assistant and them being less likely to be fully included in the class or form relationships with their peers.

Blatchford *et al.* (2009: 134) argue that pupils experiencing barriers to participation are likely to benefit from more, not less, of a teacher's time and that there is a danger that delegating responsibility to Teaching Assistants means the teacher does not feel the need: "to consider pedagogical approaches that might benefit the whole class". It is therefore important to give careful thought to the ways in which Teaching Assistants work, for example rotating groups to allow teachers to spend more time with pupils with special educational needs whilst the Teaching Assistant monitors the rest of the class and ensuring that Teaching Assistants and teachers have more time to communicate and engage in professional development, especially in relation to working with pupils with special educational needs (Russell, Webster and Blatchford 2013). In both primary and secondary schools, Vincett *et al.* (2005) used the models of Zoning and Room Management for collaborative working. Zoning involves arranging the class into learning zones usually structured by the placement of groups and allocating these to the teacher or Teaching Assistant, for example six groups could be split 5/1, 4/2 or 3/3. Within Room Management, each of the adults in the classroom occupies a clear role – that of activity or learning manager. The activity manager concentrates on the larger group and the learning manager provides intensive support to particular individuals. Staff can take on either role, depending on the needs of the class and the activities to be carried out, and can switch roles during a session if required. With each model, however, the teacher has overall responsibility for the whole class. Both of these models were found to have positive effects on pupils' self-esteem and engagement in learning, and enabled Teaching Assistants to become more involved in the learning experiences of all pupils.

The EDTA project (Russell *et al.* 2013) prompted teachers to challenge their own practice and consider how the classroom could be organised more effectively in order to ensure that pupils received equal amounts of teacher time across the school week, thereby reducing adult dependency. By the post-intervention stage, Teaching Assistants were spending much less time with low-attaining pupils and those with special educational needs, with primary Teaching Assistants spending over half their time working with middle and high-attaining pupils. Although setting was used in all of the secondary schools involved and Teaching Assistants rarely worked with higher sets, they became far more likely to work with a variety of pupils in these classes, not just those who were struggling the most. As Teaching Assistants worked with other pupils, teachers spent more time with low-attaining pupils, which enriched their understanding of these pupils' learning needs.

The Special Education Needs and Disability Review (Ofsted 2010) found that where things were working well for pupils with learning difficulties, class and subject teachers retained overall responsibility for the progress and attainment of *all* pupils in their classes as opposed to transferring the responsibility for some pupils' education to the SENCO and/or Teaching Assistants. There was also evidence of careful monitoring of progress, with timely intervention and thorough evaluation of its impact by teachers (Ofsted 2010). However, as shown in the MAST study (Webster and Blatchford 2015), teachers' confidence in teaching pupils with special educational needs can play an important part in the model of provision employed and for pupils with statements, the common practice of specifying a set number of hours of teaching assistant support can get in the way of devising appropriate methods of teaching pupils with learning difficulties.

The Teachers' Standards (DfE 2011c) stipulate that teachers must "adapt teaching to respond to the strengths and needs of all pupils". Despite this, some teachers do not feel confident or skilled in teaching pupils with complex learning needs (Glazzard 2011; Ofsted 2010). With regard to trainee teachers, initial provision in this area can vary across training providers and/or placement schools (Nash and Norwich 2010). For those already qualified, successive governments have funded a number of initiatives designed to enhance practising teachers' knowledge, skills and confidence, for example the Inclusion Development Programme and the Achievement for All Project (DfE 2011b). However, to date, only the SENCO role carries with it mandatory training in special educational needs as an essential requirement of the post, with all new SENCOs being required to gain the National Award for SEN Co-ordination within three years of taking up post (National College for Teaching and Leadership 2014). Appropriate continuing professional development must therefore be made more widely available if all teachers are to acquire skills for effective working with pupils with special educational needs and this should also include training in working with Teaching Assistants (Hartley 2010).

Where a specific pedagogy is being used, Teaching Assistants should also receive training so that they fully understand the principles of the approach and the techniques required to apply it. This will help to promote consistency and avoid the confusion that can result for many pupils when different adults in the classroom use differing techniques and methods in a given subject. In the DISS project, Teaching Assistants were found to prioritise task completion as opposed to promoting engagement in the learning process and ownership of tasks. For example, they were observed telling pupils what to do; giving them answers or physically doing work for them rather than prompting them to think for themselves (Rubie-Davies et al. 2010; Radford, Blatchford and Webster 2011). This approach may have been influenced by messages communicated unintentionally by teachers about the need to meet targets and get through the curriculum (Higgins et al. 2014), highlighting some of the tensions arising between the standards and inclusion agendas (Glazzard 2011; Runswick-Cole 2011). Radford et al. (2013: 119) stress the importance of Teaching Assistants using styles of questioning that support independent learning and advocate 'heuristic scaffolding' as a means of empowering students "by developing their awareness of relevant approaches to problem-solving", enabling them to take "responsibility for their own learning strategies". Other techniques can be found in The Education Endowment Foundation's Guidance Report (Sharples, Webster and Blatchford 2015), which makes a number of recommendations for collaborative working between teachers and Teaching Assistants and includes a framework that Teaching Assistants can use for more effective pupil questioning.

Conclusion

Many of the issues identified by Teaching Assistants in this chapter appear to be ongoing, indicating that they still need to be addressed if best practice is to be widely disseminated. It is evident that together with government-led changes related to supporting pupils with special educational needs, a continuous process of clear, constructive communication and reflective practice is needed between teachers and Teaching Assistants. However, this will only be possible if both teachers and Teaching Assistants can operate within a supportive organisational culture in which they are properly equipped to meet the wide range of needs in the classroom. Training for teachers and Teaching Assistants in inclusive practice is essential, together with training for teachers in the effective deployment of Teaching Assistants. Roles and responsibilities must be clearly defined, with time for joint planning of approaches which ensure that all pupils receive equitable amounts of teacher time and do not become separated from their peers. There is also a need for a national pay structure and management and appraisal systems that will enable Teaching Assistants to work to their strengths and identify areas for development. Finally, it can be seen throughout this chapter that valuing Teaching Assistants is of supreme importance if they are to play an optimal role in improving educational opportunities for all learners, regardless of difference.

Reflections on values and practice

1   Reflect on the relationships you have with teachers. Can you identify aspects of your work together that could be improved upon? What can you do to move towards implementing these changes?
2   How is the impact of your work measured? In what other ways might you demonstrate the positive impact of your work?
3   How might you support pupils' independent learning, rather than simply managing tasks?
4   What joint training would you and a teacher benefit from and how might this be pursued?
5   What, if any, appraisal or performance management system do you benefit from and how does this contribute towards improving outcomes for the pupils you work with?

Suggested further reading

Radford, J., Bosanquet, P., Webster, R., Blatchford, P. and Rubie-Davies, C. (2013) 'Fostering learner independence through heuristic scaffolding: A valuable role for teaching assistants', *International Journal of Educational Research, 63*(1): 116–126.
Sharples, J., Webster, R. and Blatchford, P. (2015) *EEF Guidance Report. Making Best Use of Teaching Assistants.* Online: available at https://educationendowmentfoundation.org.uk/uploads/pdf/TA_Guidance_Report_Interactive.pdf

References

Alborz, A., Pearson, D., Farrell, P. and Howes, A. (2009) *The impact of adult support staff on pupils and mainstream schools,* London: DCSF and Institute of Education.

Anderson, V. and Finney, M. (2008) '"I'm a TA not a PA!" Teaching assistants working with teachers' in Richards, G. and Armstrong, F. (eds.), *Key Issues for Teaching Assistants,* Abingdon: Routledge.

Balshaw, M. (2010) 'Looking for different answers about teaching assistants', *European Journal of Special Needs Education, 25*(4): 337–338.

Blatchford, P., Bassett, P., Brown, P., Koutsoubou, M., Martin, C., Russell, A. and Webster, R. (2009) *Deployment and impact of support staff in schools: The impact of support staff in schools (results from Strand 2, Wave 2),* London: DCSF.

Blatchford, P., Russell, A. and Webster, R. (2012) *Reassessing the impact of teaching assistants: How research challenges practice and policy,* Abingdon: Routledge.

Clayton, T. (1993) 'From domestic helper to "assistant teacher" – the changing role of the British classroom assistant', *European Journal of Special Needs Education, 8:* 32–44.

DfE. (2011a) *Support and aspiration: A new approach to special educational needs and disability,* Norwich: TSO.

DfE. (2011 b) *The National Strategies 1997–2011: A brief summary of the impact and effectiveness of the National Strategies.* Retrieved from www.gov.uk/government/uploads/system/uploads/attachment_data/file/175408/DFE-00032-2011.pdf

DfE. (2011c) *Teachers' standards.* Retrieved from www.gov.uk/government/publications/teachers-standards

DfE. (2014) *School workforce in England: November 2013.* Retrieved from www.gov.uk/government/statistics/school-workforce-in-england-november-2013

DfES. (2003) *Raising standards and tackling workload: A national agreement,* London: DfES.

Farrell, P., Balshaw, M. and Polat, F. (1999) *The management, role and training of learning support assistants,* London: DfEE.

Fox, S., Farrell, P. and Davis, P. (2004) 'Factors associated with the effective inclusion of primary-aged pupils with down's syndrome', *British Journal of Special Education, 31:* 184–90.

Gerschel, L. (2005) 'The special educational needs coordinator's role in managing teaching assistants: The Greenwich perspective', *Support for Learning, 20:* 69–76.

Glazzard, J. (2011) 'Perceptions of the barriers to effective inclusion in one primary school: voices of teachers and teaching assistants', *Support for Learning, 26*(2): 56–63.

Gove, M. (2010) *Written ministerial statement by Michael Gove on the abolition of the School Support Staff Negotiating Body (SSSNB).* Retrieved from www.gov.uk/government/speeches/written-ministerial-statement-by-michael-gove-on-the-abolition-of-the-school-support-staff-negotiating-body-sssnb

Groom, B. (2006) 'Building relationships for learning: The developing role of the teaching assistant', *Support for Learning, 21:* 199–203.

Hartley, R. (2010) 'Teacher expertise for special educational needs: Filling in the gaps', *Policy Exchange research note July 2010.* Retrieved from www.policyexchange.org.uk/images/publications/teacher expertise for sen-jul.pdf

Higgins, S., Katsipataki, M., Kokotsaki, D., Coleman, R., Major, L. E., and Coe, R. (2014) *The Sutton Trust – Education Endowment Foundation Teaching and Learning Toolkit.* Retrieved from www.suttontrust.com/about-us/education-endowment-foundation/teaching-learning-toolkit/ (accessed 17 April 2015).

Kerry, T. (2005) 'Towards a typology for conceptualising the roles of teaching assistants', *Educational Review, 57:* 373–384.

Lee, B. and Mawson, C. (1998) *Survey of classroom assistants,* Slough: NFER.

Malcolm, J., Hodkinson, P. and Colley, H. (2003) 'The interrelationships between informal and formal learning', *Journal of Workplace Learning*, 15(7/8): 313–318.

Mansaray, A. A. (2006) 'Liminality and in/exclusion: exploring the work of teaching assistants', *Pedagogy, Culture & Society*, 14(2):171–187.

Mistry, M., Burton, N. and Brundrett, M. (2004) 'Managing LSAs: An evaluation of the use of learning support assistants in an urban primary school', *School Leadership and Management*, 24: 125–136.

Nash, T. and Norwich, B. (2010) 'The initial training of teachers to teach children with special educational needs: A national survey of English Post Graduate Certificate of Education programmes', *Teaching and Teacher Education*, 26(7): 1471–1480.

National College for Teaching and Leadership (2014) *National Award for SEN Co-ordination. Learning Outcomes*. Retrieved from www.gov.uk/government/uploads/system/uploads/attachment_data/file/354172/nasc-learning-outcomes-final.pdf

O'Brien, T. and Garner, P. (2001) 'Tim and Philip's story: setting the record straight' in O'Brien, T. and Garner, P. (eds.) *Untold Stories: Learning Support Assistants and Their Work*, Stoke-on-Trent: Trentham Books.

Ofsted (2008) *The deployment, training and development of the wider school workforce*, London: Author.

Ofsted. (2010) *The special educational needs and disability review: A statement is not enough*, Manchester: DfE.

Radford, J., Blatchford, P. and Webster, R. (2011) 'Opening up and closing down: comparing teacher and TA talk in mathematics lessons', *Learning and Instruction*, 21(5): 625–635.

Radford, J., Bosanquet, P., Webster, R., Blatchford, P. and Rubie-Davies, C. (2013) 'Fostering learner independence through heuristic scaffolding: A valuable role for teaching assistants', *International Journal of Educational Research*, 63(1): 116–126.

Rubie-Davies, C., Blatchford, P., Webster, R., Koutsoubou, M. and Bassett, P. (2010) 'Enhancing learning? A comparison of teacher and teaching assistant interactions with pupils', *School Effectiveness and School Improvement*, 21(4): 429–449.

Runswick-Cole, K. (2011) 'Time to end the bias towards inclusive education?', *British Journal of Special Education*, 38(3): 112–119.

Russell, A., Webster, R. and Blatchford, P. (2013) *Maximising the impact of teaching assistants: Guidance for school leaders and teachers*, Abingdon: Routledge.

Sharples, J., Webster, R. and Blatchford, P. (2015) *EEF Guidance Report. Making Best Use of Teaching Assistants*. Retrieved from https://educationendowmentfoundation.org.uk/uploads/pdf/TA_Guidance_Report_Interactive.pdf

Smith, P., Whitby, K. and Sharpe, C. (2004) *The employment and deployment of teaching assistants*, Slough: NFER.

Symes, W. and Humphrey, N. (2011) 'The deployment, training and teacher relationships of teaching assistants supporting pupils with autistic spectrum disorders (ASD) in mainstream secondary schools', *British Journal of Special Education*, 38(2): 57–64.

Vincett, K., Cremin, H. and Thomas, G. (2005) *Teachers and assistants working together*, Maidenhead: OUP.

Webster, R., Blatchford, P., Bassett, P., Brown, P., Martin, C. and Russell, A. (2011) 'The wider pedagogical role of teaching assistants', *School Leadership and Management*, 31(1): 3–20.

Webster, R. and Blatchford, P. (2013) *The Making a Statement project final report: A study of the teaching and support experienced by pupils with a statement of special educational needs in mainstream primary schools*. Retrieved from www.nuffieldfoundation.org/sites/default/files/files/mastreport.pdf

Webster, R., Blatchford, P. and Russell, A. (2013) 'Challenging and changing how schools use teaching assistants: findings from the Effective Deployment of Teaching Assistants project', *School Leadership and Management*, 33(1): 78–96.

Webster, R. and Blatchford, P. (2015) 'Worlds apart? The nature and quality of the educational experiences of pupils with a statement for special educational needs in mainstream primary schools', *British Educational Research Journal*, 41(2): 324–342.

Whitehorn, T. (2010) *School support staff topic paper.* Nottingham: DFE.

Wilson, R., Sharp, C., Shuayb, M., Kendall, L., Wade, P. and Easton, C. (2007) *Research into the deployment and impact of support staff who have achieved HLTA status: Final Report.* Slough: NFER.

Chapter 8

How Teaching Assistants can involve parents

Michele Moore

Introduction

This chapter explores ideas from Teaching Assistants about the role they can play in helping schools reach parents. It focuses on the facilitative role Teaching Assistants can play in discussions with parents and teachers and how more could be made of this. Reflections are drawn from a range of in-schools observations made in the context of research projects, and also from experiences reported in the context of continuing professional development activities. Discussion identifies the importance of recognising ways in which Teaching Assistants can – and already do – uniquely broker relationships between schools and parents. Sobel argues Teaching Assistants are often underused; as a consequence, "they are not able to build key relationships with parents and outside agencies" and remain an untapped resource in schools (Sobel 2013: para. 2). Sobel's observations chime with my own evidence, gathered in and around schools over the last ten years, revealing a lack of celebration, and underutilisation, of the role Teaching Assistants can play in contact with families.

Exclusion of Teaching Assistants

Comments made by a teaching assistant in research I was involved in more than a decade ago continue to be reflected in discussions I take part in still:

> I've never been asked to get involved with any consultation with parents. I've often felt I've been chucked on the scrap heap in terms of what I could offer – but I've got a lot to give these children and their families.
>
> (Teaching Assistant)

Underutilisation of the skills and capacities of Teaching Assistants is, as already mentioned, repeatedly noted in research (Sobel 2013; Sharples, Webster and Blatchford 2015; Hammett and Burton 2005; Rhodes 2006). Having Teaching Assistants work in a context where frustration with neglect of all they can offer is familiar, wastes the capacity of the Teaching Assistant workforce, undermines morale and means good value for money in a hard-pressed education system is not being achieved. This is not an insignificant waste; Sharples *et al.* reported:

While the proportion of teachers in mainstream schools in England has remained relatively steady over the last decade or so, the proportion of full-time equivalent TAs has more than trebled since 2000: from 79,000 to 243,700.

(2015: 8)

The disenfranchised words of a Teaching Assistant reported in research from over a decade ago capture concern which has multiplied as the number of Teaching Assistants has grown: 'I don't want to be treated as a glorified toilet assistant or relegated to washing paint pots' typifies a frequently heard frustration expressed by Teaching Assistants, and 'We have such limited training opportunities but are not necessarily less experienced than teachers ... there is much more we could do'. In a staff room conversation during a recent school visit the point being made was 'I know we are low paid and earn half the amount teacher's take home, but still, for the hours I put in I wish I could have the chance to do my best possible job'. Time and time again Teaching Assistants can be heard expressing their wish to contribute more to school life, and especially more to the life of the school as it relates to its (and usually their) local community: 'She [the teacher] has me phoning parents when there are problems, asking them to come in and see her. ... She doesn't take a minute to think I have known most of the families around here for years and could easily have a word that might nip things in the bud'.

Much is made in recruitment drives of the value of local connections Teaching Assistants bring:

> Volunteer part-time in a local school and then train as a teaching assistant
> (www.skill.org.uk)

> Volunteering to help in a local school for a few hours a week is a good way to start
> (www.nationalcareersservice.direct.gov.uk/advice/planning/
> jobprofiles/Pages/teachingassistant.aspx)

Many Teaching Assistants are parents from the local community and so likely to be in touch with other parents of children in the school (Eyres *et al.* 2004). This suggests we can be optimistic that 'if the school really wants to improve consultation with parents then Teaching Assistants can help to do it' (Teaching Assistant). But it is not always the case that this happens. 'I've lived round here all my life and my three kids have all been through this school but no one thinks to ask me for ideas of what it would take to get families round here coming up to the school' is a remark I heard a few months ago as Teaching Assistants explored reluctance of parents to get involved with meetings about proposed conversion to Academy Status:

> Not many of the teachers are from round here. They sent two letters out about the Academy Conversion, and then another one because hardly any parents

replied … if they'd just asked me, I would have said 'Well most of those letters won't get the time of day … don't bother with the letters … say a few things about the Academy on Talent Night … that'll get people talking'. … But they don't ask TAs … at the Parents and Governors meeting they decided to send out another letter'.

(Teaching Assistants)

The financial cost of under-utilising Teaching Assistants in reaching out to families, and ramifications in terms of blocks to school development and planning, are plain to see from this example. More proactive use of Teaching Assistants in connecting schools and parents would enable Teaching Assistants to contribute hugely to the life of a school as well as increase a sense of their 'being valued' and saving the school money. A study entitled 'The Evident Value of Teaching Assistants' (UNISON 2013) similarly found extensive scope for enhancement of the deployment and management of Teaching Assistants. From my contact with Teaching Assistants it is clear their role as effective facilitators and mediators of relationships with parents is vitally important.

Teaching Assistants I meet frequently talk about wanting to share more in planning with teachers and feel they are well placed to enhance this through consultation with parents, particularly where they are already close to families through neighbourhood associations. They see themselves as ideally suited to playing a pivotal role bringing parents and caregivers into closer connection because of their own connections. They are candid about not necessarily experiencing comfortable levels of inclusion in consultation on school life themselves and feel what they know through their own sense of exclusion gives them insights into how they might work to raise the voices of parents and caregivers: 'Teachers rarely ask for my thoughts on how best to support the children so I can well imagine how families feel when they don't get asked either' (Teaching Assistant). Distinctive contributions are noted: 'Families would like being involved more and Teaching Assistants can bridge the gaps … for example I could offer more to classroom resource preparation because I know the sorts of things these families have in their homes'.

Widening inclusion of parents and caregivers

I frequently hear Teaching Assistants saying they feel more communication with parents and caregivers would help better realise the potential of children and young people, and again they feel this could go hand in hand with what they could offer. Different insights are important:

Over the years I've noticed some parents prefer to talk to Teaching Assistants. They are nervous about seeing teachers. They often seem more comfortable talking to Teaching Assistants about how the student is doing regarding personal needs or about the child's general experience of school life.

(Teaching Assistant)

Teachers might be the last people parents feel they can communicate comfortably and easily with ... Teaching Assistants might be better placed to communicate with parents – often support staff are used as conduits for getting messages between parents and the class teacher.

(Teacher)

There might even be personality clashes – at least we could give parents the choice and say in letters or when we see them *'you can talk to your child's teacher – or to any of the Teaching Assistants '* – make it clear talking to support staff is just as important and useful.

(Teaching Assistant)

It seems there are good reasons to capitalise on the willingness of Teaching Assistants to strengthen engagement with parents and caregivers. Whilst it may appear self-evident Teaching Assistants should play an active part in home-school liaison it is not necessarily easy to operationalise this. Some Teaching Assistants say they worry that asserting their confidence for effective communication with parents and caregivers might appear to imply criticism of teachers. Conversely, some teachers say they feel asking Teaching Assistants to consult with parents when there are endless classroom tasks to sort out might seem unreasonable, or imply they themselves feel reluctant to talk with parents. I have seen best practice emerge where Teaching Assistants and teachers have the opportunity to work collaboratively on the details of planned consultation with parents in a way that allows for open discussion of tricky questions such as 'what will the parents be worrying about on this occasion?', 'who has the best expertise here?', 'who would families find it easiest to talk to about this?' in a non-confrontational context. Such opportunities allow teachers and Teaching Assistants to review assumptions collaboratively and then to adjust any limitations these assumptions could place on the part Teaching Assistants can play in consultation with families. Teaching Assistants can be used to add value to contact teachers have with parents, rather than replace them, paving the way for anxious parents to think about questions they might like to ask in advance of seeing a teacher for example, or following up on actions agreed.

Acknowledging that Teaching Assistants are key to successful consultation between parents and school prompts many suggestions for good practice. In one training event it was suggested 'it could be the teacher is the best one to talk to about curriculum and 'work' matters and Teaching Assistants should be the first point of call for behaviour'. In a different discussion, about getting parents to respond to Year 7 boys missing Spanish lessons, it was felt Teaching Assistants would have a better chance of bringing parents into discussion because 'they [the parents] think the teacher is going to say 'I am afraid to say this is truancy and I will have to impose a sanction', whereas they think if they speak to me first they might be able to get things sorted with less trouble' (Teaching Assistant).

The important point is that flexibility over communications between school and parents and caregivers is helpful. Assumptions that teachers should always have foremost responsibility for dialogue with parents and caregivers can be carefully examined to expand ideas about how Teaching Assistants can contribute, ensuring their talents, local knowledge and differently perceived status offering a point for conciliation in the school hierarchy, are properly valued and not wasted.

Practical matters

In 2004 Karen Dunn and I asked a mixed group of teachers and Teaching Assistants to think about the practicalities of *how* to enhance the role of Teaching Assistants in consultation with parents and caregivers (Dunn and Moore 2004). They offered a range of ideas, frequently based on observational narratives about the reality of everyday life in the school. The ideas resonate with ideas still heard, at the time of updating this chapter, in the staff rooms of busy schools from Teaching Assistants saying they could be more usefully engaged with parents.

An insight from the research discussions was that first steps towards bringing parents and caregivers into closer relationships with schools can come from anyone – not necessarily needing to be initiated by teachers. Teaching Assistants are indispensable here and, we found, are keen to develop this role. In practical terms, Teaching Assistants know routine communications with parents and caregivers – not necessarily on the scale of formalized consultations with teachers – build confidence and help establish relationships. For those parents and caregivers who may feel they have relatively little to contribute to a discussion with a teacher, for example, Teaching Assistants might be able to use their skills to glean seemingly small insights that can contribute to improved teaching and learning. Recently a senior Teaching Assistant in a large comprehensive school gave the following example of how foregrounding engagement with Teaching Assistants rather than teachers could avoid potential pitfalls:

> It's so frustrating for teachers when so much work and effort has gone into setting up a meeting with parents, for them not to show up. Sometimes I think the parents know deep down it's a crazy thing not to show up but they lose their nerve for talking to teachers when they think their child is in trouble. Often I've noticed ages before who won't show because I've know these families for years. I could send a text home and say 'sorry you can't manage a meeting but these things are important and I could just catch up with you a bit if you could pop in for five minutes … it would help get the cart a bit back on its wheels at least … And if I made the first contact the cart might not even have to fall off.'
> (Teaching Assistant)

Teaching Assistants working one to one or in small groups with children can gather insights into parents' concerns that can help build teaching and learning in the classroom. A topical example of this at the time of writing this chapter came about as a group of Year 9 girls discussed an impending school visit to a well-known adventure park. The trip had lost its appeal as a roller-coaster crash in the same week had caused life-changing injuries to many young visitors. The girls told a Teaching Assistant they did not want to go on the trip. They said their parents did not want them to go either but didn't want to raise objections with the teacher organising the trip because it would seem to undermine the teacher's judgment for not cancelling it herself. It might make the teacher look bad in front of colleagues which could affect their daughters' relationships with the teacher in the following GCSE year, and so all in all, they felt their daughters should go ahead with the trip and 'stick to rides for younger children'. As the trip grew near, two of the girls developed considerable fear, having nightmares about crashes and leg amputations and a plan emerged to get their mums to let them stay home on the day of the trip. The Teaching Assistant who was privy to these worries and plans was able to identify one of the parents involved and talk to them briefly when they came to pick up their daughter from a Twilight session. From here, a conversation with the teacher became possible. The trip was not cancelled but reassurances given and students supported in attending. Again we see the role a Teaching Assistant can play in brokering relationships with parents; in this example the links between parents and school helped pupils manage concerns that would otherwise impede attendance and learning (the trip was linked to maths curriculum) and helped a teacher to be fully prepared and on side with families.

Teaching Assistants have significant ongoing access to communication with pupils, their parents and caregivers that offers different avenues for contact to those that teachers have. Recognition of the importance of these 'fragments of consultation' is important – Teaching Assistants often say 'I hadn't realised that sort of chitchat was an example of consultation with a parent that could improve teaching and learning'.

Sites of practice

Of course communication and consultation with parents does not necessarily take place, or need to take place, in school:

> We can't force parents to come into school – some parents have problems with transport – students come from a wide area, and some parents do not drive.
>
> (Teaching Assistant)

> If some parents are reluctant to come to the school, could the school go to the parents? Problems with this might arise – such as the question of taking up parents' time and the question of who could do such visits? Teaching Assistants would be ideal because they could maintain links between teachers, parents and any other agencies involved, but would this put loads more work on them?
>
> (Teacher)

> While Michel's in the middle of his surgery his mum can't get in to school ... perhaps someone should call round their flat each week with work he can do.
>
> (Teaching Assistant)

As Teaching Assistants also often live locally to the school, their work in home links need not be prohibitive. However, complicated issues come up over sites of consultation: on the one hand home visits might help raise participation of parents and caregivers in school life, but they might also create anxiety or inadvertent disenfranchisement:

> Well I would hate myself to have anyone from school come to the house ... I'd have to spend the morning tidying!
>   (Teaching Assistant; other participants laughed and agreed)

> Some parents may see something like this as intrusive, while others might use it as a further reason to not come in to the school or as an excuse not to see a teacher.
>   (Teacher)

'One strategy suits all' proposals cannot be helpfully prescribed to enhance the role Teaching Assistants can play in bringing families into schools but it is clear there is scope for lateral thinking. 'How long have I got to think of ideas? I'm sure I will think of plenty before the day is out' (Teaching Assistant). The take-away message here is 'Teaching Assistants should be closely involved in contact with parents and families'.

Teachers too, can think of many reasons why strengthening the role Teaching Assistants can play in developing close engagement with families will maximise school effectiveness:

> A real challenge in our school is more and more children in the classroom under the SEN umbrella – autistic, moderate to severe learning difficulties and so on. It's great to have them but a lack of funding and training for both teachers and Teaching Assistants means needs are not easily met in the main stream. If the Teaching Assistants could find out more from families they might be able to start preparing differentiated activities. We could really get much further helping the children reach their potential.
>   (Teacher)

Dismantling barriers

In segregated schools the fact of pupils having impairments can constrain a family's participation in school life as distance from school and complicated caregiving arrangements get in the way of building relationships. It is important to focus on practical ideas of how to develop inclusive practice without being straitjacketed by what is, or is not known, about impairment specific factors. This approach involves 'social model thinking'; concentrating on removing disabling barriers rather than worrying about impairment (Oliver 1996, 2013). It is not denied that some children and their families are harder to include than others but the essential task is to evolve clear and consistent thinking about how the consequences of any child's impairment – including consequential impact on how families can get involved in school life – can be managed in comfortable and enabling ways. Allan's (2003) question 'What will it take to be inclusive?' is helpful in suggesting new ways of thinking about what it might take to draw closer links between parents with complex commitments and their children's school.

Using Allan's question, thoughtful focus on the consequences of impairment can reveal blocks to home-school communication:

> A problem parents face if they are invited to something after school is finding someone to look after children – not just the one who has special needs.
>
> (Teacher)

> Another reason why parents might not come to evening or after school events is the disruption this causes to their child's routine. A lot of our students have problems coping with even slight disruptions in their normal routines – for instance Thomas, if his bath is late the whole family will be up all night.
>
> (Teaching Assistant)

By concentrating on noticing social barriers it is possible to notice ways of dismantling the barriers which shore up exclusions and find ways forward:

> Teaching Assistants could help here by providing crèche facilities, or other activities to keep students and their siblings occupied. We could use an SMS TXT service to bring in the views of families. We may be able to gear some of our strategies around informal contact so not all of the emphasis around communication with families means they have to come into school for meetings with a teacher.
>
> (Teaching Assistant)

Different strategies for involving parents may have to be tried and not all will be successful:

> We tried the idea of having meetings with parents 'tagged on' after a school event but even though parents turned up to the event, and refreshments were provided, very few stayed for the meeting.
>
> (Teaching Assistant)

Informal gathering time was then scheduled before the next big event and did indeed create opportunities for meeting more families than usual in a relaxed way. Where recognition is given to the active part Teaching Assistants can play in talking to parents and caregivers on such occasions, a great deal can be achieved:

> When we had the 'One City Many Cultures' evening I managed to talk to a few parents for ideas that would help the teacher I work with planning in advance.
>
> (Teaching Assistant)

On Sports Day I asked the Teaching Assistants to take the opportunity to talk to the parents about how best to support the children and we got loads back.

(Teacher)

These examples show how it is possible to view conversation between Teaching Assistants and parents as an important consultative mechanism. Keeping open dialogue around new possibilities for Teaching Assistants to support consultation with parents and caregivers reveals many strands of opportunity. For example, in our early research it was noticed some parents liked being invited into their child's classroom to help out. In these situations scope for consultation exists:

Perhaps class teachers could release Teaching Assistants for a few minutes to chat to parents and listen to their concerns and help let them know the school is interested in what they think.

(Teaching Assistant)

The possibility that parents and caregivers will find communication with school worrying is a frequently recurring them:

We need to find out what parents think when we invite them in to discuss how their child is doing. Many automatically think something is wrong, or their child is in trouble. Making it clear to parents why we want to meet them is important and being invited to meet a teaching assistant might be less worrying.

(Teaching Assistant)

From a parent's point of view:

Well I know they wanted to talk to me again about putting Gabe in internal isolation because he missed some lesson time that had been arranged for him in the intervention room. I know school has to be punishing or they can't improve his learning. But I felt like they wanted to see me to take a pound of flesh. I was shame-faced and didn't want to go and talk to teachers.

(Parent)

The importance of putting into place structures which encourage parents and caregivers to be involved in communications with the school early on in a child's school career is something Teaching Assistants feel they could work on to prevent distance building up:

It is vital we get a positive start with parents of children coming to us as this marks the beginning of a long relationship.

(Teaching Assistant)

Any visit a parent makes to school could include a separate opportunity to talk to their child's class TA – so they have time to reflect and get a chance to ask questions about things they might not have thought of with the teacher. Teaching Assistants could do 'follow up' discussions on the way out with parents to add to the feeling we are trying to connect with them. It would be good to have this brief from a teacher because it's often embarrassing walking a parent back through the corridors to the main entrance and trying NOT to talk about whatever their business was with the teacher. It seems a wasted opportunity.

(Teaching Assistant)

Changing practice

As part of previous action-research studies we have tasked Teaching Assistants and teachers with developing ideas for new types of consultation with parents. Different ideas included:

The school website could have a Teaching Assistants area where we can share links to information sites, other agencies, free software and invite responses from parents.

(Teaching Assistant)

A Teaching Assistant's blog might get some parents interested and be sort of less challenging than teachers' blogs.

(Teaching Assistant)

When we think about what Teaching Assistants can do to better engage parents, new critical questions constantly come up, such as how to avoid marginalising families without access to computers, what to do about ensuring access for parents who do not read or write and how to include people who find English difficult:

What will we do about the views of parents who seem to be presenting a barrier to their child's learning? Mr Hender (Year Head) spoke with some parents at length about the choice they are making to let their child miss PE but they didn't budge. I don't think they would come and see him again. But they might keep in touch with me a bit.

(Teaching Assistant)

Who will have access to knowledge gained through consultation with parents? What boundaries will be placed around the sharing of information from, and about, parents?

(Teaching Assistant)

Teaching Assistants and teachers are well aware of the importance and complexity of strong connections with parents and know this can be promoted in many different ways. Perceived Teacher/Teaching Assistant status differential adds value for families wanting to come in to a closer relationship with their child's school and it is important to recognise the power and significance of this. An excellent school is inclusive and inclusion is characterised by support staff being actively involved in all aspects of its development: 'Realising the potential of children and young people must go hand in hand with realising the potential of TAs (Report of a UNISON survey January 2013).

Conclusion

Teaching Assistants who are engaged with day-to-day contact with families are key agents for change in schools. Consultation with parents can be usefully approached as problem sharing for teachers and Teaching Assistants to work on collaboratively; best practice comes from sustained efforts to get to know what parents and caregivers feel would enable them to come into closer communication with the school. Teaching Assistants have a key contribution to make in gathering such information and raising the voices and perspectives of parents and caregivers. It seems important for schools to:

- identify possibilities for Teaching Assistants to pioneer changes for inclusive working with a range of family stakeholders;
- reflect on challenges and barriers which working to improve communication with parents throws up for Teaching Assistants and think about whole school approaches to overcoming these; and
- identify and drive through projects for developing the role of Teaching Assistants to further enhance contact with families.

This chapter has reflected upon the difference Teaching Assistants can make in bringing parents into closer relationships with schools and drawn out some recommendations for inclusive practice. Hopefully, it signifies the importance of positioning Teaching Assistants at the cutting edge of initiatives to advance the agenda for inclusion through focus on the indispensable role they can play in family contact.

Reflections on values and practice

1   What contribution do Teaching Assistants make to communications between families and the school in your own work context? How can this be extended?
2   Are there any particular concerns about confidentiality in relation to information Teaching Assistants may learn about from parents and caregivers when they are members of the local community? What needs to be done to manage this?
3   What values need to underpin thinking about involvement of parents in schools and how can the voices of Teaching Assistants help shape understanding of this?

Suggested further reading

Dunne, L. (2009) 'Inclusion', in G. Goddard and A. Walton (eds), *Supporting Every Child: A Course Book for Foundation Degree Teaching Assistants*, London: Learning Matters.

Sorsby, C. (2004) 'Forging and strengthening alliances: Learning support staff and the challenge of inclusion' in F. Armstrong and M. Moore (eds) *Action Research for Inclusive Education: Changing Places, Changing Practices, Changing Minds*. London: RoutledgeFalmer.

References

Allan, J. (2003) 'Productive Pedagogies and the Challenge of Inclusion'. *British Journal of Special Education, 30*(4): 175–179.

Dunn, K. and Moore, M. (2004) 'Reporting School Improvement: Enhancing Satisfactory Teaching'. Confidential Report to Commissioning School.

Eyres, I., Cable, C., Hancock, R. and Turner, J. (2004) '"Whoops, I forgot David": Children's perceptions of the adults who work in their classrooms', *Early Years, 24*(2): 149–162.

Hammett, N. and Burton, N. (2005) 'Motivation, Stress and Learning Support Assistants: An Examination of Staff Perceptions at a Rural Secondary School', *Leadership and Management, 25*(3): 299–310.

Oliver, M. (1996) *Understanding Disability: From Theory to Practice*, London: Macmillan.

Oliver, M. (2013) 'The social model of disability: thirty years on', *Disability & Society, 28*(7): 1024–1026.

Rhodes, C. (2006) 'The impact of leadership and management on the construction of professional identity in school learning mentors', *Educational Studies, 32*(2): 157–169.

Sharples, J., Webster, R. and Blatchford, P. (2015) *Making Best Use of Teaching Assistants Guidance Report*, London: The Education Endowment Foundation

Sobel, D. (2013) 'Teaching assistants are the unsung heroes of education', *The Guardian* www.theguardian.com/teacher-network/2013/oct/02/teaching-assistants-unsung-heroes-education-schools

UNISON. (2013) 'The evident value of teaching assistants'. Unison Briefings-and-Circulars. Retrieved from www.unison.org.uk/content/uploads/2013/06/Briefings-and-Circulars EVIDENT-VALUE-OF-TEACHING-ASSISTANTS

Chapter 9

A new role for special schools?

Gill Richards

Introduction

When the Green Paper *Excellence for All Children* (DfE 1997) announced that there would be a new role for special schools within its vision for meeting children's special educational needs, it demonstrated an acceptance that there would still be a need for special schools to provide for a small number of pupils whose needs could not be met within the mainstream sector. It argued that this new role would take account of the current context of inclusive education developments and expectations of the way that special school staff worked. This notion of retaining special schools with a role that developed in line with current initiatives has been key to later government policy and legislation, including the Children and Families Bill (2014) and the associated Code of Practice (2015).

So, what were the 'old' roles for special schools and how should these change as our schools respond to meeting the educational needs of increasingly diverse learners? Should special schools be expected to continually develop 'new' roles as mainstream schools improve their capacity to educate learners previously seen as requiring specialist teaching and facilities? What does the future hold for special schools? What are the implications for Teaching Assistants and their roles?

Teaching Assistants are often viewed as the solution to difficulties encountered with pupils identified as needing 'special' education in different environments. Understanding the social history of special schooling – where we are now and how we arrived there – is important for all staff, as these factors do affect our work even if this is not immediately obvious. This chapter will attempt to explore these issues and reflect on the impact initiatives in the past and present have had on those associated with special schools.

What was the 'old' role for special schools?

Armstrong (2003: 1) argued that "the history of special education is for the most part a hidden history. Rarely are the voices of those who were schooled in this system heard". Swain (2005: 787) supported this view, suggesting that historical views were presented mainly by "non-disabled professionals ... the history of those in power". Indeed, many historical details of special education provision have originated from official reports, medical practitioners' studies and information from other professionals involved with maintaining special education. This reflected the culture of the times where disabled people were seen as 'defective' and requiring others to decide how their needs should be met.

Historical 'facts' that originate in this way mean that our understanding of early special schools and their development is one-dimensional, drawn only from the perspectives of the 'establishment', those who worked in and managed the schools, rather than including the views of those who received the schooling. As in other areas of history where only one dominant perspective is presented (for example, one country's view of a war they fought in), careful reflection may be needed on what is presented as uncontested 'truth' about the success, or otherwise, of special school provision.

Early special schools, towards the end of the nineteenth century, were rooted in the ideology of the Eugenics movement. Eugenicists believed that the quality of the population would be improved if it contained more intelligent, educated and skilled workers. They argued that this could be achieved by encouraging 'superior' groups to have more children and by preventing 'inferior' groups from having any children. This led to policies across the world of sterilization, segregation and in its extreme version of Nazism, extermination, affecting the lives of many seen as 'undesirable' by those in power because of their race, skin colour, religion, sexual preferences or impairment. The roots of this movement can be seen in some practices with disabled people today, for example where terminations are routinely offered to expectant mothers whose baby is likely to be born with Down Syndrome; where disabled people are 'encouraged' to be sterilized or use contraception to prevent them becoming parents; and where adults with the most severe learning difficulties may still live in group settings that are run in ways that have organizational constraints reminiscent of past asylums.

During this time, intelligence was believed to be bred rather than nurtured (Kevles 1985) and so this led to commonly held views that there was no point in educating disabled people (Thomas and Loxley 2001; Mason 2005) or allowing them to have children. Consequently, disabled people were commonly viewed as defective, needing to be controlled and segregated from the rest of society. This led to significant numbers of children and adults with learning difficulties or complex needs being placed in institutions such as asylums and colonies, with the sexes kept carefully apart. Placement in these establishments required diagnosis by medical practitioners of an individual's 'defect', using for example labels such as 'lunatic', 'idiot', 'imbecile' and 'feeble-minded'.

Being able to work and not be a drain on society were also important values held by Eugenicists, so in contrast to people with learning difficulties, other groups of disabled children, for example those who were categorized as blind, deaf or feeble-minded, were provided with education to enable them to gain future employment (Armstrong 2003: 11). This early form of special education was offered in a range of special schools, classes within institutions and other settings outside of the mainstream system. Teachers in these were relatively free to decide on the curriculum they provided, although some School Boards gave them direction, such as the School Board for London (1891), which stated that teachers should offer an "extended type of kindergarten instruction, giving special emphasis on manual occupations" (Read and Walmsley 2006: 459). At this time, many special schools catered for classes of about 20 pupils while their mainstream counterparts had classes of at least 50, so despite the curriculum appearing to be a contradictory mix of childlike lessons and preparation for work, it did indicate an attempt to meet individual needs.

Generally in these times, most special schools were expected to teach the '3 Rs' (reading, writing and arithmetic) to enable pupils to gain the skills to transfer into mainstream schools. This was supplemented by work skills and scripture lessons. Work skills tended to be gender specific, with boys studying woodwork, shoemaking and basket making and girls studying cookery, laundry and needlework (Read and Walmsley 2006). Despite the 1898 report from the Departmental Committee on Defective and Epileptic Children which stated that "in many cases these children were capable of answering and reasoning almost as well as carefully taught normal children" (para. 54), society's anxiety about their need for segregation meant that pupils did not transfer into mainstream schools and progressed from school into residential training homes at 16 years of age.

Locking away disabled children and adults was seen in these times as an effective way of ensuring that they did not disrupt other pupils' learning or influence them with their supposedly potentially criminal and sexually promiscuous ways. As more children, particularly from the working classes, entered the education system during the nineteenth century, schools encountered problems with increased numbers not achieving the required standards. This pressure on schools' capacity led to more children being educated outside the mainstream system (Armstrong 2003).

During the Second World War, children returned from residential special schools to be with their families. This led to a decrease in residential provision as children attended their local schools and found work, replacing those away at war (Armstrong and Barton 1999). As the war came to a close, the 1944 Education Act had a significant impact on increasing special education provision. The aim of the Act was to provide free education for *all* pupils, but as this involved testing and categorizing groups of learners, some were still deemed 'ineducable' and placed in non-educational settings such as Junior Training Centres or Subnormality Hospitals. The following Handicapped Pupils and School Health Regulations of 1945 identified 11 categories of handicapped pupil, which was later amended to 10. When identified with a particular 'handicap', all pupils regarded as educable were then provided for within a special school. These schools had their own special curriculum so transfers back into mainstream schools rarely occurred.

The comprehensive schooling system of the 1960s and 1970s started to challenge the ideas of separate special schools. The 1970 Education (Handicapped Children) Act gave the last group of pupils, those with severe learning difficulties (previously identified as ineducable), the right to education. In practice this was often in the same Junior Training Centres which were renamed 'Subnormal Schools' and had the same staff, who were not qualified teachers, but was a great step forward in recognizing that all children could and should be educated.

Around this time it was noted that there were many more boys than girls in special schools, raising issues around gender bias, and also that children of Caribbean heritage were significantly over-represented, raising questions of racism (Coard 1972). Further criticisms of the quality of teaching and curriculum in special schools led to increasing questions about their role. Reflecting on this time, Thomas and Vaughan (2004: 31) suggested that special schools existed for the "convenience of mainstream rather than the purpose of improving the lives of those in them". This supported the views of earlier commentators, for example Goffman, who thought that segregated institutions were often presented "as the rational and humane solution to people's difficulties, [whereas] they in fact operate merely as society's 'storage dumps'" (1968: 31).

The Warnock Report (DfE 1978), followed by the 1981 Education Act, replaced the 10 categories of handicap with a new label, 'special educational needs' (SEN), and introduced the concept of statementing, identifying how and where children's specific educational needs should be met. Both the Report and the Act have a reputation for supporting the right for pupils identified as having special educational needs to be integrated into mainstream schools. However, they allowed for exceptions, which stated that education must meet children's needs, be financially efficient and not affect other children's education, so in effect, still provided the basis for mainstream schools to avoid taking on children seen as a 'problem', while maintaining a continuing role for special schools.

Although special schools were still to be required for a particular group of pupils whose needs could not be met in mainstream, the Warnock Report suggested that the educational goals should be the same for all pupils. This was later supported by the newly devised 'National Curriculum', which despite an opportunity for 'disapplication' for pupils with special educational needs, provided a defined curriculum for all children, whatever school they attended. The effects of this form of integration within mainstream school practice caused a significant decline in special schools during the 1980s and 1990s.

Developing co-operative ways of working

The developments of integration during the 1980s started to affect the stability of special schools and it was the 1988 Education Act that increased their financial support and provided them with an opportunity for working with mainstream schools. The Act delegated powers and resources from the local education authorities to schools. Special schools were funded by a formula method that was applied on the basis of the number of places available rather than the number of pupils actually attending. This ensured that special schools were not affected by fluctuating rolls or placed under pressure to recruit or lose pupils (Lee 1992). Mainstream schools were encouraged to manage support for their children with special educational needs, but this led to concerns about efficient use of finances available. As a result, special schools were viewed in some situations to be a more efficient use of resources and so led to increased placements of pupils who would otherwise have been in mainstream schools. In contrast, some special and mainstream schools used this opportunity to work together co-operatively and develop joint provision in localized areas.

In 1997, the Green Paper, *Excellence for All Children: Meeting Special Educational Needs*, set out the government's vision for raising standards of achievement for all children with special needs. This identified a new role for special schools that focused on meeting the challenge of more complex needs and supporting mainstream schools and their teachers. This all took place in the context of an increasingly political agenda about inclusion of children identified as having special educational needs, supported by the 1994 Salamanca Statement which called on governments to adopt a policy of educating all children together, unless there were compelling reasons not to do so. At this time national directives continued to affect what teachers taught and school performance became increasingly monitored. Competition between schools was encouraged as their pupils' results were compared, leading to pressure for exclusion of children who provided too great a challenge for some mainstream schools. As a result, the new role for special schools also included taking on more children identified as having social and emotional behavioural difficulties who were becoming increasing casualties of the pressurized mainstream system.

The Green Paper acknowledged that although teachers in special schools had the necessary expertise to support their mainstream colleagues, they came from a small staffing group, and so it recommended that local education authorities should consider new ways of organizing schools. Mainstream schools could be specially resourced or have special units attached. Special schools could be amalgamated and where possible linked with mainstream schools to provide them with support and training.

During the following years, schools and local education authorities developed provision to meet local needs in line with the Green Paper's plan and the following Special Educational Needs and Disability Act (SENDA) (2001). In some areas this resulted in effective support for children with special needs, but in others, there was criticism about teachers being deskilled and children's un-met needs. Some mainstream teachers began to lose confidence in their own ability to teach all children as they were persuaded by special school claims of the need for highly specialized skills and knowledge (Thomas and Loxley 2001: 26). In other situations, teachers from mainstream schools argued that although their colleagues from special schools had some specific expertise, they were inexperienced in the ways of mainstream schools and so the training they offered was not appropriate for their context. Thomas and Loxley (2001: 107) also expressed concern about the financial incentives used to place children in special schools: "While six-figure sums of money go to pay for children at some residential special schools, those sums do not accompany these children if they move back into mainstream. Nor are they available as a resource to a mainstream school in the first place". So, once again it seemed that special schools were seen to be caught in a conflicting situation; they were the key to providing innovative ways of integrating pupils with special educational needs, while at the same time their very existence was viewed to be obstructing progress.

In 2004, the government released its latest strategy for educating pupils with special educational needs, 'Removing Barriers to Achievement'. This restated previous intentions to see special schools as the providers of education for children with complex needs, while sharing their expertise with mainstream schools to support inclusion. It stressed that the future role for special schools was to focus on 'cutting edge' partnership work with mainstream colleagues through federations and cluster school arrangements.

These partnerships were expected to benefit from the strengths of each part of the sector (mainstream and special) and so make communities of schools more effective in meeting children's needs. The intention was to break down the divide between special and mainstream schools and encourage increased pupil movement across them, meeting needs with a joint sector approach. It was intended that these partnerships would reduce the need for high-cost, residential special school placements and bring provision to a localized level. Although the implications were that special schools could be working themselves out of a job in the future, the strategy stated that it was "critical to ensure that high quality provision was available locally before special school places were reduced" (DfES 2004: 38).

For the first time, a government strategy drew attention to the expertise in mainstream schools from which special schools could benefit. Special schools at this time were three times more likely than mainstream to require special measures because of poor leadership and management, inadequate curriculum, low attendance and poor teaching. The Department for Education and Skills recommended (2004) that the mainstream sector should provide training and resources to support special schools in these circumstances, laying the basis for more equal partnership arrangements. Public awareness of the quality of special school provision increased as national inspection reports became available through the internet and the media. This furthered the debate about the role of special schools and their future existence. Disabled people's voices, often absent in the past from discussions about their own education, joined this debate in larger numbers, giving them a more powerful input at national level. Criticism of special schools was made strongly by some prominent disabled people, for example, Oliver (1995), who argued that education in special schools was a failure in terms of any criteria applied to it as it lacked equity with mainstream and Mason (2000: 9) who argued that the problem about lack of resources to support learners was based in a frustrating, circular argument, where "special schools must be kept because mainstream schools cannot cope, because they do not have the resources that are in special schools". This identified one of the key problems about having a dual system of education provision (special *and* mainstream schools): if resources are limited and split between special and mainstream schools, the need will always be there for special schools, as they have resources that mainstream schools need.

A new role?

So what is the future for special schools? Should they continue to reinvent themselves and find new roles as different pupil groups experience difficulties in schools that are struggling to meet increasing numbers of national education initiatives which are seemingly at odds with inclusion? When we look back at the first part of this chapter and reflect on some of the arguments for early special schools, are there really any new roles involved, or are they similar ones, repackaged?

What about the views of those involved and how do they see the future role of special schools? What are the views of disabled people about the education provision so many attend as the result of decisions made by others? What about school staff, parents and importantly for our intended audience for this book, what are the implications for the roles of Teaching Assistants?

Clearly, the government expects special schools to develop their role to meet changing pupil needs. As medical advances enable the survival of children with increasingly complex needs, and pressures in mainstream schools create more casualties for a widening group of 'vulnerable' learners, special schools of different kinds may still be seen as the kind of benign service industry to the mainstream described by Thomas and Loxley (2001), providing access to an education previously unavailable or deemed inappropriate. Others may dispute this, either arguing that special schools provide an essential service for young people with the most severe and complex needs (Hornby 2015; Farrell 2012) or that it is these pupils who most need to be included within mainstream schools as they are the most isolated (Flood 2011; Mason 2003). When you consider groups of children put together, unable to move independently or use verbal communication, this point about isolation is clear. How can these children interact with each other? Often their main access to any action or communication is through staff rather than their peers, not the preference of many children, however wonderful we all might be! Similar arguments could be made about other groups separated because of their particular 'characteristics' – what opportunities do they have to interact with their peers being educated elsewhere?

These different views reflect a growing debate about 'special' education provision in mainstream and special schools. Ofsted, in its 2006 report *Inclusion: Does It Matter Where Pupils Are Taught?*, argued that the most important factor was not the type of provision a pupil attended, but the quality of that provision. Good and outstanding education was identified in both mainstream and special schools, although more was available in mainstream and less in Pupil Referral Units (PRUs). Advocates for inclusive education take issue with this, arguing that it does matter where pupils are educated, especially when the longer view is taken (Flood 2011). For them, 'label attribution' – the increased number of young people receiving an ever-expanding range of labels – has resulted in higher numbers being taught in segregated settings that foster greater inequality (Anderson and Boyle 2015). This reflects earlier concerns expressed by Inclusion International (2009: 40) about attempts to address the needs of vulnerable learners through separate provision rather than reviewing school practices to see how reforms could be developed and embedded to meet the needs of *all* young people: "The targeting of marginalised groups through programming without corresponding transformations of education systems results in the creation of more separate responses to the needs of separate groups – more special classes and schools".

The Children and Families Act (2014) reiterated the importance of special schools, stating that although there was to be a general presumption of mainstream education, any child or young person with an Education, Health and Care Plan (EHCP) had the right to seek a place at a special school, specialist post-16 institution or specialist college (DfE 2015). The Act expected special schools to provide for the young people with the most complex needs and to use their expertise to offer guidance and support for mainstream schools. This, in the context of the Government's view (Conservative Party 2007) that inclusive education was a 'failed ideology' and that it was time to remove the bias towards inclusion – although this was quietly dropped when challenged (Norwich 2014) – demonstrates further confused messages. The [then] Government reported there was clear evidence that many children with special educational needs made "far greater progress and were much happier in the sheltered environment of a special school" (Lauchlan and Greig 2015: 12). Where this evidence originated is unclear, as is the quality of the research carried out.

O'Rouke (2015) reviewed a wide range of evidence from research into special and inclusive education. He found that there was very little difference generally, although young people achieved marginally better in mainstream schools. This leads us to question further the Government's 'evidence' referred to above and reflect upon the place of special schools within a context of scarce financial resources – why should a dual system continue to be operated if there is no *significant* difference in outcomes for young people? We might also wonder why, in a national context driven by 'value for money' and 'evidence-based practice', there hasn't been extensive research carried out to evidence the success of special schools, or of other costly initiatives such as building 'co-located schools' (where a special school is located on the same site as a mainstream school). Griffith (2015) raises this issue, pointing out that the co-location budget was supported by a budget of £200 million, despite no underpinning evidence that this would be more effective than other provision.

Dual placements can be viewed by professionals and parents as offering 'the best of both worlds' (Griffith 2015), where young people spend part of their time in a mainstream school and the rest in a special school, enabling them to access wider resources and specialist support. The development of co-located schools could be seen to increase such opportunities. However, special schools that I know well have reported that being co-located did not ensure a good relationship with the mainstream school, nor did it replace the previously established relationships with other mainstream schools and provide better opportunities for young people: one special school reported that a mainstream school had built a fence around the special school to prevent their children 'straying' away from the school vicinity! Dual/co-located placements can also be seen as the 'worst of both worlds' – either because young people may not feel that they belong in either school as they miss out experiences in both, or because the mainstream school selected for co-location was rarely an 'outstanding' school, leading to cynicism about the criteria on which decisions were made and how association with special schools is viewed by 'high achieving' schools. In a situation without robust evidence to support any of these perspectives, we are left wondering what really does work best for young people.

So, what is the evidence that special schools work? What criteria are applied to judge their success against? We do know that the actual number of children attending special schools has steadily increased from 89,000 in 2006 to 98,595 in 2013, despite a decrease in the number of special schools, and attendance at PRUs and independent special schools has also risen from 5,458 in 1994 to 12,895 in 2013 (Alliance for Inclusive Education 2015). Equally clear is the fact that numbers differ across local authorities, indicating a very mixed response to meeting the educational needs of disabled children, reflecting the increasing range of initiatives and options available to families (Norwich and Black 2015; Mason 2006).

How long should this be allowed to continue and what about the children whose lives are affected by this? Guilherme and Freire (2015) raised concerns about young people being educated in separate schools, suggesting that schools should not just be about 'instruction' but also about the 'social world'. They described the importance of preparing young people to live in a real community together, a world where people were diverse. Their discussion of 'The Other' highlighted the dangers of young people, separated because of a particular difference, who then fail to take account of each other and so contribute to a situation where misconceptions and prejudices will grow and damage communities. In the current climate where governmental concerns focus on extremism and 'hate crimes' against our increasingly diverse community, this is something we must consider carefully for the sake of the young people with whom we work.

Conclusion

The origins of special schools were about keeping disabled people away from the rest of society and ensuring that they did not affect others' education. When we hear discussions today we might at times think that little has changed. In reality there have been many developments, but society is still reliant on this form of education despite a lack of undisputed evidence of its success. Those in favour of a continuing role for special schools suggest that these should be multidimensional, responding to localized needs. Certainly, in response to national developments for the UK education system to become more school-led, special schools have established an important role for themselves as part of Teaching School Alliances, providing support and professional development for partner schools. Others, such as the Alliance for Inclusive Education (2015), are campaigning for all special schools to close, particularly to prevent the current situation where: "Disabled young people are the only group of 'persons with protected characteristics' [as identified in the 2010 Equality Act] that can be forced out of mainstream education". The 'sticking point' appears to centre on whose responsibility it is for those students who struggle academically and socially within schools (O'Rouke 2015). This, coupled with financial constraints, affects many decisions at local levels.

Teaching Assistants' roles have changed significantly from their early days of supporting teachers with basic classroom tasks. Now, they are educational professionals whose duties require them to demonstrate a wide range of skills from supporting learning to personal care.

It is likely that as schools of all kinds develop provision for young people with increasingly complex needs, Teaching Assistants' roles will change. They will need access to high-quality professional development that focuses on support for a far wider range of diverse learning needs, to enable the pupils with whom they work to gain the maximum benefit. Many Teaching Assistants are working directly with other professionals, but as multi-agency developments increase to support pupils identified as having special educational needs, this is an area in which they may require further training to provide effective inclusion for all learners.

Whatever the future of special schools, and I would argue that this is not clear today, good practice in any education provision usually suggests that we learn best about what we should do when we ask those who are experiencing it. Such an approach is one that promotes the rights of all children to have their views valued and is the very basis of working inclusively. I would suggest that this is a very appropriate place to start discussions about what our future schools should look like.

Reflections on values and practice

1   Reflect on your own experiences of special and mainstream schools. What barriers within these schools are experienced by young people identified as having special educational needs? How could these be resolved?
2   If we know what is not working effectively in mainstream schools for disabled children and young people, why is the solution to use special school placements rather than make the changes necessary in mainstream?
3   How are disabled peoples' views included in publications about the special school and inclusion debate? What evidence is there that these are respected?
4   There is no conclusive research evidence that special schools work effectively, particularly in the long term. Why do you think this is so, and should we continue to rely on them without such evidence?

Suggested further reading

Alliance for Inclusive Education. (2013) 'How was school?' Retrieved from www.allfie.org.uk
Mason, M. (2005) *Incurably Human*, Nottingham: Inclusive Solutions.
Rotatori, A., Bakken, J., Burkharde, S., Obiakor, F. and Sharma, U. (eds) (2014) *Special Education International Perspectives: Practices Across the Globe*, Bingley: Emerald Group.

References

Alliance for Inclusive Education (2015) *Submission to the Lords' Select Committee of Inquiry on the Equalities Act and Disabilities*, London: Author.
Anderson, J. and Boyle, C. (2015) 'Inclusive education in Australia: rhetoric, reality and the road ahead', *Support for Learning*, 30(1): 5–22.

Armstrong, D. (2003) *Experiences of Special Education. Re-evaluating Policy and Practice Through Life Stories*, London: RoutledgeFalmer.

Armstrong, F. and Barton, L. (eds) (1999) *Disability, Human Rights and Education: Cross-Cultural Perspectives*, Buckingham: Open University Press.

Coard, B. (1972) 'How the West Indian Child is Made Educationally Sub-Normal in the British School System', in Richardson, B. (ed) (2005) *Tell It Like It Is: How Our Schools Fail Black Children*, London: Bookmarks.

Conservative Party. (2007) *Commission on Special Needs in Education: The Second Report*, London: The Conservative Party.

Department for Education. (DfE) (1978) *Special Educational Needs*, Report of the Committee of Enquiry into the Education of Handicapped Children and Young People, Cmnd 7212, London: HMSO.

Department for Education (DfE) (1997) *Excellence for All Children*, London: The Stationery Office.

Department for Education (DfE) (2015) *Special Educational Needs and Disability Code of Practice: 0 to 25 years. Statutory guidance for organisations which work with and support children and young people with special educational needs*, London: Department for Education.

Department for Education and Skills (DfES) (2004) *Removing Barriers to Achievement*, London: HMSO.

Farrell, M. (2012) *New Perspectives in Special Education*, Abingdon: Routledge.

Flood, T. (2011) *Response to the Government's 'Support and Aspiration: A new approach to special educational needs and disabilities Green Paper*, London: Alliance for Inclusive Education.

Goffman, E. (1968) 'Asylums', in Thomas, G. and Vaughan, M. (eds) (2004) *Inclusive Education Readings and Reflections*, Maidenhead: Open University Press.

Griffith, E. (2015) 'Exploring the definitions and discourse of co-location', *British Journal of Special Education*, 42(2): 153–165.

Guilherme, A. and Freire, I. M (2015) 'Merleau-Ponty and Buber on seeing and not seeing the Other: Inclusion and exclusion in education', *International Journal of Inclusive Education*, 19(8): 787–801.

Hornby, G. (2015) 'Inclusive special education: Development of a new theory for the education of children with special educational needs and disabilities', *British Journal of Special Education*, 42(3): 235–256.

Inclusion International. (2009) *Better Education for All: A Global Report*, Salamanca: Instituto Universitario de Integracíon de la Comunidad.

Kevles, D. (1985) *In the Name of Eugenics: Genetics and the Uses of Human Heredity*, New York: Alfred A. Knopf.

Lauchlan, F. and Greig, S. (2015) 'Educational inclusion in England: Origins, perspectives and current directions'. *Support for Learning*, 30(1): 70–82.

Lee, T. (1992) 'Local management of schools and special education', in Booth, T., Swann, W., Masterton, M. and Potts, P. (eds) *Policies for Diversity in Education*, London: Routledge.

Mason, M. (2000) 'There are only winners', *TES Curriculum Special*, 14 July 2000.

Mason, M. (2003) 'Rebuilding the walls of exclusion', *Inclusion Now*, Summer 2003.

Mason, M. (2005) *Incurably Human*, Nottingham: Inclusive Solutions.

Mason, M. (2006) 'Inclusion: The current debate', in Robinson, G. and Maines, B. (eds) *Lucky Duck*, Position Paper 13 September 2006.

Norwich, B. (2014) 'Changing policy and legislation and its effect on inclusion and special education: A perspective from England' *British Journal of Special Education*, 41(4): 404–425.

Norwich, B. and Black, A. (2015) 'The placement of secondary school students with statements of special educational needs in the more diversified system of English secondary schooling', *British Journal of Special Education*, 42(2): 129–151.

Ofsted. (2006) *Inclusion: Does it Matter Where Pupils are Taught?* London: Crown Copyright.

Oliver, M. (1995) 'Does special education have a role to play in the 21st Century?' in Thomas, G. and Vaughan, M. (2004) *Inclusive Education Readings and Reflections*, Maidenhead: Open University Press.

O'Rouke, J. (2015) 'Inclusive schooling: if it's so good – why is it so hard to sell?' *International Journal of Inclusive Education, 19*(5): 530–546.

Read, J. and Walmsley, J. (2006) 'Historical perspectives on special education, 1890–1970', *Disability & Society, 21*(5).

Special Needs and Disability Act. (2001) London: HMSO.

Swain, J. (2005) 'Inclusive education: Readings and reflections' in Read, J. and Walmsley, J. (2006) 'Historical Perspectives on Special Education, 1890–1970', *Disability & Society 21*(5).

Thomas, G. and Loxley, A. (2001) *Deconstructing Special Education and Constructing Inclusion*, Buckingham: Open University Press.

Thomas, G. and Vaughan, M. (2004) *Inclusive Education Readings and Reflections*, Maidenhead: Open University Press.

Chapter 10

'The Learning Support staff's brilliant …'

Facilitating asylum-seeking and refugee students in British schools

Mano Candappa

Introduction

This chapter is about asylum-seeking and refugee[1] (ASR) children, their experiences in British schools, and how schools could support their rehabilitation and learning in the country of refuge. The refugee experience makes these children resilient, but they are among the most marginalised in our society and the Other among their peers. Paradoxically, these students are often 'invisible' within schools yet they desperately need the school's support to help them get on with their lives. The challenge for schools is how best to support them whilst not taking agency away from them: I argue that the inclusive school is the most supportive environment for asylum-seeking and refugee students. I use the term 'inclusive' to mean including the child with his/her own culture and values in the school, within a culture that celebrates diversity (Armstrong 2008; Corbett 1999). In this model the school adapts to respond to the needs of its students, as against the integrationist model where the student has to fit into the school. It is the right of asylum-seeking and refugee children to be supported to enjoy their right to education under the UN Convention on the Rights of the Child. The nature of Teaching Assistants' work places them in a key position to support these young people rebuild their lives in Britain.

Background

A sharp rise in asylum applications in the UK since the 1990s[2] led to perceptions in many quarters of an 'asylum crisis', with applications reaching a peak of 84,130 (excluding dependants) in 2002. This number decreased to 25,712 in 2005 and to under 18,000 in 2010, before rising each subsequent year to reach 24,914 in 2014 (excluding dependants) (Blinder 2015). However, wars, persecution and related human misery in Syria, Iraq, Afghanistan and other countries today continue to drive people from their homelands to seek asylum in safe countries. Many, including families with children, have undertaken hazardous journeys in overcrowded boats to reach the safety of Europe, thousands losing their lives in the attempt (www. UNHCR.org).

The presence of refugees in Britain has attracted aggressive and hostile public attention, making it a politically sensitive issue. This gave rise to punitive legislation to curb numbers, which saw a progressive reduction in financial and material assistance to people seeking asylum since 1990, and their marginalisation from mainstream support services. Key among these was the 1999 Asylum and Immigration Act, which witnessed the compulsory dispersal of adults and families seeking asylum away from traditional areas of settlement in London and South East England to predominantly White areas where accommodation was available. Many asylum-seeking families were housed in socially and economically deprived areas; many schools in dispersal areas had little experience of multi-ethnic communities, and were ill-prepared for receiving children with English as an additional language and for diverse religious traditions. Today, people seeking asylum can apply to the Home Office for accommodation and subsistence but they have to accept an offer of accommodation in a 'dispersal' area, which will be outside London and the South East (Refugee Council, 2015).

Whilst the UK has a long history of providing asylum and refuge, previously this had been mainly for White populations, such as Jews facing persecution and dissidents from former Soviet-bloc countries. Today's asylum-seeking and refugee communities largely originate from Asia, the Middle East and Africa, reflecting countries currently experiencing political conflict. These are more visible populations, bringing with them different languages, religions, customs and traditions, and their presence has significantly increased the UK's Black and minority ethnic (BME) population[3]. It is estimated that refugees represented close to 5 per cent of all international migrants in the UK during 2010 (Vargas-Silva 2011).

Their highly visible presence and aspects of 'difference' that single them out as the Other[4] have been factors in the politics of 'race' being heavily implicated in the UK's response to asylum-seeking and refugee communities. They are pathologised in political and media discourses, associated with criminal activity, a drain on the nation's resources, and even with terrorism. The challenge for schools and TAs is how to address these negative images and celebrate the diversity these students' presence brings, and how to protect their rights as children.

Rights of the child[5]

Asylum-seeking and refugee children, as children, are protected under the UN Convention on the Rights of the Child (UNCRC), to which the UK is a signatory[6]. Whilst they are entitled to the same rights as other children, as children seeking refugee status or considered refugees, they are given additional protection under Article 22 which states that they should receive 'appropriate protection and humanitarian assistance' in the enjoyment of Convention rights.

UNCRC gives children protection, provision and participation rights based on four 'general principles': the *right to life*, including the development of the child 'to the maximum extent possible'; the *best interests of the child*; *respecting the views of the child*; and that *no child should suffer discrimination*, stipulating equality of rights for *all* children (Hammarberg 1995). Specific articles *inter alia* give children the right to education: Article 28 recognises the child's right to education on the basis of equal opportunity; Article 29 states among other things that the child's education shall be directed to the 'development of the child's personality, talents and mental and physical abilities to their fullest potential'. Under Article 19 schools need to take appropriate action to protect children from all forms of violence (which includes bullying). Asylum-seeking and refugee children are therefore entitled to a learning environment where their abilities can be nurtured and developed to their fullest without fear of being subjected to violence. These rights are all the more precious because the school as a universalist service might be the only statutory agency from which they derive support (Candappa and Egharevba 2000), and as Elbedour, ten Bensel and Bastien (1993: 812) indicate, for many children "the school serves as a second security base outside the home, or perhaps their only security base".

Under the Children Act 2004, the Children's Commissioner oversees the interests of children. The Act also places a duty on local authorities to promote co-operation between agencies to improve children's well-being, and a duty for key agencies (including Education departments and schools) to safeguard and protect the welfare of children.

Given these rights and legal protections it might be expected that asylum-seeking and refugee children's educational needs can be supported to achieve their full potential, but as we shall see, various factors operate to make this goal more challenging. First, as context, let us consider what refugee children have had to endure, using evidence from the author's research.

The child as refugee

Many asylum-seeking and refugee children have had extraordinary childhoods (see Candappa and Egharevba 2000; Stanley 2002; Chase, Knight and Statham 2008; Taylor and Sidhu 2012). Children's accounts, such as those of Sheik[7] (a Somali boy from the minority Brava community, age 10) and Bazi (another Somali Brava boy, age 11) below, tell of violence, courage, loss and endurance:

Sheik
   I was playing outside when somebody [thugs] came and tell me, 'Go and knock at your neighbours' door and speak Bravanese. Tell them to open the door or I am going to shoot you'. And then I went to knock. (They told me [that] ... because they can't speak my language.) I said, 'Don't open it, there are some robbers here'. And they [thugs] thought that I said, 'Open the door'. They didn't open the door. And I say [to the thugs], 'They don't want to open it.'
   The robbers say, 'Tell those people to open it'. And I say to my neighbours, 'Don't open the door because they are still here. They kill people'. They [thugs] say to me, 'You lie to us'. They hit me with a gun!

Bazi

One day we leave by boat ... but the boat broken in the middle of Somalia and Kenya and some of our family fell in the water and drowned. ... And we just prayed to God, and God pushed us through the sea to the land. ... It was night and everybody was praying. The boat was slowly going down to the sand, until it got to the sand. In the sand there was nobody and one day we slept on the sand. And another day, we were scared, some people came ... by small boats and they came to collect us and they took us to their island. We was very hungry that day. They gave us food. ... After two weeks, some people say that our family sent small ship from Mombasa to that small island ... and they took us and then we got to Kenya.

(Candappa and Egharevba 2002: 158)

Other asylum-seeking and refugee children have lived through dangers and trauma of war, persecution, or periods in refugee camps; some have been at the mercy of unscrupulous agents, some have fled alone, some have had to support emotionally absent parents. Their resilience is remarkable.

Once they reach a safe country such as the UK these children's troubles are far from over. Starting a new life as an 'asylum-seeker' is hard. They face dismal poverty living on state benefits which since 1999 have been equivalent to 70 per cent of income support, and since 2002 their parents do not have the right to work while their asylum claim is under consideration. Additional to their poverty is the insecurity of not knowing if their claim for asylum will be successful. Families have to get on with rebuilding their lives in the new country not knowing whether the next day, the next week, the next month, or some day in the future they will be asked to leave, putting them under great emotional stress, with implications for their physical and mental health and well-being.

Families who have been dispersed to predominantly White areas can feel even more vulnerable and unsafe because of their visibility among the local, often hostile population. Here a 10-year-old girl living in a new dispersal area in Scotland talks of her fears and worries:

There's no homework club in school – we are allowed to use help at the library, but it is too far. I can't stay because of drunks around. They shout, come and talk with you – I feel scared.

(Candappa *et al.* 2007: 25).

Their visibility makes asylum-seeking children particularly vulnerable to racism. The oppression and powerlessness this causes are here captured in the testimony of an unaccompanied minor youth: "They call me [racist] names. ... I do not respond. Sometimes I feel no freedom because people abusing us" (Candappa *et al.* 2007: 27). As Arshad *et al.* (1999: 16) point out, to be abused in a country where one had sought refuge from abuse seems "a double injustice and particularly cruel".

'Invisible' students and visible Otherness

Asylum-seeking and refugee children are often 'invisible' in schools[8] (Arshad *et al.* 1999; Pinson, Arnot and Candappa 2010). Students are not required to reveal immigration status to the school, and schools, unless officially provided this information, usually do not see it as their business to be involved with immigration issues. In multicultural schools, asylum-seeking and refugee students could blend in with the school population; in more monocultural areas their ethnicity would make them visible. In either school setting they might come to the attention of teachers and TAs only as a new arrival, a bilingual learner, or a migrant child new to the British education system. Sometimes, after trust has been established, some students or their parents might tell their stories to a sympathetic teacher or TA, but they might also choose not to talk about their experiences. Research suggests that staff members who work most closely with asylum-seeking and refugee students respect this silence and the student's choice if and when to disclose their experiences (Pinson *et al.* 2010). However, at times trying to cope with memories and effects of past traumas as well as the stresses of their new life might manifest in unruly or disruptive behaviours in the school. Kasim's account (a Somali boy who arrived in Britain as an unaccompanied minor) demonstrates the types of behaviour that have sometimes been misinterpreted because staff have not been sensitised to the experiences and needs of refugee students:

> I come to this country in 1994 [and] … I was a bit upset because of my Mum. I didn't see her … for seven years.
>   Still worried about my Mum. Can't do my homework … can't do nothing because I'm worried. When I walk [down] the street, I think about my Mum. Sometimes I cry. … Last week at school I was thinking about my Mum and I was crying in my head. And one boy hit my head. I was so angry I got him back. That's how I almost get expelled.
>
> (Candappa 2002: 232).

Too often their silence and invisibility or stereotyping have led to asylum-seeking and refugee students being penalised rather than provided the supports they need (Candappa 2002).

The decision not to disclose their refugee experiences is sometimes a coping strategy, a way of putting the past behind and getting on with their lives. Often asylum-seeking and refugee students are aware, from the media, from community experiences and from playground talk, of negative images of 'asylum-seekers' and refugees, and for self-preservation, they do not wish to reveal their pasts (Pinson *et al.* 2010). Christopoulou *et al.* (2004) suggest that silence is one of the mechanisms these young people use to handle trauma, exclusion and discrimination in their present lives. But even through this silence their peers can still identify them as the Other – the outsider, whose lack of competency in English, lack of understanding of local youth cultures and modes of dress makes their Otherness visible and excludes them from membership of the peer group until they have negotiated this painful rite of passage (Candappa and Egharevba 2002; Pinson *et al.* 2010). This often takes the form of low-level bullying and harassment directed at all newcomers (Pinson *et al.* 2010), but for an anxious asylum-seeking or refugee student such behaviour could be experienced as hostility, non-acceptance and exclusion. If they are non-English speakers these students are particularly vulnerable, as the account of Serpil, a refugee girl, demonstrates:

> I had two Turkish friends, but not that close. Sometimes they helped me but most of the time they didn't. ... When they translated anything, I think they were, like, embarrassed. ... They were embarrassed that other kids will say, 'Oh, don't talk to that girl, she doesn't speak English'.
>
> (Candappa and Egharevba 2002: 165)

It is significant that Serpil was rejected by students from her own culture, those they and the school might have expected to help her. Whilst it reveals the low status of non-English speakers within peer cultures, it also points to complexities within peer group relations that impact on developing and sustaining an inclusive school ethos.

Building inclusivity

Under the UNCRC and British law, as we have seen, asylum-seeking and refugee children have a right to an education where they can flourish and develop to their fullest potential, and under Convention rights they should be protected and supported in the enjoyment of this right. Four other pieces of legislation[9] place a related statutory duty upon schools, and together the Convention and these Acts carry the message of respecting difference and of inclusion.

The inclusive message has special resonance for asylum-seeking and refugee children. For them the trauma of war, forced migration and loss, together with anxieties of trying to settle in a new country could affect their ability to enjoy their right to education. Children from families seeking asylum have the added worry and uncertainty of awaiting a decision on their asylum claim. If their claim is unsuccessful sometimes families are forcibly removed from their homes in dawn raids. If this were to happen to someone in their community, other families fear their turn, and this could affect the children (see Pinson *et al.* 2010). The added protection UNCRC Article 22 bestows is therefore an entitlement asylum-seeking and refugee students often badly need. Here schools and TAs can play a pivotal role in helping rebuild their lives: a restoration of normality and order through schooling can in itself act as a healing agent (Bolloten and Spafford 1998).

The most supportive environment for asylum-seeking and refugee children is a school that respects its students as individuals and tries to empathise with their experiences and needs and responds to these – in other words an inclusive school. For asylum-seeking and refugee students this would mean not just seeking to respond to immediate needs, but to situate these needs in the context of their previous experiences. But these students can be 'invisible' in classrooms, so the question how to support invisible students might seem contradictory. But if a school were to provide a safe environment that seeks to address the needs of all students, identifying individual needs without resorting to stereotypes and assumptions, then many of the needs of asylum-seeking and refugee students too would be met. Indeed, as Arshad *et al.*'s (1999: 20) research indicates being inclusive means "not being picked out as different or special, even in positive ways". It means feeling included in the normal learning environment of a caring school.

To sustain its ethos the inclusive school will need to develop specific structures and practices. These could include celebrating diversity and difference; exploring and debating around social justice and humanitarian issues within the curriculum; and implementing robust equal opportunities, anti-racist and anti-bullying policies. Specific curricular and pastoral supports that could be responsive to the needs of asylum-seeking and refugee students, even without disclosure, would also need to be developed. Use of peer support and collaborative learning could be included among these. Inclusivity could also involve seeking ways of drawing parents of ASR students into the school community. Where TAs could be most effective might be in support for language and accessing the curriculum, and in fostering relationships with and ensuring communication with parents of asylum-seeking and refugee students, as discussed below.

Language and curricular supports

While some asylum-seeking and refugee children may have enjoyed uninterrupted education, conflict situations in their home countries could mean that many have had little formal schooling or that their education had been disrupted. Some could find UK schools significantly different from schools in the home country in terms of pedagogic practice and discipline, for others the school they join in the UK might be the first they have attended. Research suggests that young people's early school experiences in this country are central to how well and how quickly they adjust to their new lives. Many require help in schools for an extended time thereafter.

Acquiring competence in English is a key factor in asylum-seeking and refugee students' new lives, crucial both for accessing the curriculum and for developing self-confidence and aiding social interaction (Candappa and Egharevba 2000), and it is in this context that most TAs would come into contact with them. Many of these students are new to English on joining school in the UK and in some education authorities intensive language support is provided at the outset, with English-language acquisition seen as a basic survival need (Candappa *et al.* 2007). Many schools provide English training in separate classes or with special support in mainstream classes, and the question of the relative merits of withdrawal as against mainstreaming are often debated. It has been suggested that withdrawal allows the teacher or TA to give individual attention to the student, who could work at his/her own pace. However, the 'social turn' in second-language acquisition theory (Block 2007) challenges this argument and suggests that language learning and meaning making are products of social contexts and interactions. Moreover, withdrawal could be stigmatising and inhibit building friendships with the wider peer group. Indeed, parents in Candappa *et al.*'s (2007) study requested that if withdrawal was seen as necessary it is done in a way that did not suggest a student's difficulties with language are synonymous with academic failure. Below is a possible approach to effectively support asylum-seeking and refugee students' language needs without the need for withdrawal.

Robert Burns School: dispersal area, Scotland

The school had been asked by the education authority to place students from asylum-seeking families on class registers, though in reality they would work in a bilingual unit providing students with intensive English-language support. The school had been multi-ethnic prior to dispersal, and found this approach contrary to its usual way of working, as the headteacher explained:

> We very quickly moved away from that and began to refine our thinking – we asked, what can children do that the class was doing, e.g., expressive art, environmental studies, behind that maths, then language. We've got to get teachers and children to seek ways around that. And we also began to get peer support. ...
>
> Now ... we work on a completely different basis ... the two refugee support teachers with the EAL[10] teachers work in classrooms across the school, mainly at language times. Teachers work with groups of children, which include asylum-seekers and refugees, local bilingual and monolingual pupils. ... We feel that all children benefit from this.
>
> We had a debate within the school about 'withdrawal' ... for limited times in corners ...With joint planning with the class teacher and the support teacher ... where the support teacher takes the group becomes irrelevant.
>
> (Candappa *et al.* 2007: 41)

This is a model of team teaching with TAs working alongside teachers, and where any stigma that could attach to withdrawal is absent; children spend class time with their peers in a situation that is more conducive to learning, forming friendships and socialising.

Apart from classroom structures within which support is provided, it is important to consider the agency of asylum-seeking and refugee students and the teaching approaches needed to help them develop as independent learners. Such an approach might be seen in the account of Lena, a Year 11 girl from Nigeria:

> The Learning Support staff's brilliant, they're really helpful ... taught me to be more independent than always get help.... They kind of like, when they give you work, they make you try and do it without asking for help all the time. Like, so you can depend more on yourself than other people to help you all the time.
>
> (Pinson *et al.* 2010: 205).

This message is echoed in Sharples, Webster and Blatchford's (2015) recommendations. To help asylum-seeking and refugee students develop independent learning skills and manage their own learning TAs could, for example, give the least amount of help first to support students' ownership of a task, use more open-ended questions, and the like (Sharples *et al.* 2015: Fig.1).

Fostering home-school relationships

Asylum-seeking and refugee parents, as do all parents, are entitled to be consulted by the school and participate in their child's education, and developing links with parents and communities has long been recognised as good practice in inclusive schools. For asylum-seeking and refugee parents these links will be the more important because of their unfamiliarity with the British education system and possible lack of competency in English, on top of having to deal with the more general challenges of building a new life in the country of refuge. Issues of "discipline approaches, academic standards, ways of reporting progress and classroom methodology" were identified as issues by parents in Arshad *et al.*'s study (1999: 13). That study reported that parents "wanted to be listened to by schools ... but often felt inhibited by language or by lack of familiarity with what was 'acceptable'" (1999: 14).

TAs through their classroom interactions with asylum-seeking and refugee students and their knowledge of community languages can play a central role in developing and maintaining such links with parents. They could additionally be a valuable source of information on home and communities for schools. However, care might need to be taken to ensure that maintaining home-school links does not become a duty passed on to TAs cast in the role of 'experts', but is embraced as part of a whole school approach and an inclusive ethos[11].

Conclusion

I have contended that asylum-seeking and refugee students should be defined not by the trauma they have experienced but by their resilience, agency and courage in the face of extreme circumstances, and that inclusive schools should build on these strengths in supporting their education. However, they are often invisible within the school, and in the current political and social climate invisibility seems to be their best weapon of survival. But does not inclusivity mean that we should be encouraging safe visibility for ASR students?

Reflections on values and practice

TAs might consider:

1   How might they help foster within the school a culture of social justice and human rights?
2   How can they best support asylum-seeking and refugee students develop as confident and independent learners?

3   How might they encourage the school to actively involve parents of asylum-seeking and refugee students in the life of the school?

Suggested further reading

Closs, A., Stead, J. and Arshad, R. (2001) The Education of Asylum-Seeker and Refugee Children, *Multicultural Teaching*, 20(1): 29–33.

Pinson, H., Arnot, M. and Candappa, M. (2010) *Education, Asylum and the 'Non-Citizen' Child: the politics of compassion and belonging*, London: PalgraveMacmillan.

Rutter, J. (2006) *Refugee Children in the UK*, Buckingham: Open University Press.

Resources

Bolloten, B. (ed.) (2004) *Home from Home: a guidance and resource pack for the welcome and inclusion of refugee children and families in school*. Retrieved from www.savethechildren.org.uk/scuk/jsp/resources/details

Rutter, J. (2003) *Supporting Refugee Children in the 21st Century – a compendium of essential information*, Retrieved from www.trentham-books.co.uk.

Rutter, J. and Candappa, M. (1998) *'Why Do They Have to Fight?' refugee children's stories from Bosnia, Kurdistan, Somalia and Sri Lanka*, London: Refugee Council.

Notes

1   ASYLUM SEEKER: A person who has left their country of origin and formally applied for asylum in another country but whose application has not yet been concluded. REFUGEE: In the UK, a person is officially a refugee when they have their claim for asylum accepted by the government [within the definition of the 1951 UN Convention]. (www.refugeecouncil.org.uk/policy_research/the_truth.htm accessed 07.06.15)

2   This reflects a growth in numbers of refugees worldwide, linked to the end of cold-war politics plus ethnic conflicts in many parts of the world towards the end of the twentieth century.

3   At the 2011 census the BME population stood at 14.1 per cent of the total in England and Wales, increasing from 7.9 per cent in 2001.

4   'Otherness' is defined by difference, marked by outward signs like 'race', and often associated with marginalised people living outside the dominant social group (Onbelet 2010).

5   Refugee and asylum-seeking children are protected by a number of international, European and British legal instruments, including the European Convention on Human Rights and the UK Human Rights Act 1998. The most comprehensive children's rights instrument is the UNCRC which is reflected in the Children Acts 1989 and 2004, which I discuss here.

6   In September 2008 the UK government withdrew the discriminatory reservation on immigration it had entered when ratifying the UNCRC. Asylum-seeking and refugee children are therefore now entitled to the same rights under the UNCRC as other children in the UK.

7   Pseudonyms have been used for research participants throughout this chapter.

8   There are no accurate demographic data on the number of asylum-seeking and refugee children in UK schools, and known cases might be less than total numbers present. Rutter's estimate was that there were at least 60,000 ASR children of compulsory school age residing in the UK in 2006.

9   Under the Race Relations Amendment Act 2000, a duty is placed on schools to eliminate racial discrimination and to promote equality of opportunity and good relations between people of different groups; under section 78 of the Education Act 2002 the curriculum for all maintained schools should promote the spiritual, moral, cultural, mental and physical development of pupils at the school and of society; the Education and Inspections Act 2006

places a duty on schools to promote community cohesion; and under 'The Equality Duty' in the Equality Act 2010, maintained schools, as public authorities, have a duty to eliminate discrimination, advance equality of opportunity, and foster good relations between people who share a protected characteristic and those who do not.

10 English as an Additional Language.

11 Possible initiatives for supporting parents can be found in Ofsted (2003).

References

Armstrong, F. (2008) 'Inclusive education', in Richards, G. and Armstrong, F. (eds.), *Key Issues for Teaching Assistants: Working in diverse and inclusive classrooms* (pp. 7–18), Abingdon and New York: Routledge.

Arshad, R., Closs, A. and Stead, J. (1999) *Doing Our Best: Scottish school education, refugee pupils and parents – a strategy for social inclusion*, Edinburgh: CERES.

Blinder, S. (2015, 13/08) 'Migration to the UK: Asylum'. *Briefing*. Oxford: COMPAS, University of Oxford, Retrieved from www.migrationobservatory.ox.ac.uk/briefings/migration-uk-asylum

Block, D. (2007) *The Social Turn in Second Language Acquisition*, Edinburgh: Edinburgh University Press.

Bolloten, B. and Spafford, T. (1998) 'Supporting refugee children in East London Primary Schools', in Rutter, J. and Jones, C. (eds.), *Refugee Education: mapping the field* (pp. 107–124), Stoke-on-Trent: Trentham Books.

Candappa, M. (2002) 'Human rights and refugee children in the UK', in Franklin, B (ed.), *The New Handbook of Children's Rights: comparative policy and practice* (pp. 223–236), London: Routledge.

Candappa, M., Ahmad, M., Balata, B., Dekhinet, R. and Gocmen, D. (2007) *Education and Schooling for Asylum-Seeking and Refugee Students in Scotland: an exploratory study*, Scottish Government Social Research 2007, Edinburgh: Scottish Government.

Candappa M. and Egharevba, I. (2002) 'Negotiating boundaries: tensions within home and school life for refugee children', in Edwards, R. (ed.), *Children, Home and School* (pp. 155–171), London: RoutledgeFalmer.

Candappa, M. and Egharevba, I. (2000) '"Extraordinary Childhoods": the social lives of refugee children', *Children 5-16 Research Briefing*, 5, Swindon: ESRC.

Chase, E., Knight, A. and Statham, J. (2008) *The Emotional Well-Being of Unaccompanied Young People Seeking Asylum in the UK*, London: BAAF.

Christopoulou, N., Rydin, I., Buckingham, D. and de Block, L. (2004) *Children's Social Relations in Peer Groups: inclusion, exclusion and friendship*, The European Commission: CHICAM.

Corbett, J. (1999) 'Inclusive education and school culture', *International Journal of Inclusive Education*, 3(1): 53–61.

Elbedour, S., ten Bensel, R. and Bastien, D.T. (1993) 'Ecological Integrated Model of Children of War: individual and social psychology', *Child Abuse & Neglect*, 17: 805–819.

Hammarberg, T. (1995) 'Preface' in B. Franklin (ed.), *The Handbook of Children's Rights: Comparative Policy and Practice* (pp. ix–xiii), London: Routledge.

Ofsted. (2003) *The Education of Asylum-Seeker Pupils*, London: Author.

Onbelet, L. (2010) *Imagining the Other: the use of narrative as an empowering practice*, Retrieved from www.mcmaster.ca/mjtm/3-1d.htm.

Pinson, H., Arnot, M. and Candappa, M. (2010) *Education, Asylum and the 'Non-Citizen' Child: the politics of compassion and belonging*, London: PalgraveMacmillan.

Refugee Council (2015, March) 'Asylum support', *Refugee Council Information*, Retrieved from www.refugeecouncil.org.uk

Rutter, J. (2006) *Refugee Children in the UK*, Buckingham: Open University Press.

Sharples, J., Webster, R. and Blatchford, P. (2015) *Making the Best Use of Teaching Assistants*, London: Education Endowment Foundation.

Stanley, K. (2002) *Cold Comfort: the lottery of care for young separated refugees in England*, London: Save the Children.

Taylor, S. and Sidhu, R. K. (2012) 'Supporting refugee students in schools: what constitutes inclusive education?', *International Journal of Inclusive Education*, 16(1): 39–56.

Vargas-Silva, C. (2011) 'Global international migrant stock: The UK in international comparison'. *Migration Observatory Briefing, COMPAS,* University of Oxford, UK, March 2011. Retrieved from www.migrationobservatory.ox.ac.uk/sites/files/migobs/Briefing%20-%20Global%20 International%20Migrant%20Stock_0.pdf

www.UNHCR.org Refugee Crisis in Europe

Chapter 11

Lesbian, Gay, Bisexual, Transsexual and at school

Experiences and reflections

Colin Slater

To take part in the education of young minds – academically, socially, emotionally and physically – is a big responsibility and an enormous privilege. Teaching Assistants hold a unique position within this process. They can provide an important bridge between the student and teacher. When managed professionally, the less formal relationship between Teaching Assistant and student can be used very successfully to support the learning process. Many Teaching Assistants are employed from within the local community, which means that they are very likely to know many of the students and their families. This can once again be an advantage when interacting with students as they are aware of the wider societal implications of their performance at school. However, it is important to remember that whatever relationship you have or develop with your students, it is imperative that you respect confidentiality. All students have a right to confidentiality unless they have disclosed something that in your opinion is harmful to them or others.

Given the unique position that you as Teaching Assistants hold within a school, it is likely that you already know of or have even been the confidant for young people who are in the process of exploring their sexuality. This raises the question of the kind of support you might provide. For this reason it is important to be aware of, and understand, the kinds of experiences and issues which Lesbian, Gay, Bisexual or Transgender children and young people may face. In this chapter I discuss the wider policy context in relation to the position of LGBT students in education, and draw on the findings of a small study which I carried out as part of my MA in Inclusive Education at the Institute of Education. My underlying focus is on the perspectives of young people themselves and on the importance of listening to their voices as a means of understanding their experiences and relating these to your work in supporting inclusive education in schools and in the classroom.

Lesbian, Gay, Bisexual, Transsexual and at school – an introduction

What is life like if you are Lesbian, Gay, Bisexual or Transsexual (LGBT) and at school in the twenty-first century? As a gay man and a teacher I have a personal knowledge of the kinds of exclusion that LGBT students may experience and also the inability, or even unwillingness, of schools to acknowledge and therefore include LGBT young people and their issues as part of a wider commitment to inclusive education.

There is no question that life for LGBT people has dramatically improved over the thirty years since I was at secondary school. Huge political and social gains have been made by the hard work of LGBT organisations worldwide. This is also due in no small part to the ever increasing exposure to LGBT issues and LGBT people in the popular media. We have gradually moved from camp comedians and game show hosts, to openly LGBT movie and pop stars. LGBT people can have their relationships recognised in law firstly through Civil Partnerships and now same sex marriage. Legislation (Equality Act 2010) has been enacted which identifies sexual orientation as a 'protected characteristic' group which means people who identify as Gay, Lesbian, Bisexual or Heterosexual/Straight are protected from discrimination. The Government's white paper on education, 'The Importance of Teaching' (DfE 2010a), makes it clear that prejudice-based bullying – like homophobic bullying – must be taken "especially seriously". This is an enormous step forward from the period following the 1988 Local Government Act in which Section 28 stated:

> There is no place in any school in any circumstances for teaching which advocates homosexual behaviour, which presents it as "the norm", or which encourages homosexual experimentation by pupils.
>
> (DES 1988, para. 22)

Research both in the UK and worldwide has given us some indication of what LGBT young people experience and the needs they have (Guasp 2012; Warwick, Chase and Aggleton 2004; Robinson 2012). This research has shown the damaging effects of homophobia on young people. LGBT young people report being isolated and feeling invisible, due to the inability or unwillingness of others, especially schools, to acknowledge and address their needs. It has also shown homophobic abuse in schools is a major problem. Homophobic bullying occurs in primary school as well as secondary and is directed at those that are, or simply perceived to be, LGBT. Homophobic bullying in schools can be a problem in a number of ways. Children who experience it have their education disrupted. They may be unable to concentrate on lessons or even reluctant to attend school at all because of the fear and anger that they may be feeling. All of this is most likely to be damaging to their self-confidence, which could mean that these young people may never fulfil their academic potential.

For teenagers who are confused or unsure about their own developing sexuality, this abuse can be particularly problematic and can drive some to the edge of despair and beyond, with lasting consequences for their emotional health and development. Schools contribute to this isolation by not fully acknowledging their LGBT pupils and therefore doing little, if anything to meet their needs (Formby 2015). Governmental legislation and policies have attempted to redress these issues (DfEE 2000; DfE 2010b, 2014).

Over the past thirty years researchers have produced responses and challenges on issues relating to sexuality and gender (see, for example, Rich 1983; Stacey 1991; Redman 1994; Epstein 1994, 2000; Mac an Ghaill 1994; Mole 1995) and a strong political response has come from the Gay community, spawning most notably Stonewall, the Lesbian and Gay lobby group. Their research over a number of years has reported that bullying and attacks on Gay pupils are commonplace. However, it is only relatively recently that these issues have come to be recognised within the broader framework of social justice and inclusive education.

As part of an MA in Inclusive Education I undertook a study into the lives of eleven remarkable young people which provided a glimpse into their perspectives and experiences of being LGBT at school. This study found that all eleven young people were subjected to homophobic abuse and all felt strongly that their needs in relation to their sexuality were not being addressed: in most cases they felt it was ignored.

Other studies carried out by Stonewall in 2007 (Hunt and Jensen 2007) unfortunately give a very similar picture for LGBT young people. As a response to the 2007 study Stonewall produced a range of teaching resources and training packages for secondary schools. A further study five years later which produced The School Report 2012 (Guasp 2012) found that even though some gains had been made, most of the 1,600 young people surveyed reported that life for LGBT young people was still difficult and that their needs were not being acknowledged or met.

As an acknowledgement of, and commitment to, the needs of LGBT young people, schools will ensure that we are moving forward in the process of inclusion for LGBT young people. Schools that ignore these, or deny their existence, are thereby excluding LGBT young people. They are also not helping all their young people to develop a concern for the welfare of minorities and tolerance of difference. Discrimination against people because of their race, gender, disability, nationality, religion or sexual orientation is deeply rooted in the society we live in. Schools, which have a duty in providing a safe environment for learning, are the best places in which to challenge this discrimination. Homophobia, however, has been allowed to flourish when it should have been challenged in the same way that racist or sexist behaviour is. This would ensure that school communities are safe, supportive, respectful and inclusive environments. Schools should reach out and care for those who are different and address the social and learning needs of all students. Every member of the school community has a responsibility in this respect, and Teaching Assistants may have a particular role to play because of their close relationship with the daily lives of students and 'what goes on' in classrooms and playgrounds.

The research project and my findings

My small study into the lives of eleven remarkable young people has provided a glimpse into their perspectives and experiences of being LGBT at school. Even though their numbers are small, their 'voices' are powerful. We must sit up and take note, for what they say could possibly tell the story for the tens of thousands of other LGBT young people in our schools. This would mean that many of them are leading lonely, isolated, harassed and unsupported lives at school. A life that could drive many to despair, so much so that a large number will perhaps attempt to end it; sadly some will succeed.

In the following sections I introduce the participants in the study, and then present some of the themes which emerged from their stories, illustrated by material from my interviews with them. Through this account I hope to provide some insights into some of the feelings and issues confronting these young people.

Participants

Name	Age	Identify as	School
B	16	Lesbian	Mixed Comprehensive/PRU
Danny	18	Gay	Mixed Comprehensive
David	18	Gay	All Boys Comprehensive
Jamie	20	Bisexual	Mixed Comprehensive
Kaya	18	Bisexual	Mixed Comprehensive
Louise	19	Lesbian	Church of England Girls School
Lydia	17	Transsexual	All Boys Comprehensive
Mathew	19	Gay	Mixed Comprehensive
Mustafa	20	Gay	Mixed Comprehensive
Nate	16	Gay	Mixed Comprehensive
Richard	17	Gay	Catholic All Boys School

Coming out

'Coming out' means identifying as Gay, Lesbian, Bisexual or Transgender, it is a process of understanding, accepting, and valuing one's sexual orientation/identity. The first person that you have to reveal this to is yourself; after that you can choose to share this identity with others. For many people the coming out process is difficult mainly because it involves coping with societal responses and attitudes towards LGBT people. LGBT people are forced to come to terms with what it means to be different in a society that assumes that everyone is heterosexual and that tends to judge differences in negative ways. Most people do overcome these difficulties and come out purely because they can't stand hiding who they are any more or better still they want to celebrate their true selves. It certainly feels much better to be open and honest than to conceal such an integral part of oneself. The coming out process is, however, a very personal one. It happens in different ways and occurs at different ages for different people. Some people are aware of their sexuality at an early age; others may come to this realisation at a much later stage. No matter when or how, coming out is a continual, if not lifelong process.

Being LGBT at school

The lives of LGBT people can be difficult – not because of their sexuality but because of other people's reactions to it. Life in school for LGBT young people is particularly difficult. Students who are out, rumoured to be Gay, or simply behave in ways that are considered stereotypically Gay are sometimes victimised in varying degrees, from verbal harassment to physical violence. Many LGBT students exist on the margins of school life: an isolating and depressing situation which can lead to high levels of absenteeism and even suicide. Schools are failing to address these issues for LGBT young people as they appear to be unaware of them or unprepared to intervene into what can be, for some students, an unbearable situation.

Coming out at school

For the majority of LGBT young people 'coming out at school' is something that they do not feel able or enabled to do. However, for some their desire to be known as 'themselves' is all-powerful and can lead to them 'coming out'. For others it would appear that they have little choice.

> Nate says, "I have never had to deny it to myself. I have always been comfortable with myself and who I am". He came out in school at the age of 14. Initially this was to his three best friends. When their reactions were good he decided that he would tell the whole school.

> Danny told who he thought was a trusted friend, but by the end of the day the entire school knew.

> For David, who describes himself thus: "I am so 'camp', life at school was always going to be difficult". He said, "Everyone called me Gay because of the way my hands are moving and the way I am talking and my movement and everything".

Others make very conscious choices to declare their sexuality to the world.

> B identifies as a Lesbian and has no problem in saying so.

> For Lydia it was never about choice. As a Transsexual, her early life was marred by confusion – not hers but by others around her. She told me, "At first I just thought that it was normal, but because people were questioning me, then I thought that it wasn't normal".

Other young people are not so determined or prepared to put themselves through this sort of ordeal. Both Louise and Kaya decided, after witnessing what others in their schools had to endure due to 'coming out', that they themselves would not do so.

What are schools doing?

All the young people involved in the study felt that their schools had not done enough for them and others in similar situations. Some felt that this was because they were unable to do so. While others felt that they had in fact not wanted to.

Lydia tells of how the school arranged for her to see the school counsellor when she was 12. It was here that she told them how she was feeling and they gave her a name for it. The counsellor had told her that she was a Transsexual, but she says "they did not know anything about it and they did not have time to research it".

For Mustafa life at school after he had come out was becoming unbearable. It would take a serious attempt on his own life for the school to make an attempt at helping him.

Nate feels that some teachers are 'playing around' with the issue of homosexuality. He feels that they are not taking it seriously enough. He said that if a male student said something to a male teacher that was homophobic then the teacher is more likely to make a joke of it than to deal with it seriously. But if the same student was to make a sexist or racist joke then they would be more likely to do something about it. This sort of behaviour by schools means that LGBT young people do not tell their teachers what they are going through because they do not feel that they will be able to help or because they do not trust them.

Fortunately there are some within schools who are understanding and supportive. For Nate this was his form tutor who he describes as being very supportive. Mustafa had received support from his form tutor as well. He said she was a "really nice lady", but he did not think that the subject was comfortable for her.

Homosexuality and the curriculum

For the majority of the young people there was little or no mention at all in school of homosexuality. If there was then it was not done in a way that the young people felt was helpful. All of the young people felt that sex education they had received was not relevant to them. Louise said that in her school there was never once any mention of Lesbians and Gays in any of the sex education lessons. Mustafa said, "Sex education was about men, women and babies and that was it".

During Danny's sex education lessons he asked where the Gay sex was. He was supported by some of the girls who thought that that would be really interesting. But the rest did not think the same. Other participants in the study said that when it was mentioned in their lessons it was in relation to something else and was never discussed as a subject in its own right or in any detail. Any mention would usually be met with negative reactions from the rest of the group.

This reluctance or resistance on the part of schools to teach about LGBT issues means that the needs of LGBT young people are not being met. It also means the rest of the school population are not receiving the education that they need and which would help toward overcoming the homophobia that exists in schools and the wider community. This raises important issues concerning staff-development and in-service training, but it also underlines the importance of changing school cultures and the need to develop inclusive policies and practices throughout the school community.

Peers

School can be an isolating and lonely place for many LGBT young people. For those who have friends, many feel unable to talk to them about their sexuality. Kaya said that she did not feel secure enough coming out to her friends, as she felt that they would not understand it enough. Louise gives another reason and that is that she did not trust anyone at all with this information.

Others had told who they thought were trusted friends only to find that this information was treated like hot gossip. Richard feels that if you are going to be upfront about your sexuality in school then you have to be strong. He said, "People get murdered. I had that in my mind".

With LGBT young people fearing for their safety is it any wonder that many choose to isolate themselves from the rest of the school population. Many of the young people in my study spent all of their breaks in the one place that could afford the most protection, the school library. Mustafa signed up to be a library monitor in order to get away from the crowds. This self-imposed exile is isolating and lonely and is compounded by the reluctance on the part of other students to engage with these young people. Mustafa told me that when he came out at school people stopped talking to him and pushed him aside. Mathew also said that when he was outed at school he "lost a hell of a lot of friends". Two of his friends did stick by him, but received a lot of name calling and other abuse. Richard who was not 'out', but was assumed to be Gay by the rest of the school, had a small group of friends who were all subjected to the same assumption. David also told me in his 'gang' of five, three turned out to be Gay and the other two straight. At school, however, David said, "everyone in that group was called Gay".

It would seem that association alone is enough for assumptions to be made about one's sexuality. This is the main cause of the isolation of many LGBT young people. It can lead young LGBT people to isolate themselves from those who are out or assumed to be LGBT for fear of exposing themselves and therefore being subjected to the same abuse.

Jamie told me that at break times and lunch times he would be on his own. He would be sitting in the playground on his own doing nothing. He said, "I felt so lonely".

Homophobic bullying

This loneliness and isolation would be difficult enough for LGBT young people to deal with but they also have to deal with the homophobic bullying that is rife within schools – both primary and secondary. Renée DePalma and Mark Jennett (2010) look at homophobia and transphobia and the "subtle ways in which schools are complicit in sustaining them, even from the very earliest years". They go on to say that "the institutional culture of school must be transformed as a whole, and this must begin at the beginning, as soon as children first walk through the school gate". This view is supported by a study undertaken by Stonewall (2009) which found that 75 per cent of primary teachers report hearing the phrases 'you're so Gay' or 'that's so Gay' and that 44 per cent report hearing words like 'poof', 'dyke', 'queer' and 'faggot'.

It was also reported that pupils felt that classmates with LGBT parents would themselves become the target of homophobia. Here again, research has shown the importance of having 'supportive allies' in school, including teachers, friends, Teaching Assistants, counselors and other members of the school community (Hart, Mourot and Aros 2012).

These views are also supported by the views of the participants in my study. All of the young people said that they experienced, directed at them or at others, high levels of homophobic abuse within their schools. This ranged from name calling and verbal abuse to physical violence. For most this has to be endured on a daily basis.

David said that every day when he would go into school everyone would be saying, 'here comes that Gay-boy'. Lydia told me that she was called things like 'Man-girl' and other phrases that they would come up with. She said that there was a big competition to see who could come up with the funniest. Abuse is hardly funny and especially if it is happening constantly throughout the school day; as it was for most of the young people. Negotiating the playground and other less supervised areas would be hazardous for many of the young people. Mustafa was assaulted with a knife a couple of times on his way home from school by fellow students. Danny had his face burnt with a Bunsen burner. Lydia also told me that negotiating the stairs in her school during breaks was awful.

All the young people told me that violence or the threat of it is part of their lives at school. For some, however, this abuse by other students extends into other areas of their lives and therefore can have an effect on others. Nate told me how he had to educate his father about the names he heard his son being called. When he explained that 'Queer boy' and 'Batty boy' were names directed at those who are Gay, his father said "So that is what you are, isn't it?" Nate told me that no matter how hard he tried to explain that this was homophobic abuse his father would not acknowledge this fact.

All the young people found this abuse difficult to deal with and reacted to it in different ways. Danny feels that humour is a good way to deal with the abuse, but he also told me that in order to survive being Gay in school you have to have what he calls a 'tortoise shell'. He told me that you have to be hard because when people say things it will just bounce right off.

Unfortunately for some they do not have the same resilience and all this abuse is very difficult to handle. David told me that because of this ongoing abuse his confidence was very low and he had become very withdrawn. Even for Danny with his 'tortoise shell' there were times when it was all too much. For others the only option they feel they have is to end it all by taking their own lives. Two of the young people I interviewed made serious attempts to do so.

Help: what is being done for these young people?

It is very sad that the lives of LGBT young people are affected this way by the homophobic abuse they are being subjected to in schools. All the young people felt that homophobic bullying was not adequately addressed in their schools. Richard told me that the teachers in his school did very little about the abuse. When he told one of his teachers, who he felt was very supportive of him, that he was being abused in very subtle ways, he was told that there was nothing that could be done. Mathew said that "teachers did nothing, they had the power to stop it and yet they did nothing". Others felt that their teachers were powerless to stop the bullying. Lydia said, "The teachers did not know how to stop the bullying". Danny said, "At times it felt like I was fighting a battle that I would never win".

It would seems that the inadequacies of schools to deal with homophobic abuse means that they either ignore it, therefore making the situation worse, or they deal with it in inappropriate ways.

What would make the lives of LGBT young people better?

With many schools doing little if anything to assist LGBT young people what do LGBT young people think should be done? All the young people agreed that LGBT issues should be included in schools. How this could be done produced a variety of responses. Kaya felt that the answer is simple; education should start at a young age, she suggests five, and should consist of lessons aimed at understanding and respecting diversity. Louise feels that sex education should include Gay and Lesbian sex. Nate suggested that there should be some kind of forum, 'a LGBT forum in schools for young LGBT', so as to offer support. Mustafa feels that schools should be helping and that they have many of the tools at their disposal to do so but are afraid to do so because of what others, such as parents might think. He feels that schools are more worried about their image than about the welfare of individuals.

Conclusion

Schools are failing these young people, mostly by not even recognising and including their LGBT identity as valued members of the school community. Schools must start to include LGBT pupils by simply acknowledging their existence. They must identify their needs and address these as part of the school programme. The curriculum should include appropriate coverage of sexuality across all subject areas. Staff in schools need access to formal training and centrally produced resources in order to sensitively and successfully deal with issues for LGBT young people. Some adults will have to work hard to overcome moral, religious, and homophobic objections in order to carry out their duty of care to all their students.

Schools must tackle homophobia by adopting a whole-school approach to combating homophobic attitudes and the bullying that usually accompanies it. Schools must strive to create a positive, open, tolerant ethos in which matters of concern to young people are discussed calmly. If the response to homophobic bullying is purely reactive and short term, this may only serve to marginalise victims.

All pupils need to develop an understanding of and respect for diversity, which includes sexual diversity. As society's exposure to LGBT issues increases and the ensuing homo-acceptance that many of us encounter as a consequence grows, schools are places in which any negative consequences can be countered and positive attitudes can be reinforced.

Schools must lead the way in showing young people the possibilities and the permutations that life can present. It is important that schools include all young people, remembering that this inclusion is not about assimilation, but that it is about recognition of difference and a celebration of diversity. LGBT students, along with everyone else, must be recognised and have their needs and interests adequately and appropriately met. Doing so would dramatically improve the lives of all young people at school.

Reflections on values and practice

1   How could your own attitudes and understanding about LGBT people impact on your ability to work successfully with LGBT students? How ready do you feel to make changes in your own perspective?

2   Do you feel adequately prepared to support all young people, regardless of difference, and to challenge homophobic bullying and abuse within your setting?

3   Does your school have policies and guidelines relating to equality issues and bullying? Do these include any reference to sexuality? Is there a forum in which you can obtain this kind of information and raise issues and concerns?

4   Teaching Assistants hold a unique position within their settings. How comfortable and prepared would you feel if a young LGBT person were to confide in you about their sexuality? Would you know where to refer them for guidance, if they needed it? Would some form of staff development or training be helpful to you and, if so, what form should this take?

References

DePalma, R., & Jennett, M. (2010). 'Homophobia, transphobia and culture: Deconstructing heteronormativity in English primary schools'. *Intercultural Education*, 21: 15–26.

DfE (2010a). *The Importance of Teaching: schools white paper 2010*. London: Author.

DfE (2010b). *Reducing Bullying amongst the Worst Affected*. London: Author.

DfE. (2014). *Preventing and Tackling Bullying: Advice for Headteachers, Staff and Governing Bodies*. London: Author.

DfEE. (2000). *Sex Education and Relationship Guidance, ref. 0116/2000,*
London: Author.

DfES. (1988). *Local Government Act 1988: Section 28; DES Circular 88/90,* London: Author.

DfES. (2000). *Anti-Bullying Pack: don't suffer in silence for schools*. London: Department of Education and Science.

Epstein, D. (1994). *Challenging Lesbian and Gay Inequalities in Education.* Buckingham: Open University Press.

Epstein, D. (2000). 'Sexualities and Education: Catch 28'. *Sexualities,* 3(4): 387–394.

Formby, E. (2013). 'Understanding and responding to homophobia and bullying: Contrasting staff and young people's views within community settings in England'. *Sexuality Research and Social Policy,* 10(4): 302–316.

Formby, E. (2015). 'Limitations of focussing on homophobic, biphobic and transphobic "bullying" to understand and address LGBT young people's experiences within and beyond school'. *Sex Education: Sexuality, Society and Learning.*

Guasp, A. (2012). *The School Report: The Experiences of Young Gay People in Britain's Schools in 2012.* London: Stonewall.

Hart, J. E., Mourot, J. and Aros, M. (2012). 'Children of same-sex parents: In and out of the closet'. *Educational Studies,* 38(3): 277–281.

Hunt, R. and Jensen, J. (2007). *The School Report: The Experiences of Young Gay People in Britain's Schools.* London: Stonewall.

Mac an Ghaill, M. (1994). *The Making of Men: Masculinities, Sexuality and Schooling.* Buckingham: Open University Press.

Mole, S. (1995). *Colours of the Rainbow: Exploring Issues of Sexuality and Difference.* London: Camden and Islington Health Promotion Service.

Redman, P. (1994). 'Shifting ground: Rethinking sexuality education', in Epstein, D. (ed.), *Challenging Lesbian and Gay Inequalities in Education,* Buckingham: Open University Press.

Rich, A. (1983). *Compulsory Heterosexuality and Lesbian Existence.* London: Only Women Press.

Robinson, K. (2010). 'A study of young lesbian and gay people's school experiences'. *Educational Psychology in Practice,* 26(4): 331–351.

Stacey, J. (1991). 'Promoting normality: Section 28', in S. Franklin, C. Lucy and J. Stacey (eds.), *Off Centre: Feminism and Cultural Studies.* London: Harper Collins Academic.

Warwick, I., Chase, E. and Aggleton, P. (2004). *Homophobia, Sexual Orientation and Schools: A Review and Implications for Action.* Nottingham: DfES Publications.

Chapter 12

Challenging behaviour

Understanding the issues and providing support

Jackie Scruton

Introduction

The purpose of this chapter is to help you understand and explore some of the complex issues surrounding challenging situations and behaviour that you may experience in your role as a Teaching Assistant (TA). This role is one that has changed significantly in the recent past and you will be among a number of staff working in schools known as 'paraprofessionals' (Radford *et al.* 2013). Within this role you will be expected to support, increasingly teach, understand and have the skills to work with students in challenging situations. This chapter aims to help you reflect and develop effective behaviour management strategies which in turn will help you to extend inclusive support for all your students.

The behaviour of students in a range of settings seems to be a topic that is constantly discussed by the media. It is often the extreme behaviours such as violence and aggression that the media report, capturing "the attention of the public" (Hart 2010: 353) and I suggest, help to demonise some of our children and young people. This is not a new phenomenon. In 1996 the Ridings School hit the national headlines and more recently programmes such Educating Yorkshire (2013) gave viewers a 'snapshot' of the state of behaviour in classrooms. As far back as the Elton Report (1989) it was recognised that "bad behaviour in schools is a complex problem which does not lend itself to simple solutions" (Elton 1989: 25), and more recently Charlie Taylor, a UK government expert advisor on behaviour in schools, also articulated that managing a class effectively was both complex and essential if the children and young people were to feel safe, happy and, as a result, demonstrate good behaviour (Taylor 2011). The link between managing behaviour and achievement is one that has long been recognised (Elliott, Zamorski and Shreeve 2001; Hattie 2009; O'Neill 2011; Taylor 2012). In your role as a TA you will have a key part to play in helping to manage the classroom environment, especially given the one-to-one contact you will undoubtedly have with some students labelled as 'challenging'. Your skills, knowledge and support will be an important factor in enabling children and young people to access the learning and teaching on offer.

So, what can you do to meet such a challenge and help foster improved behaviour? This chapter will explore the historical perspectives, together with examining the latest debates and research. It will move on to identify some of the current strategies that can be used to help you develop your inclusive practice. It will also suggest ways that you can reflect on your practice, the way you support children and in so doing, compile a set of 'tips' for yourself that will help you achieve an inclusive classroom.

Taylor (2011) suggests that children are more likely to 'push boundaries' if schools do not have a 'simple' approach to managing challenging behaviour and do not recognise the importance of consistently applying that approach. I believe it is worth remembering Elton's (1989) suggestion that 'reducing bad behaviour' was realistic, but eliminating it completely was not. This seems to be as pertinent today as it was then. By the end of this chapter, I hope that you will feel more confident in your own skills and abilities in order to provide a learning environment that fosters positive behaviour and learning.

What do we mean by 'challenging' students?

Trying to define this term can be problematic for a number of reasons, some of which will be explored later. However, it is worth noting that what one TA would deem to be 'challenging' behaviour, another would not. A few years ago I was teaching a group of adult learners, all of whom worked in educational settings. I asked each member of the group to make a list of behaviours that they found most difficult to work with. As an example I indicated that the 'clicking' of pens caused me to become frustrated and indeed created a challenge for how I dealt with the situation. A member of the group said that he found students who sat on desks the most difficult to 'deal' with. At that time I was talking to the group perched on a desk! In subsequent weeks, if I sat on a desk he would 'click' his pen – all in the spirit of humour! This anecdote illustrates just how behaviour can be viewed quite differently and may depend on different levels of tolerance and the subjective experience of the teacher and indeed the TA. Roffey and O'Reirdon (2002) also comment on the fact that is the 'constant niggles' or low-level disruption that cause frustration for TAs and teachers, rather than the more extreme aggressive or violent behaviours.

Thus, I suggest that defining the term 'challenging' children, and indeed 'challenging' behaviour, is difficult. Moreover, often in the classroom the two can be seen as interchangeable. Behaviour may be challenging because it prevents you from supporting children and providing an inclusive learning environment. The challenge may also be how you alter the ways in which you approach teaching and support in order to ensure that learning takes place. In doing so, you will almost certainly have to spend time and energy 'containing and controlling' individual students and the class, rather than what you may feel is the core of your job – supporting, teaching and promoting achievement. Particular disruptive behaviour may be aimed at challenging the 'teaching', but could be as a result of other factors, such as difficulties with curriculum content, resources and use and understanding of language and vocabulary, some of which you will have control over, and some not. Remember to explore areas where you can influence change; this is discussed later in the chapter.

Some behaviour is aimed at disruption, undermining the authority and control of both TAs and teachers. Rogers (1990) suggests that this may be a challenge to their right to exercise 'leadership' in the classroom. In such cases it may be difficult to determine the causes of the challenge as these may be very complex. Additionally, in schools today there is a pressure caused by the need to raise achievement in order to look good in national league tables, so helping children and young people to engage in learning becomes even more important for you to develop your skills in contributing to this process.

A number of definitions identify possible contributory factors to challenging behaviour, including the social and emotional aspects of learning, possible low self-esteem, and specific special educational needs, such as Attention Deficit/Hyperactivity Disorder (ADHD) and Autistic Spectrum Disorder (ASD). In order to further develop our understanding of some of these complexities and to provide an inclusive approach in the classroom, we need to explore the two main models of disability – the medical and social models. The medical model has ensured that the 'blame' lies with the child, that there is something wrong with them, that they could be described as dysfunctional or 'ill' and as result, they 'own' the problem and need to be cured. This model brings with it a particular use of language which perpetuates the 'blame' approach and may lead to you seeking a solution or cure that only focuses on the child, and in doing so may result in exclusionary practices (Parry, Nind and Sheehy 2010), creating the opposite approach to the one I would advocate. The social model, which stems from the disability rights movement, takes a much more inclusive approach, removing the 'blame' from the child and suggesting that it lies with society. It is society that creates barriers that may prevent children from accessing learning opportunities. The use of the social model enables you to explore what factors might create difficulties or lead to exclusion which is beyond the child's control and seek solutions to these.

I am advocating a move from a medical-model approach to one where we consider the context, aiming to change the behaviour and not the child – one that has a stronger inclusive approach. Trussler and Robinson (2015) describe this as a transactional model, where the focus is on how the environment may impact on a child's ability to access the learning and teaching. They suggest that there is a need to focus on the child's potential and capability in order to remove barriers to learning. In attempting to achieve this, we may also need to examine our own behaviour, and we must pay attention to the voice of the child. Increasingly, practitioners across Children's Services are being required to elicit children's views as a fundamental part of their work. This agenda was driven by government through a number of initiatives, such as Every Child Matters: Change for Children (DfES 2003), the Children Act 2004 and the Children Act 2014. The most recent Act was described by Timpson (2014), the then Children and Families Minister, as key to reforming services and to give every child an 'equal chance' to make the best of themselves (www.gov.uk/government/news). Topping and Maloney (2005) and Taylor (2011) draw on children's experiences where they have indicated a teacher's behaviour affects their own. For example, they argue that if a teacher treats children with respect and has a sense of humour, for example by taking time to meet and greet children at the door of the classroom, then children's commitment would increase. They also suggest that a teacher who praises good work is much more likely to be working with class of children who are not disruptive and who engage with the learning process. Whilst these authors discuss the role of the teacher, I believe that the same is true of any paraprofessional working in the classroom setting; the lesson for us all is that our own behaviour is very likely to have an impact on that of our students.

Behaviour and learning

How do we ensure that we provide an inclusive classroom that enables all children to access the learning and teaching opportunities? We could start by developing our understanding of the links between behaviour and learning.

Hadyn (2007) and Wallace (2007) suggest that there is an assumption that all children and young people come to school or college wanting to learn. This is, however, not always the case. Hadyn (2007) also suggests that many outside the world of education view learning and behaviour as two entirely separate activities, entertaining the notion that schools will 'sort out' behaviour in the first few weeks. Developing and understanding children's 'learning agendas' (Elliott *et al.* 2001) can be viewed as an important and essential part of your role in providing an environment that facilitates learning. The Steer Behaviour Review (2008), Taylor (2011) and Shepherd and Linn (2015) suggest that the relationship between behaviour and learning is now widely accepted and there is an expectation that schools should not only monitor the impact of this connection but also develop a foundation of positive behaviour through the proactive use of behaviour polices which help support strong consistent strategies. As a TA you will need to know what those policies are and perhaps more importantly work with all staff in your setting in order to implement them.

Policies, initiatives and debates

It is important to recognise the effect history has had on the ways in which we perceive behaviour and work to promote Behaviour 4 Learning.

The 1944 Education Act aimed at ensuring that post-war Britain had an education system that all learners could access. This laid the foundation of our current education system. The Warnock Report (1978) was groundbreaking in that it marked a move away from a deficit medical model to one that could be described as positive and empowering. This report formed the backbone of various policies and legislation, including the 1981 Education Act, the 1989 Children Act and the 1989 Elton Report.

The Elton Report (1989) was a seminal work established to examine and make recommendations regarding what was seen at the time as disruptive behaviour in schools. It made the link between behaviour and learning much more explicit and as a result, the report has relevance today. This report laid the foundations for the Steer Report (2005) and subsequent review (2008). Elton (1989) suggested a whole-school approach to behaviour management through which an atmosphere would be created that would foster and promote learning. This approach would necessitate schools having clear policies and procedures, not only for when things went wrong, but also to highlight and reward 'good behaviour' (as it is all too easy to focus on the negative). It recommended the development of a school-wide ethos with regard to positive approaches to behaviour management. The significant difference in the recommendations, when compared to previous behaviour management ideas, was that of a proactive approach to teaching and learning.

Other national initiatives concerned with supporting children who may experience problematic behaviour included Every Child Matters: A Change for Children (ECM) (DfES 2003) and the subsequent Children's Plan (DCFS 2007). ECM arose following the tragic death of Victoria Climbie in 2000. It highlighted five key areas/outcomes that every child had a right to expect and that would enable all learners to fulfil their potential. The outcomes were (a) be healthy, (b) stay safe, (c) enjoy and achieve, (d) make a positive contribution and (e) achieve economic well-being. It is worth noting that these five outcomes helped guide the conclusions and recommendations of the subsequent report by Steer (2005) and much of our professional practice today.

Possible strategies

As a TA you will not be alone in helping children to achieve positive outcomes. One area of support is the development of a multi-professional Team Around the Child (TAC). Such a team has the school at the centre and as a TA, who will most likely have supported a child on a one-to-one basis, you will play an important part in helping that child, drawing on support from other members of the TAC such as the Youth Offending Team (YOT) and learning mentors. We need to be a group – all stakeholders helping children to access education and succeed.

A significant approach to managing 'challenging' children is 'Behaviour for Learning'. This theory is based on the idea that a set of three relationships should be in place which will enable the desired outcome of effective and worthwhile learning (Evans *et al.* 2003). These three relationships are:

- child and self;
- child and other; and
- child and curriculum.

This theory suggests that when there is balance between the three components, a child will learn and behave appropriately. However, if there is an imbalance, learning and behaviour may be affected.

In 2004, the 'Behaviour 4 Learning' initiative was established and used as a major component of teacher training, aimed particularly at helping new teachers to develop and foster an environment in the classroom that promotes behaviour conducive for learning. Again, whilst aimed primarily at teachers, the resources could be used by anyone working in an educational setting. This initiative was cut due to funding constraints in 2011 and the associated web resource was no longer available as a tool for schools to use. As result, a valuable resource was lost. However, in 2012, the initiative was re-launched as a social enterprise under the title of 'Behaviour 2 Learn' (B2L). This new web-based resource aims to give access to a range of materials that are helpful in developing the skills and understanding of managing challenging behaviour.

Steer's report (2005) at the time was the centrepiece of the Government's plans for tackling what was perceived to be problem behaviour, and in doing so suggested some useful strategies. These include highlighting effective practice that allows for the right conditions for good behaviour and offering practical examples of how to achieve this – for example, parental involvement and effective school leadership. Steer's later review (2008) identified what progress had been made and a further 47 recommendations were identified. The report's purpose and ideology can perhaps best be summed up by Steer's own observations:

> Consistent experience of good teaching promotes good behaviour. But schools also need to have positive strategies for managing pupil behaviour that help pupils understand their school's expectations, underpinned by a clear range of rewards and sanctions, which are applied fairly and consistently by all staff. It is also vital to teach pupils how to behave – good behaviour has to be learned – so schools must adopt procedures and practices that help pupils learn how to behave. Good behaviour has to be modelled by all staff all of the time in their interaction with pupils. For their part, staff need training and support to understand and manage pupil behaviour effectively.
>
> (Steer 2005: 12)

More recently, Taylor (2011) developed key principles for schools to help improve behaviour. We explore some of these later on, but it is interesting to note the title 'Getting the simple things right' is maybe a lesson for us all. This may raise questions for you as a TA: What approach do you take? Which of the myriad of behaviour management books and resources do you use? However, it is important to remember when you are trying to support your children and young people in managing their behaviour that "effective pedagogy can reduce problematic behaviour but cannot eliminate it" (O'Neill 2011: 44).

It is helpful for you to be aware of your own beliefs and value sets. These may be different from those of the children you are working with due to cultural and environmental factors. You will need to be able to identify what behaviours cause you the most difficulty (remember the 'clicking' pen anecdote!). From a personal perspective, once you have identified these, it is important to try and reflect on why these behaviours cause you difficulty and you may begin to change your own behaviour. At this stage, it is also very important to focus on children's positive behaviours and to reflect on how you reward them. Above all, be prepared to embark on a journey that does not have an ending!

In general terms, there are a number of strategies you could consider using in the classroom to ensure you continue to develop your inclusive pedagogy, and as a result, include all your children. These are best used within a framework which could comprise the approaches below:

- *Building trust.* This is a key element in helping the children you work with to improve and develop positive behaviour. Given the amount of time you are likely to spend with individual children, you will be in a strong position to understand their needs and build a relationship built on trust and respect. The Sutton Trust (2015) suggests that building a culture of trust in schools enables risk taking, and as a result, engenders innovative practice.
- *Good communication.* This should include positive body language, avoiding long and complex instructions, communicating with other professionals, and listening to learners and their parents.
- *Being well prepared.* Elton (1989), Hadyn (2007) and Taylor (2011), amongst others, recognised that good preparation is essential. This includes researching and sharing experiences/resources with other TAs in order to be well prepared. I would also argue that having good knowledge of (a) how to plan and prepare for one-to-one work or small-group work, and (b) the subjects you are supporting, together with knowing how your teacher 'works' so that you can engage in teamwork, will also help your preparation.
- *Establish a few simple 'ground' rules.* These are rules that everyone can understand and achieve, and they need to be firm and fair. Do not set the bar so high that achievement is impossible. This is especially important when working on a one-to-one or small-group basis.
- *Use the schools policies to support your work.* Ensure that you know what the behaviour policy is and apply it consistently with your classroom/ children.
- *Remember that you are an important part of the team in your classroom.* Consider that how you meet and greet your children, how you establish and maintain routines and how you celebrate success and good behaviour will all have an impact on your children's motivation and desire to learn.
- *Use the TAC.* Steer (2008) indicated that the development of collegiate professionalism and the sharing of good practice should have a significant impact on behaviour.
- *Develop a 'box of tricks'.* Establish activities that help you to motivate and personalise the learning. In other words, try and ensure that the activities you provide are appropriate to each individual – that they match the level at which the child is functioning. In over stretching, and indeed under stretching, a child, you may find that both situations can exacerbate problematic behaviour.
- *Involve parents wherever and whenever you can.* Sharing responsibility and planning with parents can be most effective. In order to achieve this, remember that good communication with all parties is key.
- *Decide which behaviours to focus on and which to ignore.*
- *Use the Social and Emotional Aspects of Learning (SEAL) initiative.*

This list is by no means exhaustive but should give you a starting point.

In the final part of this section I will briefly examine two strategies, SEAL and peer mentoring, together with two types of provision: Inclusion Units and Pupil Referral Units (PRUs) – now also described as Alternative Provision (AP). A number of writers (Goleman 1998; Shepherd and Linn 2015) have identified that meeting children's social needs plays an important part in nurturing and fostering an environment that enables them to access the teaching and learning that is on offer – through providing a 'climate for learning' – and to succeed as a result. Gardner (1984) discussed the concept of 'multiple intelligences', which identified the importance of being intelligent about our own emotions. Further work was explored by Goleman (1995), who used the phrase 'emotional intelligence', and suggested that emotional and social skills could be seen as more important in developmental terms than raw intelligence. More recently, Shepherd and Linn (2015) advocated the importance of social skills in ensuring children are not rejected by their peers and are able to develop relationships with both them and staff in order to decrease challenging behaviour.

As we have already identified, there has been concern, sometimes media driven, about young people's antisocial behaviour. This, together with perceived problematic behaviour in schools (Steer 2005), prompted the Government to develop a programme that supported nurturing learners' social and emotional skills. This has been translated into the SEAL initiative, which can be viewed as being of particular importance for children who are seen as both challenging for schools and at risk of educational failure.

SEAL is based on five broad areas: self-awareness, managing feelings, motivation, empathy and social skills. In supporting and nurturing these five areas it is envisaged that children will become more effective learners. In terms of challenging behaviour, it is intended that the initiative will enable children to build a foundation for managing their own emotions and hence a greater understanding of their behaviour and how it might affect others – in other words, that each child will develop a social conscience. A vast range of materials, which can be used flexibly, are available for you to support your children's understanding of their own emotions and hopefully of their own behaviour.

SEAL is not the only programme available to tackle these issues; other strategies that might help support children's development are nurture groups, circle time, buddy systems, and peer mentoring. It is peer mentoring we are going to explore in a little more detail.

Over the past 20 years there has been a growth in the availability and use of peer-mentoring schemes in the UK (Mentoring and Befriending Foundation 2010; Houlston, Smith and Jessel 2009). The original focus of such schemes was to reduce bullying in schools. They are based on nonjudgmental one-to-one relationships that can enable children and young people to tackle other issues such as bereavement or isolation, all of which can lead to challenging behaviour and possible exclusion. A clear definition of 'peer mentoring' is provided by Houlston et al. (2009):

> Peer support involves school programmes which train and use students themselves to help others learn and develop emotionally, socially or

academically. These may also be referred to as peer-counselling (or peer-listening), befriending, buddy or mentoring schemes. These schemes may be used in addition to more traditional adult-based pastoral support systems.

(Houlston *et al.* 2009: 328)

Evidence from the Mentoring and Befriending Foundation (2010) also indicates that there are a number of further benefits of running peer-mentoring schemes, such as:

- staff believe that the 'climate' in schools has changed for the better;
- the promotion and development of both self-confidence and self-esteem has improved; and
- there is a clear fit with policy initiatives, such as participation, early intervention and volunteering.

It is worth remembering that your school may run initiatives such as classroom mentors and buddy schemes, all of which could be described under the umbrella term 'peer mentoring'. It is something as a TA you are very likely to be involved in, or if not, you might like to considering introducing on a small scale with some of the children you support.

Whilst considering inclusive strategies it is important that we should also recognise that educational placement has a part to play. By this I mean that some children may be placed, or perceived as 'dumped', within an inclusion/exclusion unit that is part of a mainstream school, or in a PRU. Inclusion units are a specific type of provision, and you may find them called other things, such as Learning Support Unit, seclusion room, or some schools give them a more specific name like 'The Base Room'. In essence they provide a physical environment with particular staff and short-term tailored programmes aimed at meeting individual needs. There is little guidance on how this type of provision should be run, so schools are left to work out what they believe is right for their particular school. Whilst the aim is to keep pupils in school, it could be argued that the units themselves internally exclude and stigmatise pupils, thus becoming a dumping ground for young people seen as 'problems' and as such are not inclusive in the wider sense.

Unlike inclusion units, PRUs are an older provision and were established in 1996 in order that local authorities could become compliant with their statutory duties, providing suitable education for pupils of compulsory school age who had been excluded from mainstream provision. This type of setting is based within local areas rather than in schools. The aim is to provide short-term intervention and re-inclusion into mainstream provision. During the 1980s a number of critical reports identified that these units did not enable pupils to progress and the teaching and learning pedagogy was poor. Pupils once 'sent' to a unit rarely re-entered mainstream provision. More recently, PRUs have supported pupils in following the National Curriculum, albeit differentiated, providing a flexible approach to meeting individual pupil needs. In 2013 there were 393 PRUs across the UK. These were listed under the new umbrella term 'Alternative Provisions' (AP) – that is to say, provision physically located away from 'mainstream'. In the same year, like other Local Authority schools, APs were given greater freedom and control over budgets, staffing and how to meet the needs of their pupils. This provision is increasingly working through successful partnerships with other settings such as FE colleges, and in doing so are enabling pupils to develop vocational as well as academic skills. The more recent national changes to how schools can be run and governed, together with the introduction of academies and free schools, has meant that APs can be free from local authority control and develop their own curriculum and employ their own staff. This has allowed a flexibility of approach and tailored programmes designed to meet individual need.

Conclusion

Sharing knowledge and supporting learners to experience success is one of the most rewarding aspects of the role of being a TA. However, I recognise that working in a situation where you feel challenged is a difficult task.

Having examined, albeit briefly, some of the issues and strategies that surround the concept of children who may present a challenge, I would like to emphasise that prevention is better than 'cure' (Kyriacou 2001). I am sure that as a TA you will have worked with other paraprofessionals, and especially teachers, who make managing a classroom look easy. It is in fact highly likely that they achieve this 'ease' from having put in significant preparation behind the scenes. This is a skill you will want and need to develop over the course of your career. Observing how others achieve this, together with your continuous professional development, will help you to enhance your own skills and knowledge.

I also want to stress that you are not alone in developing your skills. There are a lot of published materials to help you, but probably one of the best support mechanisms you can use is effective communication. This works on a number of levels – TA to child, TA to teacher, TA to TA, TA to parent, TA to other professionals. Listening to others and asking for help is not a sign of failure; rather, it indicates a willingness to learn and to nurture individuals. Indeed, the DCSF (2009) recognises that in 'Building a 21st Century School System', every school should be working in partnership, because no school can do it alone. This has been further recognised in the new Special Educational Needs and Disability code of practice (DfE and DoH 2014), which has removed Statements of Special Educational Need and replaced them with Education and Health Care Plans. The aim of such a plan is to ensure that the needs of the child or young person are viewed in a holistic way. It can be seen that this, together with the policies and strategies previously mentioned, can help to ensure that support for all children is in place and that this support will enable them to succeed in adult life.

Some of the strategies discussed in this chapter will help you develop your own skills and enable you to become an inclusive TA. In order to further develop your skills, keep reading, observing, listening and talking to colleagues, the children and young people themselves.

Reflections on values and practice

1   Explore the different strategies that are available to you – which ones seem to work well and why? Conversely, what strategies have not worked for you and why?

2   Do you have you well prepared resources available to use with individuals? If not, how can you develop these? If you have, how do you change or up-date them to personalise them for individual children?

3   How do you deal with the 'stress' of working children whose behaviour you find challenging? Identify your support mechanisms.

4   Think about your relationship with other adults in your classroom. Do you communicate effectively with them? In terms of managing challenging behaviour are you all aware of the rewards and strategies you use? Are you all 'singing for the same song sheet'?

5   How well do you know the community in which your setting is placed? Consider how this may impact on children's values and attitudes and how these relate to your own.

Suggested further reading

Bishop, S. (2008) *Running a Nurture Group*, London: Sage.

Ellis, S. and Todd, J. (2009) *Behaviour for Learning: Proactive approaches to behaviour management*. Abingdon: Routledge.

Morgan, J. (2007) *The Teaching Assistants Guide to Managing Behaviour*. London: Bloomsbury.

Mosley, J. (1998) *Quality Circle Time in the Primary Classroom*. London: LDA.

Rogers, B. (2011) *Classroom Behaviour: A practical guide to effective teaching, behaviour management and colleague support*. London: Sage.

References

DCSF. (2007) *The Children's Plan: Building a brighter future*. London: Author.

DCSF. (2009) *Your Child, Your Schools, Our Future: Building a 21st century schools system*. Norwich: TSO.

DfE and DoH. (2014) *The Special Educational Needs and Disability Code of Practice: 0–25 years*. London: Crown.

DfES. (2003) *Every Child Matters*. London: Author.

Elliott, J., Zamorski, B. and Shreeve, A. (2001) *Exploring the Pedagogical Dimensions of Disaffection through Collaborative Research. Norwich area schools consortium: A final report to the Teacher Training Agency*. Norwich: HMSO.

Elton, R. L. (1989) *Enquiry into Discipline in Schools*. London: HMSO.

Evans, J., Harden, A., Thomas, J., and Benefield, P. (2003) *Support for Pupils with Emotional and Behavioural Difficulties in Mainstream Primary Classrooms*. London: EPI Centre.

Gardner, H. (1984) *Frames of Mind: The theory of multiple intelligences*. London: Heinemann.

Goleman, D. (1995) *Emotional Intelligence*. St Ives: Bloomsbury.

Goleman, D. (1998) *Working with Emotional Intelligence*. London: Bloomsbury.

Hadyn, T. (2007) *Managing Pupil Behaviour: Key issues in teaching and learning*. Abingdon: Routledge.

Hart, R. (2010) 'Classroom behaviour management: Educational psychologists' view of effective practice'. *Emotional and Behavioural Difficulties, 14*(3): 353–371.

Hattie, J. (2009) *Visible Learning: A synthesis of over 800 meta-analyses relating to achievement.* Abingdon: Routledge.

Houlston, C., Smith, P. K. and Jessel, J. (2009) 'Investigating the extent and use of peer support initiatives in English schools'. *Educational Psychology, 29*(3): 325–344.

Kyriacou, C. (2001) *Effective Teaching in Schools: Theory and practice.* Cheltenham: Nelson Thomas.

Mentoring and Befriending Foundation. (2010) *Peer Mentoring in Schools: A review of the evidence base of the benefits of peer mentoring on schools.* Manchester: Author.

O'Neill, S. (2011) 'Teacher classroom behaviour management preparation in undergraduate primary education in Australia: A web-based investigation'. *Australian Journal of Teacher Education, 36*(10): 35–52.

Parry, J., Nind, M. and Sheehy, K. (2010) 'Origins of the social model' in The E214 Team (eds.), *E214: Equality, Participation and Inclusion: Learning from Each Other; Block 1: Principles* (pp.101–181). Milton Keynes, UK: Open University Press.

Radford, J., Bosanquest, R., Webster, R., Blatchford, P., and Rubie-Davies, C. (2013) 'Fostering independence through heuristic scaffolding: A valuable role for teaching assistants'. *International Journal of Education Research, 63*: 116–126.

Roffey. S. and O'Reirdon, T. (2002) *Young Children and Classroom Behaviour.* London: David Fulton.

Rogers, B. (1990) *You Know the Fair Rule.* Harlow: Pearson Education.

Shepherd, T. and Linn, D. (2015) *Behaviour and Classroom Management in the Multicultural classroom: Proactive, active and reactive strategies.* London: Sage.

Steer Report. (2005) *Learning Behaviour: The report of the practitioners group on school behaviour and discipline.* London: DfES.

Steer Behaviour Review. (2008) Retrieved from http://dera.ioe.ac.uk/8555/2/steer%20 interim%20260308final.pdf

The Sutton Trust. (2015) *Developing Teachers: Improving professional development for teachers.* Retrieved from www.suttontrust.com/wp-content/uploads/2015/01/DEVELOPING_ TEACHERS-FINAL.pdf

Taylor. C. (2011) *Getting the Simple Things Right.* London: Department for Education.

Taylor, C. (2012) *Improving Attendance at School.* London: Department for Education.

The Children and Families Act. (2014) London: HMSO.

The Children Act. (2004) London: HMSO.

Timpson. E. (2014) Press release. Retrieved from www.gov.uk/government/news/landmark-children-and-families-act-2014-gains-royal-assent

Topping, K. and Maloney, S. (2005) *Reader in Inclusive Education.* London: Routledge.

Trussler, S. and Robinson, D. (2015) *Inclusive Practice in the Primary School: A guide for teachers.* London: Sage.

Wallace, S. (2007) *Getting the Buggers Motivated in FE.* London: Continuum.

Warnock, M. (1978) *Special Educational Needs: Report of the committee of inquiry into the education of handicapped children and young people.* London: HMSO.

Chapter 13

Bullying in schools – or bullying schools?

Neil Duncan and Bill Myers

What is bullying?

Most writing about bullying sees the problem as nastier children having a stronger tendency to bully than other children, or that victims of bullying somehow present a more inviting target perhaps through irritating or unusual behaviour, weakness or difference. However the human diversity in any group of pupils cannot explain the high levels of bullying in schools compared to other institutions. Understanding the complexities of bullying within schools is essential for Teaching Assistants to support pupils and personally contribute to a non-oppressive environment.

There is no single, perfect definition of bullying, but one popular example comes from Olweus (1993), who states bullying is an aggressive act with an imbalance of power (the victim finds it difficult to defend himself or herself), some element of repetition (these things happen frequently), can be physical (hit, kicked), or verbal (threatened, nasty and unpleasant things said) or indirect (sent nasty notes, no one talks to them).

Other definitions include *intent* and *outcome*. 'Intent' refers to the purpose of the aggressor's behaviour: was the intent to hurt or upset the target? But if a big boy barges through a group of smaller children in a rush to get to the toilet – even if this happens more than once, is that really bullying? Perhaps the bigger boy doesn't intend to hurt or alarm, but when his behaviour is pointed out to him and he doesn't understand or seem to care, is that then bullying? If the big boy has learning difficulties, does that change anything?

All this is very complicated and depends more on social relationships and feelings rather than simple acts and behaviour. One element often missed from formulations of bullying is the sense of *intimate entrapment*, of being stuck in a relationship with your aggressor or tormentor. This idea is very hard to include in a short definition, but one working definition of bullying might be 'an interpersonal abuse of power'.

What is known about bullying?

Surveys since the 1990s by Boulton and Underwood (1992), Whitney and Smith (1993) and others, show the number of pupils in secondary schools reporting being bullied running at around 20–25 per cent. Figures for children reporting that they bully others are significantly lower than this but even so, some surveys note around 10 per cent of children will admit to sometimes bullying others. Importantly, some children fall into both categories: they are bullied by some children, and they themselves also bully others. Some researchers, for example Besag (1989), refer to these children as bully-victims.

Bullying Online carried out a national survey they claim to be the biggest ever in the UK. They surveyed teachers, parents, adults and pupils and returned a figure of 69 per cent of children claiming to have been bullied (Bullying Online 2006). Whatever the actual figure, there is little doubt that bullying is widespread, takes many forms and continues to be dealt with ineffectively.

Characteristics of bullies

We dislike the term 'bully' because it is a label and suggests that the person bullying is just a bully, never anything other than a bully from birth and will never be anything else. Olweus (1997) believes that bullies have higher impulsivity – they act without thinking about the consequences, and resort to violence to achieve their goals. They are usually physically strong and powerful and have low empathy. There is little here that most teachers, Teaching Assistants, parents and pupils would be surprised at, indeed the surprise is that researchers have bothered to announce these as findings!

More interestingly, it has been shown that bullies who engage in non-physical aggression have unusually high social intelligence (Sutton, Smith and Swettenham 1999). They can cause great pain and hurt in subtle ways, manipulating and entrapping their targets unbeknownst to adults.

Bullying appears to increase with age, and people who bully regularly tend to increase the verbal attacks and decrease their physical attacks as they get older. The targets of their abuse tend to be the same age or younger. Long-term bullies justify their behaviour through the development of beliefs that they are really doing nothing bad (Rigby 1997).

Characteristics of victims

As with the term 'bullies', the label of 'victim' makes us uneasy because it can suggest a fixed, unalterable state – 'we can do nothing for him, he's one of life's victims'. Often research will categorize these children as either *passive* or *provocative*. Passive victims display vulnerability that 'encourages' bullies to attack them. They put up no effective resistance and therefore bullies repeatedly abuse them without being punished. The other common category of victim is the provocative type who does not initiate aggression against others, but teases or behaves confrontationally. Everyone finds them irritating, but bullies respond to them with violence – 'he asked for it'.

If these categories were so simple, then it strikes us as curious that so many children report being bullied in so many surveys. Take the survey where 69 per cent were victims. That's a lot of provocative or passive kids out there! This suggests that there is much more to learn about bullying than most researchers think.

Effects of bullying

One thing can be certain: effects of bullying can be long term and in some cases fatal. The modern interest in bullying originated in Scandinavia after three pupils committed suicide in quick succession following bullying by their peers. Many tragic cases have come to light, but these often are bypassed as news stories unless they are particularly awful such as the suicide of five Japanese pupils in 2006 (BBC 2006). For every suicide caused by bullying, there must be a hundred children who consider such drastic action to free themselves from their torment.

Apart from suicide, self-harm and the direct pain from being beaten up, there are many lasting problems suffered by targets of bullying. These include loneliness, depression, panic attacks, anxiety, guilt, shame and low self-esteem (Schafer *et al.* 2004). When we teach university students about bullying, many of them become tearful or embarrassed recalling, and indeed reliving, their childhood experiences.

Another important effect of bullying is on school attendance. The true figures of this effect are masked by children's excuses, sometimes backed up by parents, knowingly or not, telling the school that they are sick or otherwise unable to attend.

Cyberbullying

Cyberbullying takes the concept of bullying to a whole new place and time: everywhere and anytime. Smith *et al.* (2008) define 'cyberbullying' in similar terms to 'traditional' bullying by Olweus (1993), but the significant difference is the medium of *electronic communication,* but it is this mode that makes cyberbullying so invasive to the lives of our children. While more traditional forms of bullying have specific places which one might avoid around school, e.g. the routes between home and school, or the local meeting place for the youth of the area, cyberbullying has the potential of following the victim everywhere there is internet or a mobile phone signal. Likewise with time: places of refuge and safety exist no more.

As (Papatraianou, Levine and West 2014: 264) explain, "In contemporary society,… young people must also learn to navigate the ever changing landscape of online technologies, a place that has incredible potential for learning and communication, yet also the likelihood of increased social risk of cyberbullying". Schools want to tap into the potential for learning and encourage more online computer-based work in school and at home, but being online has the potential for increased exposure to cyberbullying. Cross *et al.* (2009) estimate 1,327,000 children in KS3 and 4 reported having been cyberbullied, with a quarter persistently cyberbullied (331,800). There is clearly a major problem with cyberbullying amongst school-aged children (Papatraianou *et al.* 2014).

Biological and psychosocial changes underlie much of the adolescent behavioural and emotional responses to the development of self-perception, esteem and group identity within. Online social activity can support and reassure the development of the child's self-esteem, sense of meaning and purpose and problem solving (Prilleltensky, Nelson and Peirson 2001) by making children more mindful of such aspects of personal development. Cyberbullying can attack all of these aspects of social and emotional development.

Schools can support home life by highlighting the dual potential of the risks and benefits of online life. Parents and siblings can make things worse by what they say and do online, but can also be a source of support to victims of cyber attack. Trust issues with regard to online permission have the potential to be both positive and negative but communication needs to be open and informed, and schools can advice on this (DCSF 2007).

Schools need to offer both prevention and support for victims of cyberbullying, but prevention is the better option. A well-constructed PSHE Education programme can increase pupil awareness of the type of sites, fora, etc., to be avoided and inform parents of the same. In the right atmosphere, for example, issues can be explored in the classroom to raise awareness of "what is meant in good humour or jest is very easily misinterpreted or can escalate rapidly, causing distress and emotional pain to vulnerable pupils" (PSHE Association 2015). This is a noted feature of cyberbullying: lack of emotional reactivity. In face-to-face dialogue we can immediately judge the appropriateness of a comment through non-verbal cues and tweak further comments accordingly. Online, this is not so easy (Kowalski *et al.* 2014), and unintentional emotional consequences can escalate as well as spread more publicly.

A clear school policy on incidents of cyberbullying is required, and the Education Act (2011) now gives schools the power to search and delete inappropriate images or files on electronic devices. Unfortunately, that may be too late as a response and, though in theory the anonymity of the perpetrator may not be as safe as they think, finding the source of an anonymous bully takes time, expertise and effort that most school staff do not have. In extreme cases the police can be informed but in all likelihood they would not act on typical cases, only the most extreme or tragic. In short, other than supporting the victim, schools are limited in their response, so focussing on prevention is key.

How is bullying dealt with by schools?

Management of bullying can be broadly split into *preventions* and *responses*. Preventions include directly discussing bullying in the classroom, thereby promoting a 'telling school' to combat a culture of 'not grassing'. Some schools use 'buddying' systems to pair up vulnerable pupils with older mentors.

Some schools use 'circle-time' where all the children in a class are involved in activities that raise empathy, improve pro-social behaviour and increase peer support (Smith 2004). Responses to bullying incidents after they have happened depend to some extent on the school's anti-bullying policy, and how rigorously staff follow its guidance. Punishment for bullying can range from school exclusion or even criminal charges brought by the police, through to a private apology and an undertaking not to reoffend.

When school responses copy processes found in the law courts they can be ineffective as there is a tendency for people to lie over things they feel guilty about. Another unwanted outcome is the increased likelihood of retaliation by the accused or his/her friends against the complainant – a genuine worry of many targets of bullying.

Some schools reduce these problems through a *no-blame* anti-bullying policy (Maines and Robinson 1992) where the teacher concerns her-/himself with making the target feel better about things, and getting the perpetrators to stop their attacks; even getting them to befriend or support the target. Anti-bullying initiatives across the world testify to the effectiveness of the strategy, and particularly appreciate the way it attempts to break the cycle of aggression and hurt. Despite these successes, the no-blame approach has been heavily criticized by numerous campaigners and press commentators who think that it is being 'soft on the bullies'. As the no-blame approach takes more time and skill to apply than simple punishment, it can also be unpopular because of resource costs as well as its non-punitive values.

Back to basics

Consideration of our own values brings us back to *why* people bully others. A view linked with the punitive approach to dealing with bullies (such as 'kick them out of school') is that some people bully others because they are just horrible people. If that was really the main reason, one might expect that once the bullies had been kicked out of school then bullying in that school would cease.

A review of the effectiveness of anti-bullying strategies and interventions revealed that, despite years of expensive research and intervention, bullying wasn't reduced significantly (Smith 2005). Perhaps researchers have been too busily looking for faults in children and not spending enough time looking at faults in the schooling systems. After all, the term 'bullying' is powerfully linked with the term 'school', even though there is bullying in other institutions, including the armed forces, prisons, hospitals and many other workplaces.

Furthermore, if bullying was entirely the fault of a few nasty kids, then why is it that similar schools have different rates of bullying reported within them? Are there simply more nasty kids in some schools or is it something else? One clue to solving this puzzle comes from two Japanese researchers who spent some time in Australia's education system. Yoneyama and Naito (2003) were struck by the powerful differences within the two schooling cultures – the West (Australia, Europe, UK, and USA) and their native Japan.

In the West, they noted bullying tended to be one or two aggressive and violent pupils causing fear and harm to a larger group of pupils. In the Japanese school system, the situation was almost reversed with the whole class picking on one child as a scapegoat and making their life unbearable. Their message is clear: if you want to stop bullying, begin with how schools operate as institutions.

Institutions, organizations and the bullying ethos

An institution is an identifiable community where its members spend considerable time together for a shared purpose. Institutions have their own way of doing things distinctive from how any one person in the institution might do them, and different from the ways other institutions do them. This ethos is a way of doing things that is perhaps hard to see or describe, but more usually it is felt by the members. The most famous study on the school ethos (Rutter *et al.* 1979) found that it had a huge part to play in school effectiveness, overriding many other factors such as size and intake, staff qualifications and curricula. Given this importance, how can we manage it, shape it and make it as positive as possible?

Schools have a formal organization that aims to do two main things: educate and *socialize*. 'Socialization' in this sense means to train people socially, so that they can get along with each other and enjoy and contribute to what society has to offer. Usually we only hear about the first purpose of schooling: to educate. However, if you have any doubts about the importance of socialization, just imagine the outcry if schools were to provide no guidance on pupils' behavior!

As well as these official rules, there are rules that are *modelled* rather than stated overtly. Through modelling, the institution's members behave according to them, but they may not be written down. In virtually every school, these modelled behaviours indicate a power structure based on a *hierarchy*, a layered structure of the staff. At the top of the hierarchy is the head teacher, then the senior management team. These are followed by middle management; SENCOs, subject coordinators, heads of year/house. Beneath this rank are the basic teaching staff followed by the Teaching Assistants, supervisors, ancillary workers and cleaning staff. At the bottom of this pyramid are the pupils.

Even between pupils, there is a pecking order. Some children will have more power than others, and we can see how pupils model their relations on the adult examples all around them. If we look carefully, there will be signs to show us what the ethos is of this structure.

In some organizations, the hierarchy is not as prominent as others, or the layers are fewer and the difference between them is less important. In other cases power is much more visible and jealously guarded by those who have it. In order to display their importance over other people they may demand that they are addressed in a different way, or they may have a specially designated parking space, a big office, and a manner that says 'you'd better watch out around me, I'm powerful'.

In schools where the ethos is one of deference to superior rank rather than warm human relationships, bullying among pupils is more likely to thrive. The way that staff bosses and their subordinates talk and behave towards each other shows the pupils how *they* should relate to each other.

How schools can bully children

Consider the almost total control schools have over children:

- punishment for speaking without permission, for not sitting in a particular position, for laughing out loud, for whispering;
- doing things they have no interest in, and then being harassed for not doing it as well as that person thinks they can;
- their ability or performance being constantly measured and compared against those of their peers; being told what to wear;
- being forbidden expressions of personality such as jewelry or makeup;
- being forced to wear their hair so it meets with someone else's approval;
- being so controlled that even your bodily functions are at someone else's discretion and you need permission to eat, drink or go to the toilet.

Put like that, it's a wonder we don't have a riot in schools across the land, but in fact, most young people cope pretty well in schools, many like it and plenty actually thrive. However, in schools with an *oppressive* ethos, bullying can become a real problem among the pupils.

From this perspective we can explore why some schools have a worse bullying problem than others (Xin Ma *et al.* 2001). There are a number of factors that reinforce one another to make schools into high-bullying schools. The obvious one, and the most commonly held, is that those schools have a higher number of nasty, aggressive children. The problem would be solved, we are told, if the school got tougher with those pupils and adopted a zero-tolerance policy against bullying to change such behaviour (Ball and Hartley 2003). But if this action was such an easy and effective one, then it's hard to understand why so much bullying persists.

The mass scale of schooling requires schools to adopt regimented approaches to discipline and organization, and all schools have some form of hierarchy in order to run smoothly (Ross-Epp 1996). In some cases, however, that hierarchy can become self-serving and lose sight of the real purpose of schooling: the education and socialization of children.

Children quickly pick up on the importance of hierarchies. A simple understanding of age-hierarchies can be checked in any primary school. The importance of who fears whom on the staff is also quickly acquired. Think about the messages hidden in very common statements: 'Any more of that attitude young man, and I'll send you to Mr Hassan'.

Most children are happy within a hierarchy as long as it is safe and fair. When they are abused, ridiculed in public, shouted at, punished as a group, or treated with sarcasm and disdain, they resent it. In the 11-year-long competition that is compulsory schooling, there are winners and losers. We all know which children rarely succeed in that competition, and for them, bossing someone else about can be the release from failure that they crave. Their predicament is described in studies of oppressed groups in other situations as *horizontal violence* (Freire 1972; Leymann 1996). This is where people are bossed around in a situation they can't change, and begin to displace their frustration and anger on the only targets available – their weaker peers. We might as well call it bullying.

Most staff are caring and intelligent people doing a difficult and demanding job. Sometimes they are less than perfect, and that can only be expected. When those lapses in their high professional standards prove effective, i.e. they achieve the right results in the wrong way and others emulate the same undesirable tactics, essentially, they are using bullying techniques to enforce discipline. I (Neil) confess to such lapses myself, and indeed used them to great effect over a period of years where I was praised for getting good behavioural results from very difficult students. It was only when I witnessed one of my younger staff copying my approach that I realized I might be doing more harm than good.

We have tried to come up with advice that would be helpful to young or new staff in managing discipline in schools. The best we came up with was to imagine in every exchange with students that their parents were present while you were dealing with them. If you could justify not only your words, but also your tone and body language, then you were pretty sure not to be bullying them. If we preach fairness and decency to them we should not then be caught out being sarcastic and mean. We must retain a professional level of dignifying children equivalent to that which we would use in dealing with their parents or other adults, and not adopting a 'might is right' attitude.

Conclusion

No one deserves to be bullied, but all schools are organizations where bullying takes place. This is due to certain factors that are virtually inseparable from schooling and that most of us don't have the power to change, for example: its compulsory nature, the vast numbers of people who need to be regulated in a small space, and the constraints on what we are allowed to do with children during the school day (which many pupils find irrelevant, difficult and boring). Once the school staff have reflected on their own contribution to the ethos, the decision has to be made as to whether their common approach will be based upon punishment and retribution, or prevention and restoration.

Most bullying is seen as the fault of particular children who are labelled as 'bullies'. Such labelling is rarely helpful, as it prevents us from looking at things staff *could* and *should* change (our personal relationships with children, our professional standards, our unnecessary or punitive rules), by focusing on things we are *unlikely* to change (individual children's personalities where bullying is a response to their situation). Interventions to reduce bullying, therefore, should be preceded by some discussion on the school ethos and culture as an institution. It may well be more comfortable and acceptable to imagine bullying in school as purely a pupil problem, but until adults engage with their own role in creating and maintaining a pro-social and non-oppressive institution, the problem will resist our attempts to make a lasting impact on bullying.

Reflections on values and practice

1   Defining bullying. Instead of using the ready-made definitions of bullying so common in books and research, listen to the range of things that kids do to other kids that they say they don't like. That way, you'll hear what really bothers them without getting tangled up in 'scientific' definitions.
2   Developing a sense of fairness. Young people have a strong sense of justice, though it doesn't always seem like it. If you have a pupil who is involved in bullying others, try to discuss occasions when s/he was treated unfairly. Consider how you can develop a sense of empathy by encouraging him or her to rethink the experience and see that s/he is emulating the unfair person in their past.
3   The acid test. You are a model to the children, so you need to reflect on your own interpersonal exchanges with pupils. Think back to an incident when you were dominating a pupil (we all need to do this at some point!). Would you feel comfortable if someone said they'd videoed you and the child's parent was going to see it? If in doubt, try to conduct yourself as though a parent was observing. Pupils will eventually pick up on the fact that you are dignified and professional and their behaviour will change accordingly.
4   To emphasize the problem of unintended cyberbullying via lack of emotional reactivity consider using blind-folded circle-time or one-to-one conversations with the pupils sitting back-to-back and afterwards ask them to reflect on how different it was compared to face-to-face conversations to highlight the importance of non-verbal cues in communication.

Suggested further reading

Most books on bullying concentrate on seeing the individual child as the problem, whether bully or victim. If you have read this chapter carefully, you'll know that we don't think that is very helpful. The best advice is to be found on websites, particularly at www.antibullying.net, which is a Scottish anti-bullying site, and at www.dfes.gov.uk/bullying, which is the UK government advice. If you are interested in gender issues of bullying, try Duncan, N. (1999) *Sexual Bullying: Gender Conflict and Peer Culture in Secondary Schools*, London: Routledge. If you wish to develop your understanding of how organizations can oppress people and create a bullying environment, then a visit to Robert Fuller's site and purchase of his book at www.breakingranks.net might just change your view on life!

A useful guide on dealing with cyberbullying in schools is DCSF (2007) *Cyberbullying Safe to Learn anti-bullying work in schools*. Retrieved from http://old.digizen.org/cyberbullying/fullguidance

A source for lesson plans on preventing cyberbullying is www.childnet.com/resources/know-it-all-secondary-toolkits/lower-secondary-toolkit/cyberbullying

And for current school policy advice the Department for Education have published *Cyberbullying: Advice for headteachers and school staff*. Retrieved from www.gov.uk/government/publications/preventing-and-tackling-bullying

References

Ball, C. and Hartley, M. (2003) *Zero Tolerance to Bullying*. Alberta: Chalk Face Project, Mentone Education Centre.

BBC. (2006) *Suicide of Bullied Japanese Pupils*. Retrieved from http://news.bbc.co.uk/1/hi/world/asia-pacific/6142816

Besag, V. E. (1989) *Bullies and Victims in Schools*. Milton Keynes, UK: Open University Press.

Boulton, M. J. and Underwood, K. (1992) 'Bully/Victim Problems Among Middle School Children', *British Journal of Educational Psychology*, 62(1): 73–87.

Bullying Online. (2006) *National Survey Report*.

Cross, E., Piggen, R., Douglas, T. and Vonkaenel-Flatt, J. (2012). *Virtual Violence II: Progress and challenges in the fight against cyberbullying*. London: Beatbullying.

Department for Children, Schools and Families (DCSF). (2007) *Cyberbullying Safe to Learn: Embedding anti-bullying work in schools*, DCSF-00658-2007. Nottingham: DCSF Publications.

Freire, P. (1972) *Pedagogy of the Oppressed*. London: Penguin Education.

Kowalski, R. M., Giumetti, G. W., Schroeder, A. N. and Lattanner, M. R. (2014) 'Bullying in the Digital Age: A critical review and meta-analysis of cyberbullying research among youth'. *Psychological Bulletin*, 140(4): 1073.

Leymann, H. (1996) 'Psychological Terrorization – The Problem of the Terminology', in *The Mobbing Encyclopaedia*. Retrieved from www.leymann.se/English/11130E.HTM_1996

Maines, B. and Robinson, G. (1992) *Michael's Story* (video cassette recording). Bristol: Lucky Duck.

Olweus, D. (1993) *Bullying at School: What we know and what we can do*. Oxford: Blackwell.

Olweus, D. (1997) 'Bully/Victim Problems in School: Facts and intervention', *European Journal of Psychology of Education*, 12: 495–510.

Papatraianou, L. H., Levine, D. and West, D. (2014) 'Resilience in the Face of Cyberbullying: An ecological perspective on young people's experiences of online adversity'. *Pastoral Care in Education*, 32(4): 264–283.

Prilleltensky, I., Nelson, G., and Peirson, L. (2001). *Promoting Family Wellness and Preventing Child Maltreatment: Fundamentals for thinking and action*. Toronto: University of Toronto Press.

PSHE Association. (2015) *Teacher Guidance: Preparing to teach about mental health and emotional well-being*. Retrieved from www.pshe-association.org.uk

Rigby, K. (1997) 'Attitudes and Beliefs About Bullying Among Australian School Children', *Irish Journal of Psychology*, 18: 202–220.

Ross-Epp, J. (1996) 'Schools, Complicity and Sources of Violence' in Ross-Epp, J. and Watkinson, A. (eds) *Systemic Violence: How Schools Hurt Children*. London: Falmer Press.

Rutter, M., Maughan, B., Mortimore, P. and Ouston, J. (1979) *15000 Hours: Secondary schools and their effects on children*. London: Open Books.

Schafer, M., Korn, S., Smith, P. K., Hunter, S. C., Mora-Merchán, J. A., Singer, M. M. and Van der Meulen, K. (2004) 'Lonely in the Crowd: Recollections of bullying', *British Journal of Developmental Psychology*, 22(3): 379–394.

Smith, C. (2004) *Circle Time for Adolescents: A seven session programme for 14–16 year olds*. London: Lucky Duck.

Smith, P. K. (2005) *BPS Seminar Series on Bullying*. London: Goldsmiths College.

Sutton, J., Smith, P. K. and Swettenham, J. (1999) 'Social Cognition and Bullying: Social inadequacy or skilled manipulation?', *British Journal of Developmental Psychology*, 17: 435–450.

Smith, P. K., Mahdavi, J., Carvalho, M., Fisher, S., Russell, S., and Tippett, N. (2008) 'Cyberbullying: Its nature and impact in secondary school pupils'. *Journal of Child Psychology and Psychiatry*, 49: 376–385.

Whitney, I. and Smith, P. K. (1993) 'A Survey of the Nature and Extent of Bullying in Junior/Middle and Secondary Schools', *Educational Research*, 35: 3–25.

Xin Ma, Len L. Stewin and Deveda L. Mah, (2001) 'Bullying in School: Nature, effects and remedies', *Research Papers in Education*, 16(3): 247–270.

Yoneyama, S. and Naito, A. (2003) 'Problems with the Paradigm: The school as a factor in understanding bullying (with special reference to Japan)', *British Journal of Sociology*, 24(3): 315–330.

Chapter 14

Disabled children, inclusion and the law in England and Wales

David Ruebain and Sheine Peart

Teaching Assistants and the law

Teaching Assistants have a key role to play for all children, but particularly for disabled children and children with special educational needs (SEN). Most legal duties rest on local authorities (LAs) and school governing bodies but staff, including Teaching Assistants, will be instrumental in ensuring effective provision. Sometimes, the legal obligations require to schools to have Teaching Assistants are required to assist in the classroom generally and sometimes to assist a specific child (for example, if the child's Education Health and Care [EHC] plan specifies individual, one-to-one support). New legal obligations identified in the Equality Act 2010, the Children's and Families Act 2014 and the Special Educational Needs and Disability Code of Practice 2014 (revised 2015) have produced significant changes to education and children and young people with SEN and disabilities frequently depend on the involvement and expertise of Teaching Assistants.

Disabled children and children with special educational needs

Background

The provision of education for disabled children and those identified as having special educational needs was transformed with the Warnock Report (1978) which established that wherever possible pupils with SEN should be educated in mainstream schools and LAs and others should promote a positive view of SEN focusing on ability and potential. Aspects of this report have since been embedded in subsequent education legislation (1981, 1993 and 1996 Education Acts; 2001 Special Educational Needs and Disability Act; 2005 Disability Discrimination Act). Prior to 1981 many children were assessed as uneducable based on a medical or quasi-medical diagnosis. Their education, including which school they attended, was often dictated by that diagnosis. For example, children with 'physical handicaps' (as it was then known) were usually placed in schools for children with physical disabilities, those with a visual impairment in schools for blind children, children with a hearing impairment in schools for deaf children and so on. There were other contestable classifications in which children were placed and some labels were positively offensive including schools for 'backward', 'delicate' and 'educationally sub-normal' children!

When the 1981 Education Act finally came into force on 1 April 1983, it transformed education for disabled children in two significant ways. First, instead of placing children in questionable medical categories (e.g. blind, physically handicapped, etc.) a 'child-centred approach' was introduced and each disabled child with additional or different needs arising from their disability or learning difficulty had their needs assessed and tailor-made provision provided to meet those needs through a 'Statement' of special educational needs. Accordingly, a child with Down's Syndrome would have their needs individually considered and would not be assumed to have exactly the same needs as any other child with Down's Syndrome. Second, the Act introduced, for the first time, a general presumption in favour of educating disabled children in mainstream (state) schools where parents wanted it, providing the school could meet the child's needs; other children would not be adversely affected and that placement at such a school did not constitute an inefficient use of the LA's resources. The Special Educational Needs and Disability (SEND) Act 2001 amended this requirement so that LAs could refuse a child with SEN a place at a mainstream school if other children would be adversely affected and there were no reasonable steps that the school or LA could take to overcome that difficulty (Sections 316 and 316A of the Education Act 1996). The Education Act 1981 was then replaced by Part III of the Education Act 1993, but the framework which it introduced largely remains intact, albeit in a strengthened form. The law was subsequently contained within Part IV of the Education Act 1996 as amended by the SEND Act 2001 and the Children's and Families Act 2014. Current guidance on how the law must be applied in schools and other educational settings is given in the government's 2015 Special Educational Needs and Disability Code of Practice: 0 to 25 years (DfE 2015). This statutory guidance strengthens educational provision and the standard of care that must be achieved for all children and young people with a disability or SEN (NASEN 2014).

Who has special educational needs?

Section 312 of the Education Act 1996 states a child has special educational needs if they have a 'learning difficulty' which includes children with a physical or sensory disability and those with challenging behaviour which calls for special educational provision (SEP). However, it does not include exceptional ability (see *S v SENDIST and Oxfordshire CC*: 2005 Education Law Report, ELR, 443) and gifted children are routinely excluded from the provisions of the Act. SEP is educational provision which is additional to, or different from, provision available to children of the same age in mainstream schools in the area. In other words, a child has special educational needs if, as a result of their learning difficulty, they *need* additional or different educational provision. However, a child does not have special educational needs solely because of having English as a second language. Under the 2015 Code of Practice (DfE 2015) LAs have a statutory responsibility to provide appropriate educational provision for all children and young people with SEN or disabilities age 0–25.

The different stages of identifying special educational needs

Many people working in education are familiar with the previous arrangements for statements of special educational needs. These statements were formal documents prepared by an LA identifying the additional support and suitable provision/placement for a child or young person up to the age of 19 to enable them to participate in education. Under the 2014 Code of Practice from September 2014 Statements and Learning Difficulty Assessments (LDAs) were withdrawn and are replaced with an Education, Health and Care plan (EHC plan). The 2014 code has since been revised and new guidance was issued in January 2015. The EHC plan differs from a statement in that it covers a child's entire educational journey from birth (or the point at which the need is identified) to 25 years. The EHC plan takes an integrated holistic approach and links education, social care, health care and other relevant services to provide comprehensive support so that individuals can realise their potential and make a successful transition into adulthood with the best possible outcomes. Rather than operating independently LAs must now work with clinical commissioning groups (CCGs) to identify an individual's specific needs and make appropriate provision for "*education, health and care ... for children and young people with SEN or disabilities*" (DfE 2015: 38, emphasis added). Previously, separate services may have been provided in isolation without reference to how different services interacted together. The new code makes it clear all services must now work together in a coordinated way for the benefit of the child or young person and to help raise aspirations of the child/young person and their family and expectations of the wider community.

The 2014 code has also replaced the old 'pre-statement' stages of School Action and School Action Plus (or, for those in early years – Early Years Action and Early Years Action Plus) with "*new guidance ... on taking a graduated approach to identifying and supporting pupils and students with SEN*" (DfE 2015: 14, emphasis added). While the Code makes it clear that LAs need to collaborate with others to meet children and young people's holistic needs, at present, schools and other settings are working to translate these guidelines and understand the logistical implications of the graduated approach. In practice, it is likely there will be some similarities with previous procedures. For example, in the first instance, the graduated response may simply require schools to reassess how they use their existing resources to effectively meet the needs of children with SEN. If more resources are required, such as help from the LA's educational psychology service, schools should make arrangements to access this additional support. While schools have some flexibility to initially interpret how a child's needs may be met, if a child does not make progress towards agreed goals this could trigger a formal EHC assessment. Without an EHC the detailed legal requirements of the plan would not usually apply and this is referred to as an 'unresourced plan', but the overarching legal duties of disability legislation applicable to all organisations and individuals still remain in place.

However, for children with more severe or complex difficulties who may require ongoing, significant additional support an EHC plan made and maintained by their LA is required. This is for children who are assessed as needing, for example, a specific amount of dedicated teaching assistant time, a specific amount of specialist teacher time or a specific therapeutic interventions (such as speech and language, occupational or physical therapy) which the LA with support from the CCG (rather than the school) has to arrange. If it is not possible to provide sufficient locally available support the LA can organise a placement in a specialist unit or school. EHC plans like statements before them are legally enforceable documents, prepared and maintained by LAs in accordance with Part IV of the Education Act 1996 as amended by the Special Educational Needs and Disability Act 2001 and the Children's and Families Act 2014.

Developing an EHC Plan

Most children will not need an EHC plan and "the majority of children and young people with SEN or disabilities will have their needs met within local mainstream early years settings, schools or colleges" (DfE 2015: 142). If it is considered a child requires an EHC plan, an EHC needs assessment must be completed. A request for an assessment can be made by a parent; a school; another agency (such as a health authority); or, for the first time ever, a young person over 16 but under 25 may self-refer and request the LA complete an assessment of their needs.

In deciding whether to conduct an EHC assessment, the LA needs to find out whether, despite previous purposeful educational interventions including providing targeted support, the child or young person has failed to make the required amount of progress and has not achieved the standards expected of a child of that age. To help reach a decision, the LA must collect and consider a broad range of evidence including:

- information on the child or young person's academic attainment and rate of progress provided by the school or other educational setting;
- details on the child's specific SEN and information about previous support provided, for example by the school, college, early years provider or educational psychologist;
- evidence from health-care professionals and clinicians which explain the child's physical, emotional, social- and health-care needs with details on what action has been taken to meet these needs; and
- information from the young person themselves, parent(s)/carer(s) and/or transition plans about the child/young person's abilities and needs.

Although LAs are allowed to develop their own local guidelines to decide when they need to complete an assessment, they cannot apply these guidelines rigidly. They are not allowed to adopt a 'one-size-fits-all' policy for categories of need and must show that they are willing to examine every case on its individual merits.

Time limits

Once the LA has received a request to complete an EHC assessment, they must notify the young person and their parents/carers whether or not they are willing to complete an assessment within 6 weeks from the date of the request. If the LA decides not to conduct an assessment, they must provide reasons and give the family an opportunity to appeal against the LA's decision. If the LA agrees to complete an assessment, they will gather all the information identified above. Any agency the LA requests information from must provide that information within 6 weeks of the request to the LA. Once all evidence has been collected, the LA will then decide if an EHC plan is needed.

If the LA does not believe a plan is needed, they must inform the young person/parents of their decision and provide information on the family's right to appeal to SENDIST within 16 weeks from the date of the initial EHC assessment request. If the LA agrees a plan is needed, it will work with CCGs and other agencies to produce a draft plan detailing what the child/young person's needs are and how these will be met and send this to the family. On receipt of the plan, the parents/young person has 15 days to comment, state what school or education provider they would prefer and to agree whether a personal budget is needed. A personal budget will be needed in lieu of special provision if a parent/carer or young person is required to make their own arrangements to access provision identified in the EHC plan. In such cases, they will receive the money directly. If all goods or services are to be supplied directly by the LA, a personal budget would not usually be required. Following further consultation with the young person and their parents/carers, the plan is amended if necessary before the final plan is issued.

The entire process from initial request for assessment through to issuing a final agreed plan should take no more than 20 weeks in total and at every stage the views, feelings and requests of the child/young person and their parents/carers must be taken into account.

The EHC plan

The content of the EHC plan is governed by the Section 37 of the Children's and Families Act 2014 and Regulation 12 of the SEND Regulations 2014. The EHC plan, which is agreed with all interested parties, can be set out in any format but must contain the 12 sections listed in the table on the next page. Each section must be clearly labelled with the letter given.

LAs are legally obliged to arrange appropriate provision identified in the EHC assessment, regardless of the cost or difficulty in doing so. Previous case law regarding statements has established this precedence and LAs remain obliged to access all necessary resources to meet a child/young person's needs (see decision in *R v LB Harrow* ex parte M: 1997, ELR 62). Previously there was some uncertainty about what could or should be included in a child/young person's statement, now EHC plan. Case law (see *Bromley v SENT:* 1999, ELR 260; and *B v Isle of Wight:* 1997, ELR 390) established anything directly connected with school,

	Section	Focus
1	A	The opinions, interests and ambitions of the child/young person and their parents. The views of the child are fore-grounded and are intended to inform and shape the development of the plan.
2	B	The child/young person's special educational needs. All needs, even those that may not require any SEP arranged by the LA, are described at this point. All needs must be identified as they may interact with one another to produce unique outcomes.
3	C	The child/young person's health needs as they relate to SEN. This may be arranged in sections such as 'Communication', 'Physical Needs', etc.
4	D	The child/young person's social care needs which relate to SEN. This may include issues such as support with forming peer friendship groups or personal care needs.
5	E	The specific outcomes the plan are designed to achieve clearly identified personalised goals including successful progression into adulthood and goals related to the young person's adult life. This section must also identify shorter-term goals such as transfer from primary to secondary school, transfer onto FE college, or other significant transitions.
6	F	The SEP needed to enable the child/young person to make progress and achieve agreed goals or targets. For example, if a child requires extra TA support, this should be set out in terms of numbers of hours of support and, where necessary, level of expertise (see decisions of the courts in a number of cases, including *L v Clarke and Somerset CC*: 1998, ELR 129 and *Bromley v SENT*: 1999, ELR 260).
7	G	The health services required arising from the child/young person's SEN or disability. If a separate Health Care Plan has been written, it should be included at this stage.
8	H1	The social care provided for under-18s as detailed in part of Section 2 of the Chronically Sick and Disabled Persons Act 1970.
9	H2	Other social care that may be provided to the child/young person as part of the Care Act 2014.
10	I	The name and type of the school, nursery, college or other education provider that the child/young person will attend, for example, 'Anytown School, 11–16 co-educational academy, specialising in sports'.
11	J	Details of how the Personal Budget (if in place) will be used to meet particular outcomes. If any direct payments are made to specific providers for example, physiotherapy services, the amount and schedule of payments must be stipulated here.
12	K	A list of all the information and advice collected to complete the EHC assessment. Where appropriate additional information on any specific service should be described in the appendix.

Note: For students in Year 9 (school age 13–14 years) or above, the plan must also specify what arrangements have been put in place to help the young person progress into adulthood, for example gaining employment or finding independent accommodation. Adapted from 'Special Educational Needs and Disability Code of Practice: 0 to 25 years', DfE, 2015: 161–162.

including teaching and teaching assistance, should be covered if deemed to be an *educational* need. In addition, speech and language therapy was usually included and physiotherapy and occupational therapy were sometimes included depending on the circumstances. However, nursing support rarely qualified for inclusion, even if a child occasionally required nursing care. Once goods or services have been identified in the EHC plan, the LA is obliged to ensure that the provision is secured.

Because EHC plans are new and it is not precisely clear what can and what cannot be legitimately included in an EHC plan: 'Case law' is currently being brought to SENDIST to set a precedent that will help determine this situation.

Choice of school

For a child without an EHC plan there are separate provisions which determine which school they attend as contained in the Schools Standards and Framework Act 1998, amended by the Education Act 2006. Broadly, the law gives parents a right to 'express a preference' for a state school and for that preference to be accepted unless it would prejudice the provision of efficient education or the efficient use of resources (which often means that the school is full) or it is a selective school and the child does not meet the admissions criteria.

For a child with an EHC plan, the '2015 Special Educational Needs and Disability Code of Practice: 0 to 25 Years' mirrors procedures for children without EHC plans. Inclusive practice principles mean the presumption is that children/ young people with SEN and disabilities will be educated, wherever possible, in mainstream settings. In common with students without special needs, young people and their parents have the "right to request a particular school, college or other institution ... to be named in the EHC plan" (DfE 2015: 172). Furthermore, a "local authority and the governing body of a maintained school shall comply with any preference" (Gold 1999: 101). However, if the stated preference "would be unsuitable for the age, ability, aptitude or SEN of the child or young person; or the attendance of the child or young person would be incompatible with the efficient education of others, or the efficient use of resources" (DfE 2015: 172) the LA may refuse the parents' choice (although this may be difficult to prove).

However, before naming a school or college in the EHC plan, the LA must consult with the governing body of that education provider and the provider has 15 days to respond to the LA's proposals. The LA is then obliged to consider the provider's comments in detail before naming them on the EHC plan. Once a mainstream provider has been named on an EHC plan, they must admit the child/ young person to that EY setting, school or college.

Families of young people with SEN may also request an independent school or college and if the organisation "has been approved by the Secretary of State and published in a list available to all parents and young people" (DfE 2015: 172) the LA must consider the request. If the preference meets the needs of the young person and does not prejudice the education of other young people, the LA must agree to the request. However, if the request would result in excessive or "unreasonable public expenditure" (DfE 2015: 173), the LA can refuse the request (section 9 of the Education Act 2006). However, other independent organisations (such as private businesses) are not obliged to admit the child or young person even if they are named in the EHC plan and usually LAs will only consider such a placement if a local, state school is unsuitable.

Occasionally, parents may seek a residential placement. Such a placement will only be agreed if the child has severe or multiple special educational needs that cannot be met in day provision; has special educational needs that require an 'extended day' curriculum; has complex social and learning needs (in these circumstances the placement may be joint-funded with health authorities); or has learning and complex medical needs that cannot be managed in local day provision. In reality, the threshold for such a decision is very high, and most LAs are likely to find suitable provision locally.

Finally, very occasionally, parents may seek educational provision other than a school. For example, some families of children who have autism seek funding through statements of special educational needs for home-based ABA (applied behavioural analysis) or LOVAAS type programmes. Currently, LAs will only fund such provision if placement at a school is not possible (Section 319 of the Education Act 1996 and *T v SENDIST and Wiltshire CC:* 2002, ELR 704).

Disputes over EHC assessments and plans

Sometimes, parents/carers will dispute decisions by LAs. If a dispute arises, the following general principles apply:

- Disagreements should be raised as soon as possible so that they can be resolved swiftly.
- Where possible, parties should arrange to meet to determine the exact nature of the disagreement and agree a local remedy (mediation).
- If a disagreement cannot be determined locally the family has the right to appeal to the Special Educational Needs and Disability Tribunal (SENDIST) or in Wales, the Special Educational Needs Tribunal for Wales (SENTW).

To support families to resolve disputes, the LA must provide independent "disagreement resolution services" (DfE 2015: 248). These services must be truly independent and involve any member of the LA. The disagreement resolution service can offer assistance regarding any aspect of the SEN provision process.

Engagement with the dispute resolution service is voluntary for parents/carers and the child/young person, but the LA must engage and is required to release any information requested by the resolution service. Parents and families should be given impartial information to help them decide whether or not they wish to use the resolution service and should not be pressured into using the service if they do not wish to. If the service cannot help the parties to reach an agreed outcome then the family can elect to use mediation. Mediation has a narrower focus than the resolution service and focuses solely on EHC assessments and plans. While not compulsory for families, it is that usual resolution and mediation are attempted before an appeal is registered with SENDIST. In any event, families can only lodge an appeal if the mediation adviser issues a certificate to the family, stating an appeal will be brought to SENDIST. However, issuing the certificate is not linked to using mediation services.

If parents decide to appeal to a SENDIST their case will be heard by a first-tier tribunal. Tribunals are part of Her Majesty's Courts and Tribunals service and have the authority to hear disputes over EHC needs assessments and plans, and disability discrimination claims against schools and LAs. Tribunals are empowered to dismiss the appeal if they find it is not justified; instruct the LA to complete an EHC assessment; direct the LA to draw up an EHC plan; amend an existing EHC plan or order additions; and correct omissions or weaknesses. Tribunals are not intended to be overtly legalistic and parents/carers should be able to represent their case without the aid of a solicitor. Parents and LAs must co-operate with the tribunal and supply any documents requested, such as EHC assessments or plans. They should also inform the tribunal of any witnesses they intend to use. Tribunal hearings are usually held as close as possible to the family's home address and may take in Her Majesty's Courts buildings.

Miscellaneous issues for children with special educational needs

Aside from this, LAs may occasionally reassess a child who already has an EHC plan. This might be because it is considered that the plan, and the evidence upon which it was made, is out of date. In addition, in any event, LAs must conduct an annual review of the EHC plan at least once a year (Section 328 of the Education Act 1996). The purpose of such a review is to consider progress and development. The annual review may or may not lead to an amendment of the plan or an appeal to SENDIST. Finally, if families of children with EHC plans move into the area of a different LA, the 'new' LA takes over the responsibility for the plan, its maintenance and review.

The Disability Discrimination Act and children at school

Apart from the SEN framework described above, since September 2002, schools and LAs have been obliged not to discriminate against children with SEN and disabilities (set out in Chapter 1 of Part IV of the Disability Discrimination Act [DDA], 1995) and amended by the Special Educational Needs and Disability Act 2001 and the Equality Act (2010). The legal framework is complex and the first thing to note is that the definition of 'disability' in the DDA is not the same as the definition of children with special educational needs.

In particular, a child is disabled if he or she has a physical or mental impairment which has a substantial and long-term adverse affect on his or her ability to carry out normal day-to-day activities. In addition, a child is disabled if he or she has a progressive condition; a severe disfigurement; medical conditions such as cancer, multiple sclerosis or HIV; or a condition that is corrected/controlled by the use of medication, prostheses or other equipment – where there would be a substantial impact if they did not have that medication or equipment. For such children, schools (including independent schools) and LAs must not discriminate by treating them less favourably without justification or by failing to make a reasonable adjustment to overcome any substantial disadvantage they may face. Case law has helped to establish what 'without justification' and 'reasonable adjustments' mean. In particular, in a case called *Buniak v The Governing Body of the Jenny Hammond Primary School*, a Tribunal determined a school had discriminated against a disabled pupil by not providing the necessary teaching assistant support identified in his statement of special educational needs. Furthermore, in *Unoajumhi v Mill Hill County High School*, a Tribunal confirmed that a school's refusal to permit a disabled pupil attending a half-term skiing trip or to make reasonable adjustments to enable attendance could constitute discrimination.

Complaints of discrimination can be brought to the same Tribunal as for SEN appeals. However, complaints of alleged discrimination about refusals to admit children without EHC plans to state schools or permanent exclusions from maintained schools are brought to an Independent Appeal Panel.

The Disability Equality Duty and other discrimination provisions

Separately, since December 2006, most state schools (some schools were given special dispensation to begin later in April 2007 and December 2007), LAs and other public authorities have had an obligation to make and maintain a Disability Equality Scheme (Part 5A of the DDA). The purpose of this scheme is to demonstrate how the school or LA will seek to reduce disadvantage of disabled children generally. The scheme must be maintained and revised periodically, and is the responsibility of the school's governing body.

In making and maintaining the scheme, a public authority, including a school, must consult with disabled people. This ground-breaking requirement means that disabled people (with all kinds of impairments) must be involved in thinking about what public authorities, including schools, need to do to ensure that they operate in a non-discriminatory, broader equalities-sensitive way.

These obligations were strengthened by the 2010 Equality Act. This was an umbrella act designed to "simplify existing equality legislation and bring coherence to the different, separate equality acts [including] the 1995 Disability Discrimination Act" (Peart 2014: 84). The Equality Act covers a wide range of dispositions and affiliations including disability, race, gender and sexual orientation. However, as the Equality Act is (in legal terms) still relatively recent, very few cases have been brought so far under this guidance.

Reflections on values and practice

1   Consider your own work setting; reflect on the extent the law requires disabled children to be included. How effectively does your workplace achieve this? How may children (even inadvertently) be discriminated against and how can staff ensure that this does not happen?

2   Reflect on your own role. How can you make sure that you meet legal obligations of including learners with special educational needs and disabilities?
3   What reasonable adjustments could be made now in your workplace to make your provision more accessible to children and young people with SEN and disabilities?
4   What other rights under the 'protected characteristics' established in the 2010 Equality Act might your school need to consider for children and young people who have been identified as having special educational needs?

Suggested further reading

Clements, L., Ruebain, D. and Read, J. (2006) *Disabled Children and the Law*. London: Jessica Kingsley.
Mason, M. (2005) *Incurably Human*. Nottingham, UK: Inclusive Solutions.
NASEN. (2014) *Everybody Included: The SEND Code of Practice Explained*, Tamworth, UK: Author.

References

Department for Education (DfE). (2015) *Special Educational Needs and Disability Code of Practice: 0 to 25 years. Statutory Guidance for Organisations which Work with and Support Children and Young People Who Have Special Educational Needs or Disabilities*. Retrieved from www.gov.uk/government/uploads/system/uploads/attachment_data/file/398815/SEND_Code_of_Practice_January_2015.pdf accessed 20 July 2015
Gold, R. (1999) *The Education Act Explained*. London: The Stationery Office.
NASEN. (2014) *Everybody Included: The SEND Code of Practice Explained*. Tamworth: Author.
Peart, S. (2014) *Equality and Diversity in Further Education*. Northwich, UK: Critical Publishing.
Warnock, M. (1978) *Special Educational Needs: Report of the Committee of Inquiry into the Education of Handicapped Children and Young People*. London: HMSO.

Chapter 15

Social justice, human rights and inclusive education

Len Barton

Introduction

The meaning and importance of schooling and schools in contemporary society has become increasingly complex and contentious. Legitimating this situation has been the emergence of a continual series of changes to the institutional structures, governance and experience of learning. For example, the relentless pressure of governments to confer academy status on as many schools as possible is reducing the influence of LEAs control on the governance, funding and access to schools. It is also intensifying the competitive relationships between schools. Encouragement will be given to critically examine, briefly, what, how and why we think about the issues involved in the title of this chapter. Thus, the question of self-critical thinking, talking and engaging with all aspects of our lives becomes centrally important. This is a relentless, disturbing process, in which part of the struggle is to seek to make connections between ideas and new alternatives, relations, conceptions and practices. These all need to be understood contextually (Swann *et al.* 2012).

This approach to life generally and education in particular is both demanding and unsettling. Two key features of education need to be recognized. Firstly, educational issues are *complex* and not amenable to quick, slick answers or responses. For example, the relationship between society, the economy and educational policy and practice is real and influential. However, understanding the relationship between these factors requires grappling, struggling with conceptual, economic, political factors and ideas. Schools and educational provision must not be viewed in a vacuum or insulated from wider socioeconomic concerns and interests. The second issue is that educational issues are complex and involve the struggles between different interest groups over meanings and interpretations. Thus, the question of the nature of the curriculum, forms of assessment, the position of support staff and the relationship between the teachers and other professionals and home and the school are all examples of controversial issues. I want to propose, therefore, that the question of inclusive education needs critical interrogation and the changes it will require will be fundamental and difficult to achieve.

When discussing the role education plays in the struggle for change, Hargreaves (1982) maintained that teachers, and I would argue in this instance, Teaching

Assistants, need to be concerned with the political functions of education and ask such questions as: 'What kind of society do we want? How is education to help us realize that society?' (1982: 92). The urgency and seriousness of such demands for change are based on an informed conviction that there is something fundamentally unacceptable about many aspects of current policy and practice in education. These barriers to inclusion involve deeply rooted patterns of inequality and disadvantage in terms of access, experience and outcomes of education that need to be challenged and changed. These inequalities are not a natural, inevitable or unchangeable fact of life. No single factor can effectively remove these inequalities and exclusionary barriers, and education, although important, cannot achieve the changes required alone. Exclusion is a complex process, involving assaults on a person's identity and self-dignity. It restricts the possibility of an individual being able to exercise the privileges and responsibilities of citizenship. It is a gravely serious issue, not only for those who are excluded and discriminated against – whether this be, for example, on class, race, gender or disability grounds, or a combination of them – but also for society generally.

Teaching, teachers and assistant teachers

In the modern classroom, teaching and learning is not merely about working with pupils. It is also about establishing and maintaining constructive working relationships with other adults, including Teaching Assistants. This is not easily achieved and it does raise the question of what 'working with others' means and to what extent do such relationships involve conflict and counter-productive processes and outcomes? Whilst it can be claimed that the role of the Teaching Assistant has changed over time, research has demonstrated that there are important differences between schools over the nature of job descriptions and actual practices. Several reasons for these have been identified including: confused aims, no clear career structure, lack of planned training and poor channels of communication (Vincett, Cremin and Thomas 2005).

Thus the position and role of Teaching Assistants raises some complex and serious issues. For example, to what extent is the Teaching Assistant concerned with specially categorized pupils in comparison to pupils generally? Mansaray (2006) argues, that where the TA concentrates his or her attention on 'less-able' children, there is a danger of reinforcing the peer group label of 'dumb'. This has an impact on some children's perceptions of adult support as stigmatizing. In order to counteract this possibility, some Teaching Assistants are also used to support pupils generally and to take more responsibility for teaching tasks under the supervision of a teacher (HMI 2002). However, this is not without some difficulties in terms of tensions over the low pay of Teaching Assistants in comparison to teachers, the lack of training for specific tasks and the overall danger of exploitation (Vincett *et al.* 2005).

Part of the task of engaging with such serious issues is to understand how decisions are made in classroom interactions between Teaching Assistants and teachers, over the distinctive and complementary nature of their roles. This involves developing clear job specifications, which will then be the subject of careful monitoring and evaluation. Making each feel valued members of staff and enabling them and teachers together to undertake staff development that will contribute to their relationship being constructively developed, are both urgent factors needing critical and continual attention.

The question of collegial relationships within schools is of crucial significance and involves teachers and other support workers learning the value of the challenges of talking to one another over issues of professional significance. Talking is important. The form of talking being advocated is the kind that is increasingly focused, developmental, a means of clarifying issues, raising questions, sharing ideas, insights, concerns and recognizing points of difference. Difference from this approach is real but also based on respect for each other. This is a demanding process and it is not easily achieved, nor is there a blueprint of how to undertake this task. Talking with one another and not *at* each other is thus crucially important. It must not be viewed as an optional extra or a task for a select few. It is an imperative for *all* of us in that it ultimately concerns the welfare of all people. It is a learning experience in which there is no room for arrogance in that we are *all* learners and given the seriousness of the issues, there is no room for complacency. In this process, the re-examination of the meaning and use of such language as 'ability', 'achievement', 'success', 'learning', 'assessment' and 'special needs' will be a vitally important task. It will demand time, commitment and a resilience that is not easily undermined. The issues and questions we have outlined so far become even more demanding when set within the context of inclusive values, relationships and practices.

Inclusive education and human rights

The question of 'inclusive education' is both complex and is shaped by historical, cultural, global and contextual factors. In an important EPPI Centre review (2002), the question of definition is discussed. Whilst recognizing the limitations of their position, inclusion for them is about three key perspectives. First, it is about responding "simultaneously to students who all differ from each other in important ways, some of which pose particular challenges to the school". Second, "it is not just about maintaining the presence of students in school but also about maximizing their participation". Finally, "inclusion is a process which can be shaped by school-level action" (2002: 7).

Significant ambiguities in the concept of inclusion have encouraged Dyson (1999) to maintain that it would be more appropriate to talk about different inclusions. He argues that these differences arise from alternative discourses at work in the field through which different theoretical definitions of inclusion are contested. A crucial reason for proposing such a position is that Dyson is concerned that particular conceptions may have an impact in terms of stifling debate and ossifying values and beliefs.

Whilst I do recognize the importance of the above approaches and concerns, I would argue that inclusive education is not an end in itself but a means to an end.

It is about contributing to the realization of an inclusive society with the demand for a rights approach as a central component of policy-making. This perspective raises some important issues with regard to the question of inclusive education. First, it encourages the issue of change to be foregrounded. Unlike integration, the change process is not about assimilation but transformation of those deep structural barriers to change, including the social base of dominant definition of 'success', 'failure', and 'ability' within education as well as schools (Whitty 2002; Gillborn and Youdell 2000). Nor should we underestimate the difficulties of the task. Secondly, inclusive education is a "distinctly political, 'in your face', activity" (Corbett and Slee 2000: 136) and it involves a political critique of social values, priorities and the structures and institutions which they support. This is both a disturbing and challenging activity, which is an essential feature of the struggle for change. Lastly, inclusive education is fundamentally about how we understand and engage with difference in constructive and valued ways. It is a public process of naming and celebrating differences and engaging with the identification of what it is we value about one another. To do justice to the differences between pupils, to utilize these differences and to approach such factors as a resource, an opportunity for learning and not a problem to be fixed or excluded, becomes a crucial dimension of an approach that is working towards inclusive education (Ainscow 1999).

When trying to understand what constitutes inclusive values, thinking and practice, it is necessary that the focus of attention should be directed at the nature of the varied barriers to inclusion, both within education and society generally. The interest in inclusion is not solely about the position and experience of particular categorized individuals. It is about the participation of all pupils. This approach involves a perennial struggle for change and we must not underestimate the extent of the changes that are required. It is about much more than attitudinal change. The critique involved and the efforts for change need to be informed by a human-rights approach. Human rights, as Armstrong and Barton note, involve "a set of principles based on social justice, a statement by which the conditions and opportunities of human life can be evaluated" (1999: 211).

Education, from a rights approach, is not a privilege for a select few, nor a matter of charity. No child is viewed as uneducable. All children are entitled to high-quality education. A human rights approach to education entails issues of access, fair treatment with regard to learning, and fair access to the outcomes of education (Unterhalter 2006). The question of rights is derived from the qualification of being human. However, recognizing the formal equality of citizenship rights does not necessarily lead to quality of respect, opportunities and resources. Too often there is a gulf between laudable rhetoric and practice. A commitment to human rights in education demands the highest form of expectations with regard to the learning and well-being of all pupils.

One of the dangers that we need to be constantly aware of and seek to resist is engaging with these concerns in an unquestioning manner. Gibson (2015) reminds us of this with regard to the subject of human rights, in which she offers several criticisms of unacceptable ways this issue has been dealt with in relation to inclusive education.

Outstanding issues

One of the starkest exclusionary issues needing serious and urgent attention concerns the position and involvement of pupils in decision making in schools. Pupils have extensive knowledge of change within schools, both in terms of the organization, teaching and curriculum, but they are never seriously consulted over new policy initiatives, their implementation, nor are their views sought with regard to the purpose of education. An inclusive approach to education will give priority to the voices of pupils and the possible and essential contributions they can make to the struggle for change. Former Secretary of State for Education David Blunkett called pupils 'co-partners' in the pursuit of inclusive relations and practice (DFEE 1997). Pupils, from this perspective, need to be viewed as a rich resource whom future developments in schools must engage with in serious and respectful ways. How far is this a significant feature of relationships and practices within your school? What does it mean to listen to the voices of pupils?

Another key feature of working towards inclusion is a recognition of the absolute necessity of developing good and effective legislation, which supports the removal of all forms of exclusion and discrimination within education and society generally. Both the specific nature of the legislation and the degree to which it is enforceable are of paramount significance. Understanding children's entitlements under law and our responsibilities to meet those requirements within our institutions is an urgent task, which needs to be part of a carefully supported, monitored and evaluated staff development policy and approach. The extent to which we have an informed knowledge and understanding of the latest legislation and its effective impact on our daily practice is thus an issue of perennial importance.

Conclusion

In this brief chapter I have highlighted some contentious issues concerning the question of inclusive education and the position and practice of the Teaching Assistant in schools. This is an extremely important topic involving particular values, relations, practices, conditions and desired outcomes.

Inclusive education is about the maximization and continual participation of all members of the school community, staff and pupils. It is a learning process in which developing mutual respect, identifying, understanding and overcoming all forms of exclusionary values, relationships and practices as well as the generation of positive views of difference, are all essential features of this engagement.

Reflections on values and practice

If we are to contribute to this process of change, then we need to continually ask ourselves critical questions about our own perspectives, experiences and work contexts. These could include, for example:

1   What do we understand by inclusive education?

2   How far do we think pupils can contribute to the development of a more inclusive culture within schools?
3   To what extent and in what ways, do we value our working relationships with teachers and how far do we feel valued by them?
4   What can be changed within schools and in particular, the ones in which we work, that will enable learning to become more meaningful and engaging for all learners?

Suggested further reading

Armstrong, F. and Moore, M. (eds) (2004) *Action Research For Inclusive Education: Changing Places, Changing Practice, Changing Minds.* London: RoutledgeFalmer.
Barton, L. and Armstrong, F. (eds) (2007) *Policy, Experience and Change: Cross-Cultural Reflections on Inclusive Education.* Dordrecht, NE: Springer Books.
Swann, M., Peacock, A., Hart, S. and Drummond, M. J. (2012) *Creating Learning Without Limits.* Maidenhead, UK: Open University Press.

References

Ainscow, M. (1999) *Understanding the Development of Inclusive Education.* London: Falmer Press.
Armstrong, F. and Barton, L. (1999) 'Is there anyone there concerned with human rights? Cross-cultural connections, disability and the struggle for change', in F. Armstrong and L. Barton (eds), *Disability, Human Rights and Education: Cross-Cultural Perspectives.* Buckingham, UK: Open University Press.
Corbett, J. and Slee, R. (2000) 'An international conversation on inclusive education', in F. Armstrong, D. Armstrong, and L. Barton (eds), *Inclusive Education: Policy, Contexts and Comparative Education.* London: David Fulton Publishers.
DFEE. (1997) 'Excellence for all children: meeting special educational needs'. Government Green Paper. London: Author.
Dyson, A. (1999) 'Inclusion and inclusions': Theories and discourses in inclusive education', in H. Daniels and P. Garner (eds), *Inclusive Education.* London: Kogan Page.
EPPI Centre. (2002) 'A systematic review of the effectiveness of school-level actions for promotion, participation by all students'. Institute of Education, University of London.
Gibson, S. (2015) 'When rights are not enough: What is? Moving towards new pedagogy for inclusive education within UK universities'. *International Journal of Inclusive Education,* 19(8): 875–896.
Gillborn, D. and Youdell, D. (2000) *Rationing Education Policy, Practice, Reform and Equity.* Buckingham, UK: Open University Press.
Hargreaves, D. H. (1982) The Challenge for Comprehensive School. Culture. Curriculum and Community. London: Routledge and Kegan Paul.
HMI. (2002) *Teaching Assistants in Primary Schools: An Evaluation of the Quality and Impact of Their Work* (A Report). London: Ofsted.
Mansaray, A. A. (2006) 'Liminality and in/exclusion: Exploring the work of teaching assistants'. *Pedagogy, Culture and Society,* 14(2): 171–187.
Swann, M., Peacock, A., Hart, S. and Drummond, M. J. (2012) *Creating Learning Without Limits.* Maidenhead, UK: Open University Press.

Unterhalter, E. (2006) *Gender, Schooling and Global Social Justice.* London: Routledge.

Vincett, K., Cremin, H. and Thomas, G. (2005) *Teachers and Assistants Working Together.* Maidenhead, UK: Open University Press.

Whitty, C. (2002) *Making Sense of Education Policy.* London: Paul Chapman Publishers.

Index